The Political Power of Visual Art

Also available from Bloomsbury

Aesthetics, Arts, and Politics in a Global World, by Daniel Herwitz
Cosmopolitan Aesthetics, by Daniel Herwitz
The Aesthetics of Imperfection in Music and the Arts, edited by
Andy Hamilton and Lara Pearson
The Curatorial, edited by Jean-Paul Martinon
The Philosophy of Curatorial Practice, by Sue Spaid

The Political Power of Visual Art

Liberty, Solidarity, and Rights

Daniel Herwitz

BLOOMSBURY ACADEMIC
LONDON • NEW YORK • OXFORD • NEW DELHI • SYDNEY

BLOOMSBURY ACADEMIC
Bloomsbury Publishing Plc
50 Bedford Square, London, WC1B 3DP, UK
1385 Broadway, New York, NY 10018, USA
29 Earlsfort Terrace, Dublin 2, Ireland

BLOOMSBURY, BLOOMSBURY ACADEMIC and the Diana logo are
trademarks of Bloomsbury Publishing Plc

First published in Great Britain 2021

Copyright © Daniel Herwitz, 2021

Daniel Herwitz has asserted his right under the Copyright, Designs and
Patents Act, 1988, to be identified as Author of this work.

For legal purposes the Acknowledgments on p. vii constitute an extension
of this copyright page.

Cover design by Louise Dugdale
Cover image: Tyeb Mehta painting, Indian painter, Dinodia Photos / Alamy Stock Photo

A catalogue record for this book is available from the British Library.

A catalog record for this book is available from the Library of Congress.

ISBN: HB: 978-1-3501-8238-7
PB: 978-1-3501-8237-0
ePDF: 978-1-3501-8240-0
eBook: 978-1-3501-8239-4

Typeset by Newgen KnowledgeWorks Pvt. Ltd., Chennai, India

To find out more about our authors and books visit www.bloomsbury.com
and sign up for our newsletters.

Contents

List of Figures   vi

Acknowledgments   vii

 1   Introduction   1
 2   The Politics of Visibility: Lurie and Rancière   27
 3   Art and the Mining of Diamonds: Kentridge, Modisakeng,
     and What Is Meant by Politics   41
 4   The Politics of the Witness: Georges Gittoes   63
 5   Virulent Nationalism and the Politics of Offense: The NEA 4   75
 6   Literature and the Politics of the Truth Commission:
     Dorfman and Coetzee   89
 7   Identity Politics in a Consumerist World   129
 8   Art Market Politics: Manet to Banksy   143
 9   Autonomy as Negotiation: Mozart Reconsidered   159
10   Film, the Individual, and the Collective   173

Notes   189

Bibliography   195

Index   199

Figures

1.1 Alexander Rodchenko (1891–1956), VAGA@ARS, NY,
     Emergency Ladder (from the series "The House on Mjasnitska
     Street"), 1925   14

2.1 David Lurie, *Free Palestine* (from *Undercity: The Other Cape
     Town*, Hatje Cantz), 2017   31

2.2 David Lurie, *The People Shall Share in the Country's Wealth*,
     2015, Khayelisha, Cape Flats, mural by Faith47 (from
     Undercity: The Other Cape Town, Hatje Cantz), 2017   35

2.3 David Lurie, *Woodstock, Lower Main Road* (from
     Undercity: The Other Cape Town, Hatje Cantz), 2017   35

3.1 William Kentridge, untitled drawing for *Mine*, 1991   49

3.2 William Kentridge, untitled drawing for *Mine*, 1991   50

3.3 William Kentridge, untitled drawing for *Felix in Exile*, 1994   61

4.1 George Gittoes, *The Preacher*, 1994   69

4.2 George Gittoes, *Blood and Tears*, 1995   70

4.3 George Gittoes, *P. Souljah, Love and Pain*   72

5.1 Andres Serrano, *Piss Christ*, 1987   78

7.1 Judy Chicago@ARS, NY. Installation view of Wing Two,
     featuring Elizabeth R. Artemisia Gentileschi and Anna van
     Schurman place settings from *The Dinner Party*, 1979   131

7.2 Judy Chicago@ARS, NY. *The Dinner Party*, Emily Dickenson
     plate, 1979   132

8.1 Andy Warhol, *One Dollar Bills* (fronts), 1962   148

8.2 Banksy, *Girl w/Balloon* after shredding, begun 2002, shredded
     at auction 2018   153

8.3 Banksy, *Walled-Off Hotel*, opened 2017   154

8.4 Banksy, interior guests eat in the dining hall of Banksy's
     Walled-Off Hotel, December 21, 2019   156

Acknowledgments

It is bizarre to complete a book in lockdown isolation, at this summer moment of 2020 with a global pandemic raging and the ugly face of inequality laid bare by the ravages of disease. For this book is about the tension between two roles that art has played—and philosophy has encouraged—since the eighteenth century. One being that of aesthetic isolation, a completely individual experience between self and artwork whose purpose is the experience itself. The other being the aspiration to solidarity and politics deeply engrained in art since Mozart's operas, Dickens's novels, the painting of Manet and Pissarro, the polemical writings of Marx, the avant-gardes.

Writing is tailor-made for solitary confinement since it happens alone. But it is also a plea for solidarity (or at least conversation) with others courtesy of the printed page. And whether in lockdown or not, writing requires (at least for me) the help of others. May I thank Lydia Goehr, who has almost become my writing partner, each of us pouring over the scribblings of the other in a way that has helped to commute loneliness into an ever-deepening friendship. Lydia's scrupulous attention to detail, and equally subtle ability to square the lopsidedness of overall argument, has proved invaluable.

Michael Steinberg, carrying forward our intellectual conversation of a lifetime, proved invaluable in his sympathetic grasp of my project, making his criticisms all the more telling. Other friends have also been important for the making of this book: Vassilis Lambropoulos, Imraan Coovadia, Akeel Bilgrami, Elisa Galgut, Nicholas Delbanco, David Lurie, George Gittoes, Marjorie Perloff, and Paul Kaiser. A workshop at the American Academy, Berlin, organized by Michael Steinberg and Rosalind Morris in January 2019, allowed me to present early versions of this work. There, I particularly benefited from the comments of Miriam Tichtin. My editor at Bloomsbury, Colleen Coalter, has provided clarity and encouragement. Lisa Ballard of Artists Rights Society has been invaluable in the securing of images. Artists George Gittoes, David Lurie, and William Kentridge have graciously offered rights and photos.

This book is written in honor of Lucia Saks, with whom I have had the privilege of sharing a life and a daughter, not to mention decades of loving hilarity, dazzling adventure, and critical advice. Long may our cornucopia last.

Introduction

Part I

Visual art has nearly a ubiquitous political cast today. If one reads daily art blogs like *Hyperallergic*, they are almost entirely dedicated to installations, video productions, paintings, work in new media, curated exhibitions, and the like, addressing humanitarian issues of broad global concern: refugees, global inequality, virulent nationalism, repressed or marginalized identities, environmental degradation and climate change, violence, decolonization, race. And when not on the job addressing these global conundrums, art is busy chipping away at the artworld, its institutions, branding, marketing, economy for the one percent, its auction houses, and curatorial practices. And when not on that second job, there is a third—the critique of aesthetic legacies: the nude, the voyeur, the consumerist nature of visual culture, the way the beautiful serves as a veil of power, the sublime as a conduit for ideology.

If politics are a currency of art today, then which politics? The avant-gardes arose largely from a singular vision of political history, and at the end of the First World War, when Europe lay in ashes, the world order was believed to be capable of radical transformation, and the Russians had stormed the ramparts of the Kremlin, with Germany believed soon to follow a similar path. According to Marx's overarching framework for utopian emancipation, the history of the world had a single shape, destined for a single, emancipatory conclusion. Thanks to the rise of new forms of technological production, tectonic shifts in the social and economic formation erupted, leading from feudalism to mercantile capitalism to industrial capitalism, to the degradation of the proletarian and the class struggle, understood to be a political struggle for control over the state and its mechanisms of power and authority. The avant-gardes in some cases (Italian futurism) embraced politics on the right, carrying forward the fascist banner of endless war (Italians in Ethiopia), the beauty of speed, energy, and bombardment, a celebration of brutal state power and historical grandiosity for a lost, mythic past capable of regenerating the (Italian) nation into a newly minted Roman empire.

These utopian political aspirations for art have mostly fallen away since the days of the avant-gardes when radical alternatives to the political order were believed possible—and on the horizon. We no longer quite believe in such radical powers of art, because art is no longer linked to a united front of battle underwritten by a rational scheme inherently pressing history forward at a moment of necessary change. Indeed, it is no longer possible to approach society, economy, inequality, class, culture, and art from the point of view of a single, overarching political narrative. This was the point of Jean-Francois Lyotard's *Postmodern Condition*, published decades ago in 1979.[1] Then how should one seek to understand—much less critically engage—the many political practices of art today? I think while this very obvious question follows about political culture from Lyotard's book and from the entire postmodern questioning of grand political narratives, it hasn't been directly asked about contemporary art. Rather, writing on art in relation to politics has tended to set forth one view of politics, then another, then another—each concept meant to provide a general political framework through which art and the aesthetic should be approached. The domain, range, and limitation of a particular political concept is never explored, much less specified.

If one were to make a brief list of some of the various concepts of politics people bring to the understanding of art today, it might look like this. We have Hannah Arendt's notion that politics is a matter of declaring a point of view in the agora, the public space where the conversation of democracy happens. This is to think of art as a form of dissent within democratic culture. Against that, we have Jacques Rancière's notion that democracies today are totalitarian systems of control, what Rancière called "the police," precluding rational consensus around questions of justice and policy. For Rancière, dissent within the system is not possible. Democracies today are forms of exclusion. Dissent must take place at the margins of the democratic state, or outside of it entirely. And the aim of dissent must be a disruption of the system rather than a new point of view within it, causing the system to tremble, thanks to what Rancière calls the setting forth of new forms of visibility, new ways in which those aspects of reality that the system has ignored, repressed, rendered invisible, covered over with ideology, or (in the case of persons) thrown in jail may emerge into sensuous, perceptual, and cognitive views. Dissent is the production of new, alternative forms of visibility posed against the police.

Add to these concepts political ideas about global decolonization that veer between seeking to include new nations within the global system and seeking to change the global system to make room for (those) resource-poor and moderate nations in a way that does not simply rely on them for cheap labor and the extraction of resources but brings global resources to their empowerment (development). Add the idea of the importance of human rights and the witnessing of atrocity as a basic humanitarian condition of our time. Add debates about which rights should be understood to be absolutely necessary and universal, which culturally specific, and which a matter of global debate/argument. Much of the culture of humanitarianism is about such a conversation. Add issue-based politics into the mix: solidarities around the degradation of climate, the ultranationalist turn, racial politics, and the security and liberty of women. These solidarities may be formed across many political divisions. Add identity politics in the mix, the claim of marginalized persons to change the power of representation, erasing stereotypes, allowing new voices to be heard, achieving rights within the democratic culture. Add the question of the state: those who believe it has been weakened by globalization and seeks compensatory strength through right-wing nationalism versus those who believe it is stronger than ever before, thanks to its efficiency and power of control. And finally, turn to the politics of financial capital, which exerts a controlling influence on art markets (their choice of product, their mode of branding and marketing, their circulation of cultural commodities, their selling power and consumer base) and much else in the world. Leading, as Piketty has shown, to an ongoing spiral of greater and greater class inequality.[2]

And what does one have?

A conundrum. Especially if each and every one of these political ideas (and there are more) begins from a conception of the kind of conditions from which emancipation is demanded, along with what has to happen for emancipation to take place. And these conditions are various and subject to disagreement.

Even more of a conundrum if one also admits that any work of art (or cultural object) can be understood as political in the sense of being an object of *political analysis*, the kind of analysis that seeks to uncover its ideological function, the way it articulates racial, gendered, class or other forms of systemic power, and so on.

This book is dedicated to thinking about art practices in relation to aesthetics and politics and from the perspective of a world in which we no longer have a single overarching political theory capable of driving emancipation, or, related, any single idea of what emancipation is, but many, and these in partial contradiction. The point is not to interpret the world, as Marx said, it is to change it, but where can art enter the game? There is wild variation in claims made about the political efficacy and agency of art in our time. About the kind of job it can or might do. I am of two minds on the subject. In a dark mood, I am prone to think visual art today fetishizes politics. A fetish is meant to replace the sense of powerlessness with a symbolic agent of power, which can be worshipped and manipulated in the hope—more likely the illusion—that the fetish-object empowers, even if all it does is confirm powerlessness. Anything from a foot, to an article of clothing, to Art Basel can serve. Political art is a way of converting demoralization by those who, because they can't change the world, place all their aspirations instead in the currency of *symbols*, into illusions of agency. The market thrives on this fetish, turning political art into a branded commodity of edgy and important value, all of which is about inflation in price.

In a brighter mood, one might say: But political art is a genuine aspiration today, not simply an illusion, a genuine way of responding to national ills, global markets, and, importantly, global humanitarianism. And who can really say what a work of art does for human empowerment, perhaps even years after its encounter? Perhaps for an audience that wasn't even born at the time.

The question of political aspirations for visual art has a particular resonance given the germ of a fine idea that, loosely and somewhat creatively, derives from the Hegelian tradition of thinking about art in relation to the potentialities of the medium. Namely the insight that not all things are possible in every medium of art. (One might say the same thing about research. Not every genre of research is capable of gaining all manner of knowledge.) To know a medium is to know its limits, as well as what it is good at. Visual art lacks the articulateness of language. It is therefore far less dialectical in encompassing different points of view into a larger synthetic whole than literature, film, nonfiction writing, media podcasts, or the like. One wonders if it is beyond the resources of the visual medium to address political issues as complex as climate change, financial capital, and equity. If one wants to propose a new solution to the refugee crisis affecting the globe today, it will hardly do to make an abstract painting, write a flute solo, or weave a basket. Abstract painting lacks the verbal articulateness demanded of the task. But then so does a great deal of visual art. Only when a shared iconographic background is in place, such as the Christian story, can a painting *depict* with the subtle brilliance of a Leonardo or Raphael. Only when theory empowers the avant-gardes with political principles and utopian aspirations can their magnificent experiments "speak" to the world. It is for this reason that at the center of avant-garde practice was the *Manifesto*, which proposed the terms through which visual experiments should be understood aesthetically, and in relation to utopian ideals. Much of contemporary art today has gone in the direction of the installation, whose various parts have a better chance of speaking dialectically and reflectively, of capturing the mind as well as the senses. But even installation lacks the suppleness of language without the piston of theory behind it. Hence the importance given to the "curator's statement," or "artist's text."

On the other hand, photography can bring home searing realities in a way no book might be able to do. The drawings of Weimar artists underscored a society of suffering and collapse and were a siren screaming out against the darkness. Goya's depictions of war are unparalleled. Picasso's *Guernica* is iconic of fascist destruction and the power of bombs to unravel a world of human and animal. Visual art can bring home the raw intensities of reality, in a way that cries out for action. Even if its analytic and diagnostic capacities may be limited. Given these facts about the medium or media of visual art, we might then refine the question a little by asking about the kind or kinds of contribution to politics that such media can make. To state the obvious: It is deep in the history of visual art that depiction is acknowledgment of suffering, loss of dignity, of the brave and the mighty, of reality seldom noticed until art forces it upon one, of daily banality and indifference.

Moreover, art's deep connection with the human imagination makes it a scion of liberty, which can be awakened in the right circumstances. Art engages what is most free in us, our minds, imaginations, feelings, inner life. It cultivates our capacity for imaginative sensibility. This was a core idea of the aesthetics of the eighteenth century. The problem is that once awakened in the imagination to liberty, a person may act in various different ways, leaving the question of politics unresolved. It takes more than individual experience to turn the imagination into a political instrument. The left and the right will encounter the same artwork, and both believe they are acting on the basis of the ideal of liberty it awakens.

Since there is no formula for how the awakened mind becomes a political mind, much less what the politics are which that mind embraces, there can be no *theory* of what makes art political: insofar as the role of art is to awaken the mind. Which is part of the reason why there are so many such theories. It is better, therefore, to consider a series of *case studies*, each of which might imply, aspire to, or hold the illusion that it produces a different kind of political approach. That is how this book is organized. As a series of case studies linked together in various ways.

I actually think the absence of an overriding political framework for emancipation is an advantage, even a political strength for art, since it allows for a multiplicity of ways in which art may be charged with politics, or charged as faulty politically, or recharged as challenging a received point of view inside or outside of art. It is my own political belief that emancipation demands such multiplicity of tactics and political concepts and utopian aspirations and forms of solidarity. This point will be brought home through the case studies that follow. I also think it is vital to democracy to keep any single one from settling. Politics remains alive when political concepts are in flux, deftly negotiated in the process of becoming. I think Rosa Luxemburg held an idea similar to this (while remaining wedded to the overall Marxist framework), and so did Herbert Marcuse and Theodor Adorno (also Marxists), and more recently Jacques Derrida (less clearly of any single political position), not to mention Gilles Deleuze and Richard Rorty. I think it a good idea still. And an idea that privileges art because art has the flexibility to drive, and be driven by, multiple and different political perspectives. Its innovative plasticity allows it to set and aspire to multiple ends. Rather than believing that contemporary art needs a single guiding politics, I think its strength consists in the fact that it doesn't, and can't.

On the other hand, in the absence of a shared framework for thinking about equality, rights, sustainability, and justice, political agency is rendered inefficient, sometimes weakened to the point of nothingness, and this at a moment when the dignity of the human race is at stake, most people being impoverished, without access to proper education and health care, their security under threat, and when the survival of the planet is in question.

Finally, it is my own view that the political power of visual art largely consists in its capacity for aesthetic innovation. I refer to art's ability to create shocking, new, indelible, productive visions of reality that seep into the imagination and remain, that challenge, excite, and even at times catalyze. Art's political force largely arises from its aesthetic power; even if in the name of politics, art constantly tries to shed the ease of aesthetic pleasure in favor of tougher, edgier, more ballistic rhetoric. It is in this tension between the power to reveal the world from innovative perspectives that deepen the imagination, proving unforgettable, and its desire to shed aesthetics in favor of tough rhetoric and incendiary weapon that political art lives. But this does not determine whether, or in what sense, the art in question achieves genuine politics. That thought runs through the book.

Part II

A second theme of the book, implicit throughout and explicitly addressed in the final two chapters on philosophical aesthetics, is that contemporary art is the inheritor of two opposing legacies of thinking about the proper role of art in relation to politics. Between these opposing legacies, much art practice takes place today. The first is the tradition of eighteenth-century aesthetics; the second that of the twentieth-century avant-gardes. The inheritance is uneasy and fragmentary. But in some very interesting ways, it is through a recombination of these traditions in part or whole that the making and interpretation of art largely takes place today. So, it is important to get this background story of genealogies right in order to deepen the understanding of art practice today.

The first inheritance celebrates art as an icon of individual liberty. This thinking about art arose in the wake of the modern nation-state and the articulation of natural rights. The second is an exemplar of political solidarity and arose in the wake of the First World War and the Russian Revolution. The first eschews politics, while the second courts politics, aiming to stand in the forefront (the avant-garde) of the battle of history. Each celebrates innovation, but under different terms. Both traditions celebrate the value of aesthetic experience, but under very different terms.

The first cultivates personal intimacy; the second, anti-bourgeois solidarity. The tradition of aesthetics eschews the social and political world seeking autonomy so that art may stand as an experience without an "end" or purpose in the world beyond its own reveling/revelation. The tradition of the avant-gardes despises the bourgeois culture of art markets—buying, selling, owning, and enjoying—aiming to break out of this encomium to engage the masses with the goal of eventually destroying such bourgeois infrastructure. The first tradition is about pleasure taken in an art object (or natural subject) in and for itself and the transcendent power of sensuous, aesthetic experience that follows. The second tradition aims to alienate the viewer from ordinary habits of taking in the world, in the service of heightened perceptual and intellectual self-consciousness, heightened and reflective awareness that is meant to create a politically motivated subject or enhance their motivation.

One tradition is part of eighteenth-century liberalism, broadly construed; the other aims for radical alternatives to liberal ideology (on the left or the right). Both propose and depend on a relation between the individual and the collective, but again very differently.

Between them the political spectrum of art can be found.

As to the first: Aesthetics—a distinctive way of thinking about and practicing art—arose in the context of the articulation of individual liberty at the end of the seventeenth century. This modern emphasis on the individual was at the time innovative and emancipatory. The late seventeenth and eighteenth centuries set forth for the first time in history the concept of natural rights, what John Locke, in his *Second Treatise of Government* of 1689, called the rights to life and liberty. By liberty, Locke meant the freedom to offer one's labor in the marketplace for compensation—the freedom to acquire property and to hold titled estates.

Locke's natural rights, to which Thomas Jefferson added the "inalienable" right to the "pursuit of happiness" in the *Declaration of Independence*, were meant to be universal and equal, applying to all persons in virtue of their existence as persons. Such rights Locke believed come from God. Natural rights could not be taken away by any government or religion; they answer to a higher calling.

Crucial to Locke's idea of natural rights was that they existed prior to any individual's relation to government. Since humans were free prior to government, they had the right to enter freely into a relation with it. This gave rise to Locke's famous contract theory: The sole purpose of government is to secure and sustain the liberty of its citizens. That is the *only* legitimate purpose of government. Should government fail in its purpose, descending into tyranny or even overwhelming ineptitude, individual citizens have the right—indeed the duty—to leave or to revolt.

It should be noted that although Locke articulated liberty as a universal right, he himself was an exemplar of its restriction from the colonies, since as a colonial administrator he had himself written the slaveholding constitution of the Carolinas. This was typical; colonialism preached universal rights, then restricted them to European citizens.[3]

Even in Europe, freedom of the individual was inevitably fraught, since state power tended to express itself as control. The proper condition of individual liberty, therefore, became understood as that of *autonomy*— autonomy in the negative sense of a safe space free from the encroachments of state and other forms of coercive power. And autonomy in the positive sense of the conditions under which an individual could discover and write their own life script and live freely according to it. In fact, the concept of autonomy was subject to variation across Europe. If Isaiah Berlin is right,[4] England emphasized the negative formulation of autonomy—autonomy from the state. Whereas Germany emphasized the positive formulation, which it rewrote as the freedom to actualize oneself through the idealized/ enlightened nation. Both traditions believed liberty and citizenship were connected, in that the point of liberty is not simply to live a life of one's own on one's own terms, but to contribute—thanks to one's own experience—to the general Commons of moral, aesthetic, and epistemological truth, each understood citizenship differently: that is the relation between individual freedom and national belonging/duty.

Now aesthetic experience was seldom *merely* about the self and its freedom of choice. It always contained the added value of building a community of taste (Immanuel Kant's "sensis communis"), a common set of experiences capable of bonding persons together under the national framework, of building a national heritage, even, for some (David Hume) establishing an objective standard of taste on the model of a jointly established legal standard tested, tweaked, and confirmed by multiple individual experiences and aesthetic judgments.[5] The eighteenth century discovered the philosophical importance of *sensibility* in the broadest sense: sense experience and its role in knowledge production, sensuous experience and its role in the experience of beauty and the sublime, taste (sensuous pleasure taken in an object). And then the creation of a moral community, thanks in part to the cultivation of shared sensibility or taste.

And so, art took on two related roles.

First, to symbolize and celebrate individual liberty by standing as an icon of freedom of choice. There could be no more central expression of liberty than the liberty to enjoy what one wanted, to choose freely whom to love, whom to consider a friend, where to live, what to collect, which experiences of art and nature in which to take pleasure. These are matters of taste, which became an icon of what Jefferson called the "pursuit of happiness." Taste is central to what makes me the person I am, you the person you are, and so on. Differences in taste mark individual differences between us. For the eighteenth century, taste was more than an expression of liberty. It was an *icon* of liberty. Since taste was a freedom to experience and enjoy things for the sake of the experience as an end in itself, taste became a symbol of liberty: symbol of a life lived in and for itself, as its own end, according to its own moral goals, its own aspirations for work and property, and so on.

Second, taste and aesthetic experience were meant to play a role in the creation of a Commons—a shared set of values, interests, ways of looking at the world, a set of imaginative bonds between citizens. My individual liberty, while my right absolutely, does not take place on an enchanted island apart from the community, but within the community and in part shaped by it. Locke understood this well, which is why he was concerned to show how individual interest could incorporate a common sense of cooperative bonding between individuals—a Commons in which each is concerned for the freedom of the other. The basis of experience is individual experience, but from the individual experiences of many, each partly confirming those of others, a common stock of belief and bond was meant to accrue, deepening the community and its common nationhood, creating national heritage, linking persons through the bonds of Common life.

There is more. If one reads a book like McPherson's *The Political Theory of Possessive Individualism*,[6] it is clear that liberty arose with a consumerist edge and in relation to markets: as the right to sell one's labor and acquire property and estates. With empire, the colonies, and the emergence of modern market economy, the focus on taste is linked to expanding wealth and consumption. The ability to collect things, indulge in pleasures, enjoy nature and art was the exercise of an individual in a world that became his oyster. In the men's clubs of London, oysters were readily available on the half shell, to be eaten with port and followed by a fine cigar with musical accompaniment throughout. This class adored wine taken in the men's clubs, in objects bought, eaten, smoked, caressed, and consumed. Since there could have been no equivalent rise in bourgeois consumerism without empire in place, the pleasure of sampling, trying, tasting, owning was occasioned by colonialism. Markets grew, thanks to the extraction of goods from the colonies and the exploitation of labor therein. Europe became loaded with new, exotic objects of pleasure and fascination.

The new aesthetic thinking of the eighteenth century formed a sharp departure from the thinking and practice of art before it. In the Renaissance, to take an example, the purpose of art had been to link the beauty and sublimity of the pictorial image to the Christ story. The frescoes painted in churches told the inner truth of Christianity to a largely illiterate population capable of "reading" it visually (through iconography) in a way that deepened their devotion. The Renaissance fresco had its proper home not in an autonomous space but a space of public power and authority. It *spoke* and was certainly *not made* for the pursuit of individual happiness or pleasure, although we may treat the Renaissance fresco like that today. The theory and practice of taste changed all that. The key to taste is that it is experiential, not representational. A work of art, considered as an object of taste, does not speak, or if it does, this does not really count aesthetically. The very judgment of taste was conceived of as a matter of pleasure felt, not propositions understood. The aesthetic judge did not have to have intellectual support for their judgment, merely the experience of pleasure in the right circumstance. Sensibility provided the grounds of judgment. This shift from judgment based in concepts to judgment based in sensibility is basic. One can see it in the way the eighteenth-century person approaches the Renaissance fresco— not as an object for religious instruction but as a conduit for intense rapture (pleasure). The Titian painting of the "assumption" of the virgin in Venice was now approached as an object of pure contemplation. That was when all Europe turned into a museum, and objects lost their primary roles, becoming artifacts of the past for the aesthetic pilgrim on the Grand Tour.

This shift in the purpose of art was a paradigm change in which sensible experience replaces the social/political representation and aspiration, allowing representation back in only as a correlate of experience, always secondary. Aesthetic experience is purely about the pleasures and intensities of contemplation. These the eighteenth century categorized as the beautiful and the sublime. What art was *about* became less important that the *experience* it generated in a willing and competent viewer, reader, or listener.

There is far more to the eighteenth century than any brief survey can do justice. May I mention the revolutionary character of that century (the

American and French revolutions), its clerical and anticlerical debates (about religious truth and doctrine of high moral consequence), the rise of science, as well as what Theodor Adorno and Max Horkheimer call the culture of instrumental reason associated with the rise of modern markets.[7] My point is that although one can hardly presume to encapsulate an entire century in a few sentences, the historical legacy of that century for aesthetics and art is the link between the autonomy of aesthetic experience and the cult or culture of individual liberty. A link provided by the theory of taste. That and the related idea of the role of aesthetic experience in the creation of a *Commons* or community of taste. These are of genealogical importance for our time.

Now the theory of taste arose in relation to the museum and the concert hall, where art was meant to be enjoyed apart from any other public function. Art, music, and theatre began to be made, which was meant only to be seen or heard—seen in the museum or home, heard in the concert hall or private chamber. Colonialism extracted objects from the empire, wrested them from their social roles, and placed them in the museum, where, emptied of their meaning and use (in which Europe was uninterested), they became mere conduits for disembodied contemplation. They became aesthetic objects. Without these public spaces dedicated to the autonomy of art, it is unclear whether aesthetics could have arisen.[8]

Nineteenth-century Romanticism began to deepen the notion of aesthetic experience from abstracted (and sometimes "disinterested") contemplation to a more fully embodied engagement with art, to the point where Nietzsche envisioned aesthetic experience in terms of the dynamic/erotic/Dionysian force of dance, a tremulous power, Nietzsche believed, capable of compelling nations into a state of becoming. This idea of the communal power of art to forge nations had its apogee in Bayreuth, where the operas of Wagner were meant to be experiences of sufficiently sublime and communalizing power to bring about the birth of the German nation in idealized form. This tradition of politics gained through the power of aesthetic experience became as central to the history of Europe as that of aesthetics. At its most horrifying, it led to fascism, with its concept that history is in effect an aesthetic power unleased within the people, compelling it onwards to all manner of invasions, wars, and atrocities. At its best, it led to the avant-gardes.

Part III

This is the second of the pair of legacies that inform art practice today. Let me turn to the avant-gardes in relation to radical collectivity.

The avant-gardes arose out of the ashes of the First World War. Against the fact of a decimated Europe, they preached radical political change, wishing to play a role in bringing it about. It was with the avant-gardes that plastic experimentation became linked to the goals of consciousness-raising and revolutionary political change. With an entire generation wiped out, and Europe in ruins, many sought radical change in the social, political, and economic formation—change that at that time was believed to be not only possible but already announcing itself on the scene of history, thanks to the Russian Revolution on the left and the growth of fascism on the right. Enter the avant-gardes, dedicating themselves to utopian political and social change. The goal of the new art was consciousness-raising. By designing a better world, the idea was that human beliefs and aspirations would correspondingly improve, the clearest example being architecture, where it was widely thought that by placing persons in identical housing, their sense of equality and shared rights would be sharpened.

But consciousness-raising was also meant to flow from experimentation in art through shock, defamiliarization, and presenting the world anew. Here the goal was to wrest the viewer from his or her complacent and habituated ways of seeing and knowing the world, to whisk the viewer away from their comfort zone so that the most ordinary things—a building, a woman sitting on a bench, a day in the life of a city—could be reframed as strange, distant, anthropological, unfamiliar, but also fresh and magical, as if reality, the most ordinary reality were suddenly encountered for the first time. The key was to shock the viewer into a new reflection on their relation to the world— to force the viewer to see the world differently, in a way that allowed the viewer a new recognition of agency. The shock had to be an *aesthetic shock*, a way of suddenly revealing the world in a sublimity previously invisible. And from a perspective uncertain enough to require reflection. The viewer was meant to become aware that the world is capable of being known and constructed afresh in some radically new ways, that it could be seen, known, and produced differently.

The avant-gardes most often refused the autonomy of taste (surrealism being a possible exception), and some movements refused taste altogether (Dada). All were against the reigning norms of taste and autonomy that they felt were co-opted by bourgeois culture and there to celebrate it. And their enemies were the institutions of art, the museum, concert hall, gallery, collector, critic, the connoisseur, the man with money to burn who wanted to own commodities. The cultural home of the avant-gardes was meant to be the street, the building, the political gathering, the rampart.

To take an example: Alexander Rodchenko, a photographer associated with the revolutionary constructivist movement in the Russia of the revolutionary 1920s, would photograph an ordinary building from a nearly inscrutable visual angle of such shock and beauty that the viewer of his photo disrupted what should have been a totally ordinary scene. A high-rise building is shot upwards from between the vertical fire escape and the building's side with a man curled on the ladder. The camera is tilted to the point where the high rise looks horizontal. The man on the emergency ladder (fire escape) is contorted around its rungs, so one cannot easily tell on which side of the ladder he is located. In fact, he twists through both sides.

These photos were meant to enthrall and disorient the viewer and excite the viewer by the prospect of the ordinary urban world seen differently, from a vibrantly strange perspective demanding reflection on point of view, camera angle, and so on. The point was to heighten the viewer's perceptual capacity by posing dissonance between eye and mind, perception and cognition, what the viewer knows (the building rises, it is not horizontal) and what the viewer's eye tells them. Dissonance places the viewer in an unresolved situation demanding a process of resolution between mind and eye. The lesson was meant to be: you are in a world that is processive, can be encountered and known differently, as if reality were not stable but rather in the process of becoming, based in part on how we see it. To achieve this recognition, one has to learn to live with, and thrive on, dissonance. Dissonance alienates one from ordinary and unchallenged habits of perception and cognition. The keyword being the Russian "Ostranenie," or German word "Verfremdung"—both meaning in avant-garde theory and practice the disruption of ordinary habit in a way that aims to break the viewer from the bourgeois world, thus raising the viewer's consciousness.

Now the photo could not by itself instruct the viewer in the right kind of historical change. This further politicization of the viewer demanded language to chart and prompt the path—hence the manifesto, with its theories linking aesthetic innovation to historical conclusion. Visual experimentation is by itself too abstract to carry a determinate political message, much less shape the human mind in a way that "raises political consciousness." There is a reason why the manifesto was at the core of avant-garde practice—a hybrid text combining the announcement of a new aesthetic (to be shared by the movement), lambasting all other art, especially that of the past, and promulgating a politics meant to derive from aesthetic/experimental innovation. The manifesto is almost always cast in the ecstatic language of the poet-prophet. It is meant to exemplify the aesthetic principles of the movement, their sublimity, ecstasy, transparency, constructivist utopianism, their shattering force. Deriving from the pages of Marx (the *Communist Manifesto*), the manifesto was felt to be charged with an electric current, creating a movement of disparate artists, yoked together in solidarity and

Figure 1.1 Alexander Rodchenko (1891–1956), VAGA@ARS, NY, *Emergency Ladder* (from the series "The House on Mjasnitska Street"), 1925. © 2020 Estate of Alexander Rodchenko/UPRAVIS, Moscow/ARS, NY.

with aesthetic/political purpose. *Theory* took on a formative role in art practice at this time because a visual object is incapable of "speaking" with the clarity, rhetorical intensity, and incisiveness required of political art without propositional content behind it (or a shared iconographic language as in the Renaissance, which was out of the question for the avant-gardes given their demand to bring about radically new). And so, the manifesto had to come into being as the central defining condition of an avant-garde movement in order to proclaim, prophesy, and explain avant-garde terms. Through the manifesto and its aesthetic/political theory, art sought to become the specter that haunted Europe.[9]

This fusion of experimentation with the theory and prose of the manifesto was a paradigm change in artistic practice from the eighteenth century with its canons of taste and autonomy. Concepts, rhetoric, theory were now meant to be central to aesthetic experience, challenging the autonomy of the artwork by turning it into a political cauldron.

The manifesto seeks to turn individual experimentation into a collective project, defined under its auspices. And so, turn a collection of artists into a collective movement.

Now, it is not for nothing that Rodchenko's work took place in the thrust and parry of the constructivist movement, formed in 1917, the year of the Russian Revolution. In point of historical fact, the avant-gardes were mostly ignored by Lenin, who believed them to be too intellectual and experimental to play any real role in the education of the masses or the construction of the Soviet state. Stalin then shut them down. Generally, they were the object of lambaste, violent attack, or at best indifference. Ironically, the only nation-state to embrace the avant-gardes was Italy, whose fascist leader Mussolini saw in Italian futurism a mirror of what he believed he was doing. As to avant-garde architecture and public work, it ended up becoming the expedient tool of the real estate builder, or worse, the drab, faceless apartment blocks of Eastern Europe and inner-city New York. The *actual agency* of avant-garde art was historically underwhelming.

But avant-garde practice did reshape the world of art. Its legacy can be felt to this day. Many of the styles art relies on for its political projects derive from the avant-gardes: the critique of representation, the aim of systemic political disruption, the recruitment of theory to empower a work with political meaning and force, the aspiration to solidarity through the symbols of art, the creation of new forms of visibility, and the alienation of viewers from the old in the name of raising their consciousness. The avant-gardes remain under invention, thanks to the political aspirations of art. Even if we no longer quite believe in the utopian visions that motivated that art—and those struggles.

There have also been a number of spin-offs from the avant-gardes, including the populist-driven art of resistance and solidarity in the Global South: art meant to be made by the people on the streets and for the streets, that is, in the name of popular resistance and emancipation. Here, simplicity of image and clarity of image-rhetoric are paramount (the rising fist, the people united in demonstration). Then there are those degradations of avant-garde practice: propaganda art and kitsch, both on the left and the right. Populist art has aimed to energize an oppressed population through symbols easily understood, and through the manning of the barricades by making art on the streets, on walls, in public places. Propagandistic kitsch is the inverse of populist resistance art, since it too aims for easily comprehensible symbols but, in this case, advertising state triumph or state capture in the name of what Gramsci called "hegemony," meaning the art is meant to hook the masses into the revolution by causing them to believe it is all about *them*, that they are the larger-than-life workers bulging from the political posters, that the revolution is in their name and for them when the revolution, in fact, serves the interests of the statist class (the "Party"). Kitsch featuring workers with larger-than-life fists and faces, chiseled from granite, eating the fruits of springtime or dynamizing the workplace with industrial-quality flowers is meant to convince the working class that they are the main actors and beneficiaries of the revolutionary state, its bounty. Hence art critic Clement Greenberg's horror of kitsch, which he understands to be both an aesthetic and a political degradation.[10]

In its more consumerist, less overtly statist form, kitsch drips with gold-plated sculptures of puppies, forty-foot plaster casts of Paul Bunyan complete with ax and he-man smile; it features zirconium-studded quilts of Michael Jackson, purple pillows embossed with pink angels, images that turn popular attachments into maudlin reliquaries. Real emotions are dampened into ersatz devotion.

Part IV

While it would be impossible for this or any single book to take up all the various things meant by politics in relation to contemporary art practices, I do mean for the book to provide a catalogue of significant range. And so, the book is arranged thus:

Chapter 2, "The Politics of Visibility: Lurie and Rancière," considers Jacques Rancière's notion that the politics of dissent are about issuing forth new forms of visibility to challenge the state by bringing to light its fault lines and forms of exclusion. This Rancière calls dissent. Emancipatory politics are always also an aesthetics for Rancière, since the substance of dissent is for him changing the terms of the sensible (of sensibility). Through a close reading of the work of the Cape Town photographer David Lurie, the chapter seeks to show that, once suitably revised, Rancière's idea finds its perfect home in characterizing one of the great possibilities of photography—its ability to render visible that which is otherwise consigned to darkness within a democratic (or other) dispensation.

Chapter 3, "Art and the Mining of Diamonds: Kentridge, Modisakeng, and What Is Meant by Politics," explores visual art's capacity to encompass a system as complex as that of mining in South Africa. Drawing on the work of William Kentridge, but also on the installations of his younger South African colleague, Mohau Modisakeng, the chapter asks in what kinds of ways their arts are capable of "addressing" or encompassing this complex socioeconomic system, and what it might mean to think of these forms of "address" as political. A variety of political concepts of relevance to contemporary art come into play, from notions of agency to those of disturbation, and to the claiming of a voice in public life. I try to distinguish these from what I think Kentridge really does, which is to make work that ruminates on political violence and its traumatic afterlife rather than staking any political position beyond a clear anti-colonialism and skepticism about the grandiose certainties of the colonizer. Rumination carries political hope.

Chapter 4, "The Politics of the Witness: Georges Gittoes," concerns the difficulties of visual art in taking up the humanitarian position of *witnessing*, given the domination of the media (TV news, the internet) to flash the world in all its traumatic intensity across the screens of the world in the manner of "sound bites." What kind of struggle is at stake in visual art to achieve an alternate and perhaps better way of claiming the witness position? What kind of innovation is required? I ask this of Australian artist George Gittoes. I also ask: What does it show about the political limitations of visual art that he has gravitated to film and digital media?

Chapter 5, "Virulent Nationalism and the Politics of Offense: The NEA 4," begins with the case of the NEA 4 in the 1990s—four edgy American artists who had their grants taken away by the National Endowment for the Arts on account of what the (right-wing) American Senate and Congress at the time considered the offensive character of their work. The interesting part is that each of these four artists *aimed to give offense*—this in the name of pungent dissent. So, these questions follow: When and how is offense justified? How may it be negotiated? What is its relation to democratic dissent? What are its aesthetic liabilities? What should best be the role of the state with respect to freedom of expression when offense is on the table? (And what kind of offense, since there are many.)

Chapter 6, "Literature and the Politics of the Truth Commission: Dorfman and Coetzee," is the only chapter concerned with literature, whose political capacities are sharply contrasted with those of visual art. The chapter reads J. M. Coetzee and Ariel Dorfman in relation to the democratic transitional instrument of the Truth Commission, asking what literature is called upon to do at a moment of democratic transition. The chapter seeks a new way of understanding the complex demands of transitional justice, which, of necessity, idealize the democratic future and the role of the instruments of transition in bringing that future about, generating utopian energy. But which also leave the lives of many of those victims of the earlier regime these instruments are meant to help, unacknowledged and even more traumatized in spite of best efforts. This calls for the corrective mechanism of literature, whose debates with these transitional instruments may be called political, while also placing politics to one side in the name of the acknowledgment of private life. This corrective mechanism is also crucial to the forging of new canons of free speech at the end of censorship. Especially when the books in question generate national debate.

Chapter 7, "Identity Politics in a Consumerist World," is an interrogation of the role of identity politics in contemporary art. The chapter begins by acknowledging the importance of identity politics for the project of emancipation. And in this regard focuses on the derivation of contemporary identity politics from earlier, politically utopian avant-garde practices. The chapter then turns to the America of the 1970s and 1980s, which remakes the avant-gardes in the light of identity politics, focusing on the *critique of representation* and solidarity building for stereotyped, marginalized, and/ or excluded groups. (Judy Chicago's *Dinner Party* is brought to the table of this dinnertime conversation.) The chapter then turns to a basic liability of identity politics today, which is to turn identity into a *form of capital*, a currency which is meant to guarantee value in the cultural marketplace in virtue of who you are. This inflation of capital, or self-capitalization, meant to replace aesthetic excellence by *self* as the source of value in art, then may fuse with narcissism and consumerism, not to mention celebrity culture to turn identity into a brand or market value.

Chapter 8, "Artworld/Art Market Politics: Manet to Banksy," the second about markets and art, explores the Gramscian idea of hegemony—how capital markets are able to incorporate that which criticizes or eludes them, rebranding political edginess as market value. It is also about the way markets create celebrity and how this cashes out in terms of price and prestige.

The final two chapters of the book turn back to the history of philosophical aesthetics considered in relation to politics that is initially explored in Chapter 1. Chapter 9, "Autonomy as Negotiation: Mozart

Reconsidered," explores the legacy of thinking about autonomy that has come down to us from the eighteenth century, and how this legacy is, in fact, out of sync with some of the greatest aesthetic work of the eighteenth century, which can stand as a model for aesthetics in relation to politics today. Through a reading of Mozart's *Marriage of Figaro*, I seek to show how that opera presents a better idea of autonomy than the philosophical traditions I discuss, which have their origin in the same century as Mozart's. On my reading, Mozart's opera presents autonomy as a condition achieved through struggle (in the opera, largely through subterfuge) and measured in relation to the quality and character of human relationships as these encode power (in the house of the Count). Autonomy is forged contextually through dialogic relations of a sociopolitical nature (in the opera, relations of servitude and family under a single roof). Autonomy is about how individual liberty squares with collective life, even if the domain of the collective is restricted to the house of the Count. The moral: There is no individual freedom or autonomy apart from the collective. Autonomy is always dialogic.

Chapter 10, "Film, the Individual, and the Collective," the book's final chapter, pursues the avant-garde position that emphasizes the collective over the cult of the individual. The chapter is partly a conversation with Walter Benjamin, who argued that new technologies of reproducibility would permanently wither that aesthetic cult, replacing it with an art dedicated to the emancipation of the collective. This would have to do with the withering away of what Benjamin called the aura of individual things and individual experiences. I argue that film, the most relevant example of reproducibility for Benjamin, rather remakes the aesthetics of the aura in a way that continues that aesthetic cult, instead of permanently degenerating it as Benjamin thought and prophesied. Or rather film can go both ways, either remaking the old aesthetic cult of the individual in a way that makes it mass producible, or eschewing it. The chapter explores Hitchcock in contrast to the Russian avant-garde idea of film pursuant to this matter.

Running through these chapters is the question of the limits, as well as powers of the visual medium. But also, four other equally central ideas:

The first is about the *form* politics takes. Politics is about individual liberty posed in relation to the collective and its demands, and both in relation to the nation-state and market economy, or what is otherwise called political economy. This triad—liberty (or not), the collective (for whatever purpose), and the state/market (in whatever form)—is the domain of politics, the structural relations through which politics in modern societies play themselves out. And this is true for art as well as anything else. A basic assumption of this book is that we are unavoidably political animals;

everything we do or make, whether art, ideas, or manufactured goods, is made or imagined within the triad individual liberty/collective power/state and market or political economy. This book is structured around different situations in which this triad emerges in art. All art is, in one sense or another, political simply because everything in life is. The question is *how*, to what extent, with what degree of importance, for whom, and in what way exaggerated or deflated? Which is simply another way of asking: In what kind of ways (situations) is art political?

Second, art (like all other cultural items) gains political agency or force not in and of itself, as if it were a magic potion or bullet, but instead, only in virtue of a larger context that catalyzes it. It is the fit between the work of art and a larger context of trust, institutional commitment, state control, or global distribution that lends the artwork political power, whether direct agency to change the world or simply ideological power (which keeps the world order in place or shifts it but usually more slowly). Without that broader context, a work of art may be eloquent but without power, although its eloquence may play a role in empowerment.

Third, it is not simply that any work of art can become an object of *political analysis*, the kind of analysis that seeks to uncover its ideological function, the way it articulates racial, gendered, class, or other forms of systemic power, and so on. It is also that political analysis extends to entire aesthetic traditions, and not simply the avant-gardes that were obviously political in intent. Eighteenth-century aesthetic theory was set forth in alliance with the articulation and practice of individual liberty. Taste—the capacity for an individual to take pleasure in an object for its own sake—is meant to mirror the ideal of individual liberty, of a life scripted autonomously and valued for its own sake, as a natural right. Aesthetic experience, so understood as an encomium of pleasure, becomes an icon of individual liberty, a way for persons to take pleasure in their own capacities for life, liberty, and the pursuit of happiness. This is why the two final chapters each takes up an entire aesthetic tradition or legacy.

Fourth, contemporary art is not simply in the business of inheriting political traditions. It is about changing the very relation between aesthetics and politics. Which is why the writing of this book is an adventure, and not simply an exercise in moderation or restraint.

These four guiding ideas are variously emphasized by the book's chapters. Not every chapter takes up all of them, each focusing on some aspect or another.

I consider these guiding ideas for my book to be commonplaces. Many people will probably agree with them in the abstract. But sometimes, as the philosopher Ludwig Wittgenstein was at pains to point out, persons need to be reminded of what they already know by drawing out the implications of what they know in context. This is what I try to do in the book.[11]

Part V

A good part of my life has been lived in the fray of art and politics. My family collected modern art of India and had been embattled for decades in their quest to bring it to the serious attention of museums and galleries in what was then called "the West." I recall the great Indian modernist painter M. F. Husain visiting a New York gallery in the 1960s when abstract expressionism was the signature art of the moment and believed to be the culmination of art history with a capital H. The work is good, the gallery owner said, you can paint. So why don't you paint abstract? Why paint figurative? It's out-of-date. To which Husain replied: There is nothing abstract about 750 million people (now over a billion). Another gallery person told him: Your work will never sell; they'll think you're Jordanian (at that time King Hussein was in the public eye).

These guys were interested in what was selling in New York City. But I think behind their blithe write-off was something more insidious. A neocolonial belief widely held in the artworld until recently, a residue of colonial ideology according to which the native, once colonial now postcolonial, is destined to occupy a derivative position in modernity. For she exists in an endlessly repeated past, mired in tradition, and in a way that compromises her capacity to achieve innovation in modernity. The gift of European heritage and civilization that the colonizer offered the colonized was a gift that (according to colonial belief) the native could never master. Except by aping the master, that is, in some imitative way. The native would always occupy a degraded role in modernity. This ideology was a strategy to attach the native to the path set by Europe. Were the European to acknowledge that the native could be capable of finding her own path into modern life, this would empower her independence, which was exactly what colonialism did not want. And so, the native was taught that she was destined to a menial position in modern life. Taught by being treated that way—as a menial. This treatment of most of the world by the European (and later the American) remained in place in the cultural systems of most of the twentieth century. Husain's use of figurative art when the "serious world" of art history had moved on (to abstraction) was taken to be an example of a man condemned to lag behind the times.

My family encountered this attitude many times during the 1970s and well into the 1990s, although there were exceptions. And, I have to say the standard narrative of modernism believed at the time was Euro/America-centric. To the point where a famous art critic in New York, whom I will not name, once said to me: Diego Rivera doesn't count. Doesn't count for what, or whom, I asked. For Mexico? For cubism? For Latin American innovation? Answer: for the narrative of art history that defines what is of importance. Which has no interest in those things. I am pretty sure this critic held the stereotype of the inept and hysterical Hispanic, worthy of imperialistic conquest, which was exactly what America was doing at the time. Imperialism meant colonialism remained in place in a new form—that of Cold War territoriality. Or of talent off in a corner. Rivera could not count because Latin America didn't. This all computed to a refusal to countenance Rivera's voice, a voice that fused what he mastered in Europe (cubism, surrealism) with pre-Colombian culture and the Italian Renaissance fresco, the project being to call forth the emergent Mexican nation-state.

This problematic reception of modern Indian art in the halls of Europe and America was my personal introduction to the way larger ideologies shape artworld politics down to fine-grained details of interpretation: of what a work of art is about, its terms of originality, receptivity, imitation, the larger project into which it might partly or completely fit—in the case of modern Indian art, the interrelated projects of recovery of past traditions in new forms creatively melded with what was learned from European modernism, of nationalism, and later of national critique.[12]

My instruction in the politics of art continued through the three decades I have lived between America and South Africa, beginning in 1991, when I, American-born, began to spend time in South Africa with my wife, a South African–born, naturalized American who wished to return to her home country. 1991 was the moment when the talks between the African National Congress and the then National Party (guardians of the Apartheid state) began in Kempton Park, inaugurating the democratic transition and leading to the writing of the Interim Constitution of 1994, the first free and fair elections of that same year, the writing of the final Constitution of 1996 and the Truth and Reconciliation of 1996–9 (for more on these events, see Chapters 3 and 6). From 1996 to 2002, I held the post of Chair in Philosophy at the then University of Natal and wrote about the events of transition in real time. We remade the university, opening it to persons of color who quickly became two-thirds of the student body. At issue was the transformation of curriculum, research, and governance for a newly decolonizing African university in a context of inclusion (those formerly bereft of the chance to attend such universities on racist grounds), of massification (as majority populations poured into universities, overwhelming their capacity by number), of linguistic diversity (one-third of our students were native Zulu speakers), and of research (how should the university's commitments to social engagement be recalibrated with its abstract knowledge production or "blue sky research" for post-Apartheid South Africa, in what ways should the legacy of European thought be challenged and also preserved given the history of Eurocentrism) proved energizing and nearly intractable.

Those were years of high-risk-high-gain, approximating the permanent condition of modern art. South African art at that time found a variety of ways to respond to these tumultuous events, one of which was cross-pollination. The work of art became a laboratory for the fusion of materials assembled from across racial, cultural, and class divides into shimmering, hybrid wholes, as if art's border-crossings could serve as utopian exemplars for new and improved relations between formerly stratified peoples (across racial, cultural, and class lines). I have written at length about this in both *Cosmopolitan Aesthetics* and *Aesthetics, Arts and Politics in a Global World*.[13] I still write regularly for the South African newspapers (mostly online) and, since my wife and daughter live and work in film in Cape Town, I consider Cape Town my home, even if my other home is in Ann Arbor, Michigan. (For me the question of what a home is demands recalibration given the terms of my life.)

What I learned during thirty years of South African/American life is not merely a good deal about cultural politics at moments of regime change, but also something of how the globe looks through a *southern lens*. This lesson is in part that of necessity generating originality, as should be clear from the chapters in this book on South African art and on literature and the Truth Commission (Chapters 2, 3, and 6). But the lesson is also one of dependency—about how a place like South Africa, at the margins of the globe, moderately resourced, formerly colonial, depends on the global centers of Europe, America, China for markets and circulation in a way that puts special pressure on artists and cultural institutions (I wrote about this in *Cosmopolitan Aesthetics*, ch. 2).[14] Dependency is also about drainage, since the Global North continually extracts South Africans of talent to its far greater resourced institutions, creating a vacuum within the country constantly demanding to be filled. I have also written about this in *Aesthetics, Arts and Politics in a Global World* and *Cosmopolitan Aesthetics*.[15] But brain-drain also has its own silver lining, since it creates a diaspora of persons betwixt and between South Africa and the first world, who, being cosmopolitan, contribute original, hybridized, and critical ideas that are the result of their experiences betwixt-and-between. And South Africans who do not end up in the first world are nevertheless often highly globalized, since they have to look to the rest of the world for so much. This can also lead to cosmopolitanism.

Dependency is also a legacy of settler society (South Africa's) in which the English or Dutch settler gained authority over the native by claiming the badge of being European. Although most settlers would never visit the home country, they still identified themselves as *of it*, in a way that entitled them to "superiority" and power over native populations. Eurocentrism means dependence on elsewhere for identity, which proved deflationary for the settler's independence and innovation, since the settler usually thought of himself or herself as an adjunct to the home country (England, Holland). This sense of being a supplement or add-on from the margins led to a fair amount of happy cultural imitation. You wanted to paint like you were a Brit living in Dorset; it was what made you who you were or at least who you thought you were. This while the true condition of being a settler, also acknowledged in the history of South African art and culture, was that of being unsettled both in Europe (one was no longer of it) and in Africa (one's life there was naturalized but also alienated since one was permanently at odds with most of the population).

"Europeanness" became increasingly understood in the eighteenth and nineteenth centuries as a racial idea—the settler's badge for being white. During the Apartheid regime, segregated beaches, restaurants, toilets, universities, and so on, were referred to as "European" or "for Europeans only." The segregationist American south never referred to its whites-only facilities in this way; it would have been "un-American." But for the South African, European heritage remained the badge of self-recognition and authority, the key to racial identity. Even while the settler was often looked down upon in London or Amsterdam as a second-rate throwback, necessary to colonial rule but hardly au courant or capable of making new things. A kind of throwback.

The settler's internalized sense of being an add-on to Europe was very much in play when I worked at the University of Natal during the 1990s, since Eurocentrism was considered part of the problem, the thing that needed to change. Yet, dependency remained. We used to invite whoever was the current first world star to lecture us about the kind of theory and method we would need to advance ourselves down under (as it were), as if we were children in need of first world instruction. What we should have been doing was actively challenging the authority of such persons to respond to our context and aspirations. We existed in a state of misrecognition, thinking ourselves in need of instruction when, in fact, we were creatively responding to the tenor of the times with all kinds of new ideas and ways of doing things. These ideas and practices were at their best (as in the South African Truth and Reconciliation Commission and the Final Constitution) developed through global influence innovatively remade (again see Chapters 3 and 6).

Influence goes in both directions, north–south and south–north, or better, in every direction, like wind patterns. South Africa's Constitution and its Truth and Reconciliation Commission have both stood as moral exemplars to the world. While its failure to address horrendous inequality has not. Nor its post-Apartheid history of corruption.

More recently, the moral culture generated by South Africa and radiating out to the first world has been the Rhodes Must Fall campaign initiated at the University of Cape Town in 2015. Rhodes Must Fall began as a refusal of the culture of institutional racism, especially the legacy of colonial and Apartheid monuments. The highpoint of the student movement, before it turned into a fight around free education and then became violent, was the removal of the statue of Cecil Rhodes from its pride of place fronting the main hall of the university. This movement influenced Black Lives Matter in the United Kingdom (which is now removing its Rhodes statue from Oriel College, Oxford, where Rhodes scholars are housed). And in the United States, with its tearing down of statues to the Confederacy, its renaming of buildings and the like.

My point is that there has been a mismatch between the fact of innovation in post-Apartheid South African society and South Africa's sense of itself as marginal, imitative, and diminished. Even if now a new generation of Africans approach their land with a sense of sovereignty, confidence, and ability. Learning about how legacies of misrecognition play themselves out even in times of innovation was part of my political education, since it is about larger contexts of empire, colonies, and race. Politics are not simply about what you aim to achieve by making art, or creating new ideas or practices. They are about how the production of new things takes place in larger cultures of recognition or misrecognition that are the result of larger political shapes.

Husain used to say art follows politics, by which he meant that as soon as a nation-state achieves global significance on the economic and political stage, suddenly everyone looks at the art and culture with fresh eyes, finding signs of national power and authority in it in ways that they had never sought to do. Power conveys cultural authority, cultural excellence. The signature year for India was 1987, when Christie's brought the imprimatur of the London Auction House to Bombay with an auction of contemporary Indian art, having decided that India now had sufficient wealth and prominence on the international stage. Immediately, the prices of the art rose ten times and kept rising. And suddenly the art was no longer seen as second-rate, imitative, destined to fail on the international stage, because the nation was no longer seen that way, and the prices were too steep to ignore the issue of quality. And so, the neocolonial attitudes of the art world my family had encountered for decades quickly began to evaporate with India's ascendency as a state. The same would happen in China a decade later. This was also true of the Mandela years (the 1990s) when I lived and worked in South Africa, a country that had emerged from its Pariah status into moral flavor of the month, thanks to this saintly and stoic icon (Madiba) and the democratic transition. Suddenly, traditional and modernist South African art became of interest to Germany and the UK. And then it was dropped sometime late in the 1990s.

This surge of national power and international interest has contributed to the overcoming of the sense of abjection of which I spoke. African art is right now flavor of the month, this time continent-wide because global art markets have turned to it. But this is also about markets seeking new products for the global market. Art does not simply follow politics: it follows markets.

Between art, politics, and markets, this book is written. It is a product of my personal life, not simply my writing.

2

The Politics of Visibility: Lurie and Rancière

Part I

One of the reasons we need photographs is because we should meditate on things we pass every day in the city but do not notice. We do not notice because we are in motion or because we pass them every day and are acclimatized, or perhaps because they are not "framed," that is, highlighted. It is the stillness of a photo that solicits reflection on the shape of the everyday, its unique way of transposing visual intensities into questions of meaning. As if looking at a photograph, we see for the first time. This is one of photography's great possibilities, among the medium's great themes.

This ability to make visible that which eludes the social grasp is one of photography's chief ways of becoming political. And also, one of its chief ways of becoming *aesthetic*, since no one is interested in that which is made visible unless it is done in a compelling, absorptive, shocking, weirdly beautiful, and quite possibly innovative way. Not prettified of course, removing the dark blemishes of the world with a nail polish remover, as in Detroit ruin-porn or those too-too beautiful pictures of suffering (dogs and humans alike) that appear on charitable Christmas cards. But beautiful or striking enough to cast the ugliness of the reality portrayed in an uncanny way. Beautiful or striking enough to break through the surfeit of images about which Susan Sontag writes (see Chapter 4), an oversaturation that dulls the receptive mind.

> There are those who live in darkness.
> And those who live in light.
> And those who live in darkness.
> They quickly drop from sight
> (Bertolt Brecht, *The Threepenny Opera*, my very loose translation)

In what sense is the bringing to light of those dropped from sight political? Not in the sense of agency (photos usually have little), nor of proposing specific political solutions. A photo of degradation may challenge complacency but is not as a norm something that *asserts* a specific political position, unless words are also there, or in the background context, to give the photo added propositional content. Then in what sense exactly?

Jacques Rancière, whose work is an excellent invitation to think through these particular photographic possibilities of the medium, puts it in this way:

> Suitable political art would ensure, at one and the same time, the production of a double effect: the readability of a political signification and a sensible or political shock caused conversely, by the uncanny, by that which resists signification. In fact, this ideal effect is always the object of a negotiation between opposites, between the readability of the message that threatens to destroy the sensible form of art and the radical uncanniness that threatens to destroy all political meaning.[1]

The work of art (here, photo) must balance political ideas, concepts, and narrative with aesthetic character—the character of an uncanny arrangement of the world into strange stillness, where space, figure, materiality become lopsided, strange, resisting concepts altogether in the manner of the beautiful or the sublime conceived by the eighteenth century. The photo compels and succeeds at the task of making the invisible visible only if it compels the imagination, shocks, deranges, threatens to obliterate meaning in the strangeness of its form. Art is political in virtue of its aesthetics.

In framing this idea, Rancière is among the few to have tried to reconcile avant-garde and eighteenth-century aesthetic thinking. On the one hand, he returns to the central eighteenth-century notion of the aesthetic, a term taken over from the ancient Greek term "aeskesis," meaning sense perception, as part of that century's reframing of aesthetic experience as first and foremost sensual experience, the activation of the senses into the capacity for taste, the ability to take pleasure in an object. For the eighteenth century, aesthetic experience is, we have already seen, apolitical, because an encomium detached from the world outside it, a way for the free agent to celebrate their capacity for free choice by deploying it in an experience that shares the absolute autonomy that their freedom demands. The autonomy of sensual experience from all else, what Kant calls pleasure taken apart from a concept, allows the field of aesthetics to mirror that of individual liberty (and is in this unique sense ideological).

Rancière returns to this notion of the aesthetic but completely changes its meaning in the light of the avant-gardes. The aesthetic demands a shock, something defamiliarizing to perception, a whirl of reality formed into a work of art that unhinges, but also proves magnificent, beautiful, sublime, uncanny, weird, given the darkness of the world the work is meant to reveal if doing a political job. This emphasis on shock, defamiliarization, the challenging of perception in a way that demands cognitive reflection is a hallmark of avant-garde theory and practice. It is the combination of shock and beauty, along with political significations subliminal in the work of art, that is, the avant-garde ideal.

There is much more to the intersection of aesthetics and politics than this in Rancière's thinking. At bottom, there is no politics without an aesthetic for him. And the politics of emancipation are totally dependent on the creation of new forms of aesthetics, that is, new forms of sensuous/emotional visibility.

Rancière comes from the Parisian left, from 1968 Jolie Mai with its anarchist refusal of French politics and culture and its celebratory hallucinations of utopia. An early contributor to the 1965 volume *Reading Capital* (with Louis Althusser, Etienne Balibar, Roget Establet, and Pierre Marchery).[2] Rancière broke with Althusser over May 1968, perhaps the defining political event of his intellectual generation. To those like Rancière who grew up on student demonstrations, taking to the streets, manning the barricades, proclaiming the future in the manner of anarchic prophecy, politics is understood as resistance to "the system." "The system" is a political form understood as essentially a form of oppression, in which inequality is built into its very structure, along with control.

Rancière calls this form of oppression "the police." Its enforcement of structural inequality manifests itself in two ways for this French intellectual (and others). First, the system kills thought, imagination, the ability to think otherwise/against it. This is the brutal function of ideology. It grinds the spirit down, the inquiring mind, the imagination with its capacity to envision alternatives. Second, the system creates and sustains inequality in part thanks to forms of visibility and invisibility—who is foregrounded, who remains invisible or unacknowledged, whose world and work can appear in the right light, whose can't. These politics of visibility are related to those of enunciation. Who can speak, what can they say, whose words do not make their way into social realities, who is capable of speaking within the system.

Politics, by which Rancière means opposition politics, is not a matter of debate of the kind guided by regulative ideas of rational consensus *within* an institutional system of democratic norms. Aims of rational consensus of the kind embraced by liberals and social democrats from John Rawls to Jurgen Habermas are considered by him as ways the system diffuses challenges to it by bringing criticism within its political control. This ideal of speaking within the system in the name of its perfectibility is precisely what Rancière and much of Paris 1968 rejects. For Rancière, politics happens when, and only when, the system is challenged by new visibilities or forms of speech, which disrupt its principles of exclusion and indifference and invisibility and subaltern voiceless-ness. And also disrupts its *manner* of making things visible: the joint contribution of Fox TV, Reality TV, and the cult of celebrity and the omnipresence of wealth, the aggression, and oversimplification of Instagram, not to mention the pageantry of churches and schools, to the American vision of justice, the good life, and so on. Here "visibility" goes beyond the literal meaning of what you actually see, to become something like what Ludwig Wittgenstein calls "seeing-as," a way of knowing, encountering, imagining, viewing the world. This is the Althusserian idea of ideology—less a system of beliefs (although that is part of it) and more a way of encoding persons into a way of imagining and doing things. Ideology is action informed by a sense of things. At the core of every political system is a visual system or what he calls "distribution" of the sensible. Aesthetics is at the core of politics. It is this that must be rescripted for political change to take place.

Rancière believes this is why art plays a privileged role in the politics of dissent because it shares with the political a capacity to make visible those realities otherwise unseen, unknown, unconscious, or bypassed.[3] To put them front and center as a public challenge. It is for this reason that aesthetics must play an essential role in any political emancipation. For part of the project of emancipation is to make visible that which is repressed or ignored or under the radar screen.

I want to suggest that his view is particularly suitable for the medium of photography, since *making visible* is a hallmark of how photos become political gestures or instruments. No doubt this is one of the key ways in which *photography can and does become political*. Even if he himself mostly writes about avant-garde painting when he turns to art.

Part II

I will raise questions about Rancière's view later in this chapter. First, I'd like to illustrate its power by turning to the work of a photographer I much admire—the Cape Town artist David Lurie. One could choose any number of others if one wished: Salgado, Gursky, David Goldblatt, Shirin Neshat. Let Lurie's work stand for the kind of thing this genre of artist does. But Lurie's art is particularly apt, at least his book of photos *Writing the City*, because it seeks to make visible not only life otherwise less noticed but also political inscriptions that arise organically throughout the city of Cape Town, and which demand meditation. And remember Rancière's remark: "Suitable political art would ensure … the readability of a political signification and a sensible or political shock caused conversely, by the uncanny, by that which resists signification."[4]

May I begin very concretely with a single photo: David Lurie's capstone image in *Undercity: The Other Cape Town*. The photo is of an abandoned lot in Woodstock (a mixed-use industrial area of the city). The photo is mostly of the lot, with a bit of weed growing in the dirt, empty apart from a tire and piece of pipe that seem to have formed a "relationship" (the pipe "touches" the tire). At the back of the lot is the side of Cassiem's shop, with its signage painted on the first story of this three-story building, along with an oversized pair of blue lips. Above the signage for the shop on this bare concrete side of the building is painted an enormous hand (it is plastered onto the upper two stories). It's finger points to a flag of Palestine (a faded tricolor), plastered below. The flag has "Free Palestine" scribbled onto it. The hand is absurdly large relative to the size of the building, an odd building because of its top, which resembles a fairy tale version of the Arabian Nights, with a latticed stone balustrade on the turrets like a royal crown. Along the back of a row of shacks to the right of the abandoned lot are painted childlike images of animals and people. The houses or shops across the street from Cassiem's shop on the left are in better repair and painted an orange-red. The photo is a meditation on idiomatic city architecture in disrepair, but also on public protest—at least for those in the neighborhood who might walk past this corner of Woodstock.

Figure 2.1 David Lurie, *Free Palestine* (from *Undercity: The Other Cape Town*, Hatje Cantz), 2017, hand-painted mural by Gaia. Image courtesy of the artist.

Lurie's concern with architectural idiom and how meaning is locally broadcast in the city has a long tradition in film, photography, and painting dating to the nineteenth century, to Baudelaire's *flaneur*, that denizen of the arcades and public parks, of restaurants and the effervescent entertainment of Paris at night, a wanderer who tastes, samples, and consumes the city in a kind of intoxication. Lovers of modernity include the impressionists who thrive in the frisson and energy of the city, tracking its crowds, boulevards, department stores, its women with parasols, summer fetes in the Luxembourg Gardens, turning of leaves in the Tuilleries. Impressionism is dazzled by the speed of horses, the arrival and departure of trains, the steam glazing the sky as the train disappears toward a country destination, above all by the day in the country at the boathouses, on the banks of rivers, and in the forests outside of Paris where the city dweller might go for the day, bringing home memories on the night train that can then become eternalized by the impressionist's brush.

Lurie is a flaneur with a difference. For there was little urban darkness in the French artists' lexicon. The art historian T. J. Clark pointed out long ago[5] that the impressionist removed the grit and poverty from their portrayals of the dank environs of Paris, from that Parisian Woodstock through which the Sunday devotees of the country would have passed on the train to reach their cheerful destination. The impressionists (with the exception of Degas) seldom painted the working classes and their dwellings and workplaces. Abandoned lots were never featured.

Darkness entered photography in the anguish of the America of the Civil War whose wounded were photographed by Matthew Brady; later, in the New York of Jacob Riis and Alfred Steiglitz who photographed the city's immigrant poor in their tenement houses, their rough and unrewarding labor, their faces full of strain but also aspiration. Steiglitz showed them arriving on the bows of ships, past the Statue of Liberty to a New York where they hoped to achieve lives unimaginable to their elders. They reveled in dreams that with luck their children might actually realize but that to these new immigrants would be challenged by disease, poverty, and brutality, the brutality of a city of skyscrapers Steiglitz so powerfully photographed like glorious, but also implacable cathedrals of power.

South African modernity has had plenty of brutality, from the Boer War through the Apartheid state to the present, and there is a long tradition of documentary and journalistic photography aiming to capture another kind of modern architecture than the soaring cathedrals of New York— the architecture of the Apartheid state. This architecture included the pass laws, the Bantustans, and the forced removals; it included the detentions without trial, the executions, the banning and burning. It was the subject of Santu Mofokeng, David Goldblatt, Paul Weinberg, Jurgen Schadeberg, Ernest Cole, and other photographers who gave documentary art a moral and political end—that of exposure, placing negatives in developing solution until images otherwise invisible or ignored became dislocating calls to acknowledgment.

David Lurie's fascination, or duty, is to capture the raw, unyielding nature of Cape Town, a city set between two dazzling oceans against a mountain covered in floral abundance and pristine, azure light. Cape Town is as multilayered as Paris was in the nineteenth century, a city of the spume of enjoyment but also poverty, leaking sewage, underfed children, homelessness, violence. Cape Town is a place of immaculately refurbished heritage buildings and company gardens, of high design elegance and world-class cuisine, a city filled with advertising shoots and fashion models, a city of coffee, wine, and the guided tour. But Cape Town is also a scrappy city, disheveled, unyielding, and melancholy. It has the melancholy of homeless people asleep in the company gardens, people whose leathery, angular faces are the spectral remnants of disappeared Khoi and San peoples. Its melancholy is the bulldozed, empty area that used to be District Six from which a generation was forcibly removed, sometimes to shacks now decaying like leaking batteries. This is the Cape Town where the azure light does not reach, or reaches in unbearable intensity: abandoned lots, underpasses, of raw and decrepit concrete whose very texture bespeaks roughness, brutality, implacability, cheap labor, the Cape Town of gloomy days and weeks when the Mediterranean light disappears and the city is blanketed in dank cloud and bone-chilling rain. The mountain then becomes invisible, as if the city had lost a limb.

David Lurie is a photographer of the melancholic city, a Cape Town apart from the touristic Five Star Hotel, designer chef and architect, the fashion shoot, model and the beautiful white mansion. Their cheerful inhabitants pass by degradation every day when they drive into town or Woodstock; we all do. The mountain helps; it is a narcotic, dulling the moral conscience into an intoxicated, mesmeric haze. Cape Town is a city of contrasts between the splendid and the decayed.

Shot mostly in cloud or after rain, with brown water seeping into mud, his Cape Town is a place of deserted spaces, of homeless people living in drainage pipes or underpasses. Lurie will photograph a building, a sign, a highway from midrange, often leaving a space of disheveled pavement, empty lots overgrown with thin grass, dank water between the buildings or figures photographed and the viewer, as if separating the one from the other. It is the way buildings and people are set off, or contained, by dead space at the front of the photo that matters. Sometimes the space is so empty that one feels he is photographing a city from which everyone has fled.

Lurie's study of signage is precisely a way of tracing the human voice, the public gesture, as it broadcasts itself across the divide. As if to say: *I too am part of the world, I too exist.*

But to whom are these voices speaking when they paint on walls and write on flags? To whom are these public gestures of graffiti, poster, and drawing addressed? And do they make it across the divide of empty or dead space? To live in a city is to be part of its cries for communication while also as far from them as the living are from the dead. The visual question is whether the speech, the signage, crosses these divides to reach a larger colloquy of listeners, or whether empty space atrophies the message, dampening it, turning its mighty phraseology into gestures contained by neighborhood or freeway or underpass. Sometimes I feel Lurie's camera is a medium whose purpose is to be a spirit guide getting us in touch with those voices "on the other side of the urban divide" as if in a photographic séance. South Africa was always a place where the comfort zones of cities were artificially separated from the centers of pain and dilapidation, even if, Lurie shows us, you stop at any underpass on Orange Street or downtown and find someone asleep wrapped in an old blanket in the midday heat. Millions live in shacks on the Cape Flats. The township is an Apartheid creation to which populations of color were forcibly relocated during Apartheid to remove them from contact with cities declared white/pristine. Many—or parts of many, since the townships are now economically variable, with middle- and even upper-middle-class neighborhoods—remain impoverished. Their residents lack access to water and sanitary facilities.

And so, the signs "declare" at the edge of the highway: "The people shall share in the country's wealth."

This quote is from the Freedom Charter of 1955, which declares that the land and resources of South Africa belong to all the people. Rights are being demanded that are yet to arrive.

Lurie's photo *Woodstock*, also from *Undercity*, shows us the back of a building plastered with a people's mural of fists raised—a mural of a multitude struggling for freedom and prosperity. The mural is reflected in the dirty brown water in back of this building, as if the echo of this peoples' tableaux finds itself dampened or drowned in the brown muck. The image seems to say, *the people speak, but this is as far as their voices travel. To the dank water behind the timber factory where it is painted.*

The photo's formal arrangement is strange and unnerving because of the beautifully abstract and asymmetrical angles of the building reflected in the water. It is a transient relationship that, unless caught by his lens, might quickly disappear as the light changes or the water evaporates. In its own way, this *pas de deux* between building and water is an *impression*

Figure 2.2 David Lurie, *The People Shall Share in the Country's Wealth*, 2015, Khayelisha, Cape Flats, mural by Faith47 (from *Undercity: The Other Cape Town*, Hatje Cantz), 2017. Image courtesy of the artist.

Figure 2.3 David Lurie, *Woodstock, Lower Main Road* (from *Undercity: The Other Cape Town*, Hatje Cantz), 2017. Image courtesy of the artist.

for an impressionist painter (although not in the blithe spirit of the impressionists).

A photographer is always a denizen of chance. It is what makes his or her work arresting and inviting for reflection. We feel we are discovering a strange and momentary revelation of meaning when we study such photos and are lucky to do so. It is through this imaginative encounter with a chance moment eternalized in the photographic frame, rather than through some didactic statement, that Lurie's moral questioning arises. His questions are about who speaks, how far their voices go in this city, about who bothers to look, and what they see when they do, about the omnipresent invisible. These are also political questions.

To compel recognition is an artistic achievement, having to do with the strange stillness of the photo and its visual arrangement of parts. But a photo can also offset a face, a person in a way that compels the study of them. Lurie's homeless people are often photographed full frontal and close-up, their faces unyielding, and not without dignity.

It was Eduard Manet's purpose when he wished to disturb the cheerful consumerism of the bourgeois art world, to bring us confounding figures about whom the more we study, the less we seem to know them. His clochards (street people) are painted full frontal, like a Lurie photo. Manet alternately called these figures "Ragpickers" and "Philosophers," inviting ambiguity. Are they really "philosophers" he was asking, cynically in retreat from the world, choosing to live in caves like Diogenes because of some dark knowledge of the world they possess? Are they aggressive, or sullen, bold, or simply hung over and beaten down? Is their gaze a challenge? Or are they past caring? Manet's point was that we do not know who these people are, across the divide. They live off remains and we treat them like remains. Lurie is, I think, making a similar point about these motherless denizens of the mother city. To acknowledge that one doesn't know these people is the first part of respecting them.

Lurie's photos share one thing with the posters, graffiti, and wall paintings they so often picture. It is size. Size matters, and Lurie's photos are expansive, sometimes one and a half meters in length, enough to give a sense of panorama. His photos are anything but intimate wallet-sized pictures of wife or child, friend or parent. Nor are they photos to be studied up close and personal, in the manner of certain abstract art photos. You study them horizontally as if reading a street sign or wall poster from across the street. They mirror the city and are part of it. A Lurie photo could be expanded and then placed on the side of a building in downtown Cape Town almost like an advert. But its point is the opposite, to turn panorama into an object of slow and quiet reflection, to interrupt the bustle of time with a kind of solitude, revealing a city that is empty or slow, abandoned or shut down for the night, or waking to early-morning light, not yet strident. Lurie's city sleeps or exists in a state of late-night insomnia, unable to drift into unconsciousness, awake in the dark.

In most of the photos, there is no sun but rather dull cloud, or dank water after rain. *Morning after Dark* captures the city before the intensity of daylight has had a chance to arise, at that moment when night gives way to the soft oranges and bluish-grays of the early morning. These pictures have a color palette that is very unusual for the Cape, which is usually photographed (and likewise experienced) in the vivid reds, purples, yellows, and pinks of the Bo-Kaap (the Cape Malay Quarter), in the kaleidoscopic colors of a mountain view, as the pure, vivid, and highly saturated light that Cape Town shares with San Francisco, Morocco, and the Italian Amalfi coast. Here the light is subdued, uncertain, clouded. The palette is of dull concrete and subtle green and orange. Sometimes it is off-white sky against gray concrete. But in some of these photos, there is recompense, a sense—when the city is seen panoramically from the Tafelberg Road that runs along the highest point of the city like a mountain's shoelace—that these soft colors in an incipient, early-morning sunlight are grace for the weary, for the multitude of people who have not been graced with the rewards of the South African democratic dream.

Part III

These people who paint walls behind shops and on the sides of the highways of Cape Town aim for visibility. Their languages are those of public dissent from a democracy that does not otherwise pay them attention, refusing to share its goods, consigning them to voices spoken apart from the usual democratic channels of parliament, provincial government, or newsprint. Their desire is to make their concerns and aspirations—their world—visible to a larger public, so as to be able to say to themselves, "I refused to be consigned to the indignity of silence even if those driving to work may pass my signage every day without seeing." This desire is a kernel of democratic dissent from a system that offers little. It is politics by other means than those of institutional democracy (voting, parliament, government and its ministries, point of view voiced in the mainstream media).

We have seen that for a philosopher like Jacques Rancière, such dissent is true and only real meaning of politics, namely a refusal to lay down and die and instead to urge new forms of visibility on a society.

My problem with Rancière's position is not its emphasis on visibility, but rather his monolithic vision of the closed concrete walls of a democracy. I am never quite sure who speaks from *within* a system, demanding inclusiveness, and who speaks from outside it, as if outside the front doors of a police station where there is no more access to real democracy (rights, opportunities) than there is entry into Kafka's law. Nor is it so very clear who speaks in the name of crashing the walls of the democracy down, and who for transformation from *within*. (This theme will be amplified in the next chapter.)

There are two ways one can take the idea of a police state, usually combined in any totalitarian dispensation. First, the police create and enforce walls, clearly demarcating inside versus outside the state. Albert O. Hirschman long ago wrote in a number of books[6] about the central fact of closure for nondemocratic states, which either restrict entrance or exit on the basis of ideological conformity, usually barring persons from leaving at all. As a person who risked his life to get European Intelligentsia out of France during the early days of the Second World War, Hirschman knew about this first-hand. A fascist or totalitarian state turns its borders into the walls of a prison. The obvious example being the USSR and, until the collapse of the Berlin Wall, Eastern Europe. Few democracies can claim this degree of control over populations, in spite of Donald Trump's desire to "build a wall to keep them out," an aspiration taken directly from Germany and Russia of the old days.

Second, the idea of democracy as a police state is in a Foucauldian sense about the endless inventions of new systems of knowledge and power, from law to ideology to ritual to the mythologization of heritage in order to subdue, intimidate, tame, and control populations through arrest, stereotyping, exclusion, fear, and such tactics of bullying with an aim to subdue dissent from within, virtually crushing it.

As to the first, few *democracies* close borders in this way, nor can they.

As to the second, the claim that democracies ever come close to achieving panoptic control, or even entirely aim to, is undefended and frankly indefensible. It is a fantasy of a monolith where rights, urban life (which resists control), and markets are subservient to—or secretly articulate in spite of themselves—police authority. Even Foucault was clear that no society is ever complete in this form of control; it is always generating resistance and in a way that blurs the borders between resistance from the inside or the outside. Democracies seek walls and internal controlling mechanisms, but usually only totalitarian regimes such as the Soviet Union succeed in creating them. And that is just the physical part. One requires, in addition to the police, a security system capable of identifying and capturing those who "speak against the system" and an entire system of knowledge and power of the kind alluded to above—something not even the most horrifying regimes could entirely succeed in doing (East Germany with its Stasi, Nazi Germany with the SS). Once a democratic dispensation of any kind is in place, the porousness of dissent within, as opposed to without, is capable of being neither identified nor policed, given any modicum of free speech.

So, I really don't know if Gaia, the painter of "Free Palestine," is speaking from the inside or outside, indeed if that is the best metaphor for radical dissent—inside versus outside. One should rather say this. There is at any time some kind of systematic form of exclusion operative with any given democracy (short of its complete emancipation, which has never happened). Along with hidden forms of control deep in the state apparatus. At any given time, some persons and some ideas *are* on the outside; somebody is prevented from speaking, from exercising rights and opportunities; somebody is marginalized and arrested. Somebody, not everybody, and this somebody must become visible to the society if it has the slightest interest in being better: in emancipation. Insofar as art participates in this goal of acknowledgment, of making something visible, it is political in that way.

This is really all Rancière needs to make the point about the importance of art in "making visible." (Although it is insufficient for his own monolithic view of democracy.)

The voices Lurie discovers in exclamation point across the city do *not* find representation within South African democracy, three decades into its history. These are excluded persons. I think Lurie intends to make that case photographically and succeeds. Government has done far too little to create conditions of social mobility and dignity for the majority of citizens in spite of the rights mandated by the South African Constitution, which include the right to health, a house, a job, and far more. The failure of multiparty democracy twenty-five years into the South African dispensation has licensed astonishingly deep corruption within the African National Congress, which has governed the country without serious opposition during this period, thanks to its struggle credentials from the past. South Africa remains the most unequal society in the world, with the largest GINI coefficient. Land reform is stalled and uncertain. State President Cyril Ramaphosa has vowed to end corruption and to redistribute land in a way that is viable. He may just succeed in doing so, but the jury is out as to if and when. Public infrastructure is collapsing, thanks to long years of corruption and mismanagement. There is no serious plan on the table for job creation, for boosting the quality of primary education (which in rural areas is beyond degraded), or for the creation of a banking system friendly to aspiring entrepreneurs without means, which are keys to the build-up of a broad middle class. Powerful forces within Ramaphosa's own party fiercely resist the curtailing of corruption.

And so, at this moment in time, Rancière's picture of a closed system is correct for *these people in this democracy.*

The jury remains out as to whether the voices Lurie photographs are voices for revolutionary change, or rather for democratic inclusion. I think they can be taken either way, as can many voices of dissent at the margins, depending on one's view of what a democracy is and what it includes. One way to take these voices is to say: They speak from outside the system, aiming to disrupt it. But one can also say: This is what South African democracy is—that which veers between parliamentary/formal process and the voices of the outcasts or invisible. Let's say we are unsure of their politics, of their conceptions of what a democracy is and should be. But let's also say these are voices that desire inclusion, by way of dissent, and also significant social change. Their purpose is to achieve visibility, which means *to be listened to* and to do so apart from the institutional systems of the South African democracy that have little interest in them—ministries, government, parliament, the media, and the like. Photography is perhaps even more clear about politics than Rancière, because it understands that one need not take sides on this question of inside-outside to make visible that which is demanded in the name of justice.

Lurie's photographs are not unlike the street messages and graffiti he shoots. They are a plea to make a fault line in South African democracy visible. They do not take sides about more luminous political questions of "the fate of democracy," revolution, and so on. Lurie's photos also are acts of dissent from the democratic margins. Whether outside or inside, "the system" is, contra Rancière, unclear. And perhaps finally not so important. More important is the question of who listens.

3

Art and the Mining of Diamonds: Kentridge, Modisakeng, and What Is Meant by Politics

Part 1

I begin with an insight loosely derived from the Hegelian tradition: the now commonplace thought that not all things are possible in any given medium of art. To know a medium of art is to know the kind of things it can do and what is beyond its limits. If one wants to compose a work of art speaking to the way inequality is built into global capitalism as markets search for cheaper and cheaper labor, abandoning one location to ruination in the search for the next, it is unlikely that one will choose to write a flute solo. Maybe a documentary film or novel or perhaps installation art with video might do better.

The idea (loosely derived from Hegel through his very creative twentieth-century interpreter Arthur Danto) is not simply that different media have different possibilities. It is also that at a certain point in modern life, reality becomes too complex for art in *any* medium to express, represent, embody, at which point art gives the job over to philosophy. Or, one may add, to history, economics, political writing, and so on. This is interesting because one might think a system of extraction—and here my example is South African mining—has exactly that level of complexity. Too much for art to capture except obliquely, since the system involves labor, sometimes racially coded, international economy, profit, inequality, and what I call the aesthetics of the diamond. Too much for visual art anyway, if not for documentary film or the novel.

But let's assume that visual art will have real difficulty addressing a system as complicated as extraction conceptually. Or let's assume that, for visual art, even work as complicated as visual installation with various components, some textual, in order to address complex conceptual questions of this kind head on, the work will end up something closer to a philosophy or economics or history book, in which case why bother with the installation? What does it add? There has to be some value addition that makes it worth the effort as some kind of art. Meaning has to be, in Arthur Danto's words, embodied in the work's visual texture, not added on like a price tag. I will return to this point toward the end of the chapter. Here the question is rather: In what ways may visual art still speak to that system with political force without turning itself into a proxy for philosophy, economics, or history? There are various things to unpack here.

Since I will unpack them in the light of South African art, a bit of context is wanted for those not familiar with the events of the democratic transition.

The history of modern South Africa is in many ways a history of extraction. Diamonds were discovered in 1871 on Colesberg Kopje at Vooruitzigt, the farm belonging to the De Beers brothers. Almost immediately after the discovery of diamonds on the De Beers farm, the great pit in Kimberley began to be excavated, leading to a free for all of Rhodesian proportion, and in 1899 to the Boer War, an invention of Cecil Rhodes to claim the diamonds and the gold from the independent Boer Republic in the Transvaal.[1] When the Boers successfully resisted the redcoats marching through the Veldt wearing the plumage of war like white and red peacocks (all they lacked were diamonds on their lapels), Lord Kitchener was brought in to sort matters out for the British. Which he did through his brutal policy of slash and burn, ruining Boer farms so that nothing would ever grow again and placing Boer women and children in concentration camps. The concentration camp, originally called, euphemistically, "refugee camp," was invented by the British for this war. Ensuing Boer ruination would then lead to the resurgent politics of Boer resentment and finally to the Apartheid state.

In order to build a workforce of black labor for the growing mining industry at the beginning of the twentieth century, the Land Act of 1913 was passed, which disallowed black Africans from owning 90 percent of the land of their country. Apartheid would later compound their misfortune by disenfranchising them from South African citizenship, thanks to the tactic of declaring black Africans citizens of the "Bantustans," empty tracts of land far from cities and employment. This led to the pass laws and the creation of the Dompas, the pass book that all people of color were required to hold and have stamped, in the manner of a travel visa, should they wish to work in the cities or travel the country. The Land Act led to the breakup of African families as men were forced to make the long journey to work in the mines, staying in bleak single-sex hostels far away from families visited once a year. These hostels later became breeding grounds for HIV/AIDS (thanks to prostitution). Those who worked in the alluvial diamond fields of Namibia, owned by De Beers and fenced off with razor wire, were strip-searched every night before being allowed to leave. The mining industry was an act of Foucauldian control.

If the diamond is radiant light the process of mining it occurs in sooty, dank mineshafts miles from the earth's surface, by miners whose lungs are as black as their faces. In South Africa, miners are almost all black, to the point where Sol Plaatjie, founder of the African National Congress (ANC), was astonished to discover, on a trip to England in the early 1920s, that English miners were white (although this would not have been entirely easy to determine if one watched them emerge exhausted from a day's labor in the mines, covered in black grime resembling blackface).

When the Apartheid state came to an end in 1990, a power-sharing government led by Willem de Klerk (former president) and Nelson Mandela was entered into with the purpose of designing terms for the political transition. These terms were ironed out in the Kempton Park negotiations between the ANC and the National Party of 1991–4—talks that led to the Interim Constitution, the writing of the Final Constitution, the first free and fair elections, and the establishment of the Truth and Reconciliation Committees. The crucial sticking point of the democratic transition had to do with nationalization of the mines, which the ANC supported and the National Party, with business behind it, refused. The talks might well have broken down had not Nelson Mandela managed to convince the ANC to relinquish its demand for nationalization.

The decision to retain a private sector for the mining industry (and other forms of capital) meant that South Africa's democratic transition would be what Antonio Gramsci called a weak revolution, with capital remaining in place. It signaled a broad neoliberal turn on the part of the ANC, which expressed itself in GEAR—the Growth, Employment and Redistribution Act of 1996. GEAR forced the state to take on measures of structural adjustment demanded by the International Monetary Fund of debtor nations even though South Africa had no international debt. It took on these stringent measures in the hope of readying itself for foreign investment, which South Africa believed would happen now that, in 1996, it had shape-changed into a democratic state and was an international moral exemplar. But GEAR failed miserably: foreign investment went to China, including South African textile production that relocated its workforce there. (The textile industry only returned to South Africa a decade later under Chinese ownership.) GEAR led to a loss of two million jobs. GEAR did have the benefit of requiring white monopoly capital to shed 20 percent of its assets to black ownership, therefore instantaneously creating a new economic ruling class consisting of a small number of black elites. But redistribution stopped with GEAR. No general improvement in the quality of work or of pay for the vast black African working class followed.

Then there is the violence of the mines—Jan Smuts, when president of the Republic of South Africa, firing on South African miners during the 1922 miner's strike; the Marikana Strike and massacre of August 2012 when thirty-four miners were shot for demanding a decent wage from their bosses. That their boss was Cyril Ramaphosa is all the more egregious, since Ramaphosa achieved his corporate position, thanks to GEAR. He is now the state president.

In some sad or cynical way, one might say the miners are among the lucky ones. At least they have jobs in a society where 27–30 percent of the population is unemployed, the vast majority being black Africans. This is in spite of the South African Constitution's bill of rights that mandates the right to work for all citizens, requiring the government to "make a reasonable effort" to bring about full employment.

Part II

Then, what can art do to play even a small role in the correction of this moral and political injustice?

Since the topic is gold and diamonds, a word about their aesthetics. Most of what I will say pertains to diamonds, but gold will make its entry in due course.

In two earlier books of mine, I explored the idea of what I call aesthetic synergy or fusion.[2] This came to me watching Lady Diana's funeral on September 6, 1997, on TV in Durban, South Africa, where I was teaching at the time. As her bier click-clacked its way slowly toward Westminster Abbey, the BBC announcer kept comparing Lady Diana and Princess Grace of Monaco—Grace Kelly a film-star-turned-princess; Diana a princess with star quality. It seemed that in the announcer's plummy imagination, the pair fused together, as if, by osmosis, Diana had taken on the qualities of the Kelly Hitchcock blonde film star, even though Diana had never acted in any film. The fusion took place on account of their shared stories: each a princess, each seen continually over film or TV, each leading a melodramatic life culminating in their car crash. Both were classical beauties—although Diana's face was far more expressive. Both possessed the illumination of a glowing star, distant from ordinary mortals—Grace Kelly in virtue of her place on the silver screen, Diana in virtue of the distance acceded to royalty, and her natural reserve, even if Tony Blair would dub her "the peoples' princess."

This synergy or fusion of aesthetic types or personae seems to me a general principle of aesthetics today. It is central to American politics. Famously J. F.

Kennedy appeared—thanks to TV and magazines—before the American public as a dashing war hero, tough Irish now bred to the bone, and finally a kind of Jay Gatsby star. The attitudes we project onto public figures are variable, depending on who they are, how they look, and what they represent. And so, Obama in the 2008 presidential campaign was elevated to Lincoln, while Sara Palin took on the pert, aggression of the American cheerleader from the happy family on your TV screen, not to mention the status of an *American Idol* contestant for whom we were all supposed to cheer, that is, vote.

Synergy also happens between things, indeed between persons and objects. I think the diamond takes on the allure both of modern art and of the film star. This is central to its aesthetics. A word of background is in order. Modern art was plagued from its inception in the Paris of the nineteenth century by the tension between religious and consumerist attitudes, attitudes that began to arise in the eighteenth century (see Chapter 1) and even earlier, but dramatically increased as the art world took modern form in the mid-nineteenth. The museum made art eternal, beyond the frame of temporality like a diamond: "forever." But modern art also depended upon the rise of the middle classes in the nineteenth century who, having expendable money for the first time, wanted to flaunt it by purchasing everything in sight, buying art, drinking champagne, and renting women by the hour or year, broadcasting their money and taste with paintings hanging on their walls. This turned art—not to mention women—into a consumable item at the same moment when the culture of the museum eternalized art as beyond time and price. There is nothing like *pricelessness* to jack up the price of goods, which points to the confusion endemic to modern art, sitting uneasily between these valuations.[3]

Diamonds are an epitome of femininity and should be understood in the light of the nineteenth century's fusion of women, art, and the male imagination as things of beauty, voyeuristic pleasure, consumption, and display. It is a commonplace that diamonds and women also go together. When a man is decked out in diamonds (in some Hollywood movie, for example), it usually means there is something fishy about him. The laws of gender decree that women are the proper bearers of diamonds—a fact that the Gilded Age of American wealth took to such heights that certain wives of captains of industry were so decked out in jewels that they required bodyguards to guard them as they jangled their way down the Fifth Avenue in New York.[4] Women became museums of wealth. Properly decked out, they alchemized with their diamonds to become objects of aesthetic allure.

And so, the diamond synergized various characteristics of modern art: display, pricelessness, museological allure, commodification, femininity.

The allure of the diamond also fused with the attraction of the film star after film was invented in the 1890s. A short definition of a film star is that all eyes gravitate to that person as soon as they appear on screen and remain fixed on him or her by an alchemy of attraction.[5] If the star uniquely attracts the eye, so does the diamond. The gem diamond exists in a state of permanent close-up. We have to bend down and look at it in the jeweler's case, or on the finger of someone's hand. Close-up is required for viewing. Like the entrance of the Hollywood star in a classic movie, where suddenly the forward march of the film stops and we get the limpid full frontal of the actress, her face filling the screen. As in Ingrid Bergman's appearance in *Casablanca*, or Greta Garbo's in *Grand Hotel*.

The clearest example of this fusion is *Gentlemen Prefer Blondes*, Howard Hawk's film musical of 1953, in which Marilyn Monroe (aka Lorelei Lee) sings, "a kiss on the lips may be quite continental, but diamonds are a girl's best friend," adding, "talk to me Harry Winston, tell me all about it," Harry Winston being the iconic Beverly Hills jeweler. Monroe sings like a French Chanteuse with throated, cooing effervescence, her voice taking on the dazzle of a diamond. Women want diamonds; they wear them and glitter in the eyes of men, who pay to own and enjoy both. A diamond is also a protection against the fickleness of men, of love. As the song from the movie goes: "Time rolls on and youth is gone and you can't straighten up when you bend. But stiff back or stiff knees you stand straight at Tiffany's. Diamonds are a girl's best friend."

And so, the dynamics of ownership are complicated. The man buys the woman a diamond to have her glitter as his (she is mine); she wants it, in part, to glitter for him and as herself, but also in defense against him and the brutality of his presumption that because she is his property he could drop her in a minute when something better (younger) comes along. There is no workers' union for women like Lorelei Lee to represent her interests, such as the mine workers' union in South Africa. She is left to her own devices, which turn out to be ample. This drama around ownership and power runs throughout the culture of extraction and its aesthetics.

The gem diamond may be the purest icon of capitalism. Diamonds are plentiful; they can be found alluvially on dried river beds in vast tracts of Namibia as well as extracted from mines in South Africa, Canada, Russia, Australia, and so on. To create and maintain the illusion of their rarity, flow was restricted. Marx calls this the fetish of commodities. By this he means that to disguise excessive profit built into the valuation of goods, their excess value is naturalized—mythologized as in the nature of things. Here the disguise is that the diamond is expensive because it is so rare when it is not.

At the same time, the beauty of the diamond depends on the invisibility of the labor that produced it—all that sweat and grime and lung disease, lack of pay, and black soot covering the body of the miner. Balzac says that at the bottom of every story of wealth, there is a crime. Which wealth has the means to conceal. This is also true of the apprehension of objects. Place the i-Phone you buy back in the Asian sweatshop where its parts were made and its white elegance is tarnished aesthetically.

While the aesthetics of gold and of diamonds overlap, there are also differences. Gold has a long history as currency (the gold sovereign conveying financial sovereignty) or as the standard on which currencies were based (the United States went off the gold standard in 1976). Gold is linked to the history of greed, accumulation, possession in a way diamonds are not, given its status as currency. Its relation to power is told in stories from Wagner's *Ring of the Nibelungs* to Tolkien's *Lord of the Rings*. Gold has a mythology that diamonds lack; even if in the Harry Winston store, they may appear similar as objects of aesthetic attraction. This although the diamond's aesthetic is that of dancing, prismatic light (akin to the allure of the film star), while gold's allure is more dulcet, closer to that of a late-summer sunset.

Part III

I think it is reasonable to say that visual art is not capable of encompassing the system of extraction as a whole; for that, documentary film or some kind of writing is required. One needs a language-driven medium.

However, visual art can undercut the repression of labor on which the aesthetic of the diamond is based by creating an aesthetic in opposition to the world of Harry Winston and diamonds-are-a-girl's-best-friend. It can return perception to the brutality of labor, making that visible. It can show the daily encounter with danger, the exhaustion and anxiety of the miner. It can picture the devastation of the mining process, its environmental degradation. It can seek to give recognition to the laborer. It can expose the profit-driven owner. It can uncover concealment. It can acknowledge the racial nature of exploitation. That is a lot, and there is more.

Consider two examples of South African art addressing mining. Both are of high quality. I suggest they form an ensemble. One is about the mining of gold; the other about the mining of diamonds. But many of the issues of the labor, culture, and economy pertain equally to both. One work is by William Kentridge, about the mining of gold on the Johannesburg reef; the other by Mohau Modisakeng, about the miner of diamonds. What then of their relations to the politics of the mining system? Are these best called political works, and if so, in what ways? How might the word "politics" apply?

The gold mines are no longer individually owned and/or controlled as they were in the days of William Kentridge's randlords. And the mining on the Johannesburg reef gave out early in the twentieth century. Both gold and diamond mines are now public companies listed on the stock exchange. Those earlier days of rogue capitalism on the Johannesburg mines are brilliantly evoked in Kentridge's masterpiece from the Soho Eckstein series, *Mine* (1991). *Mine* was made the very year the Kempton Park talks were beginning. Kentridge had gone off to study mime and theatre at the L'Ecole Internationale de Theatre Jacques Lecoq in Paris during the previous decade, after a youthful career doing intensely expressionistic drawings and paintings along with theatre. Upon return to South Africa, he began to toy with a new form of film that would arise from drawing, and also that rely on the silence of the mime. The series he created was based on two characters: Soho Eckstein, a mine owner/capitalist boss with a Central European/Jewish background; and Felix, the beautiful soul who pines for and then becomes the lover of Soho's wife. The theme returned to the days of early Johannesburg capitalism, when "randlords" could own the mines and rule the city like bosses of old, and when racial capitalism produced the exploitation of black miners, who thread their way throughout his films like silent reminders.

Kentridge's work is actually film or rather the fusion of film and visual art, but, since it is not documentary, does not claim the resources of that medium.

Mine, the third film in the series, is titled so because it is a play on words. For Soho Eckstein, the mine is all his, meaning from his point of view: mine and mine alone. This claim of absolute ownership, control, and of course profit is expressed in Soho's size. He is a hulking Middle European randlord towering over his desk, dwarfing his breakfast, who goes to bed completely dressed, his pet rhinoceros on his bed, as if size is reversed and he is the rhino in a heavy gabardine suit, while the rhino a being in miniature, as if he has tamed the fiercest of animals into his personal house pet.

Thick-skinned, blunt, crude, all powerful, this icon of rogue capitalism plunges his morning coffee (French-pressed); and to the music of Dvorak, the plunger plummets down the mine shaft thousands of feet into the earth, to the distraught world of the miner. As if Soho himself physically plunged his mine into being with his own hands.

Kentridge's films are build up painstakingly frame by frame through charcoal drawing, erasure, and redrawing in the manner of animated Disney features of old like *Fantasia* of 1940, whose every frame was meticulously painted. The key to frame-by-frame animation is to sync the twenty-four frames per second so that each follows the next in a way that leads to continuous motion for the viewer—no easy task. Working at an enormous

Figure 3.1 William Kentridge, untitled drawing for *Mine*, 1991. Image courtesy of William Kentridge.

easel, Kentridge draws a frame, then rubs out parts of it, and changes the shape to allow for the flicker of motion frame-to-frame. Charcoal is easy to erase because of its thick, dusty opacity to begin with. His partial erasure of each image to make way for the next leaves a residue of more opacity to the succeeding frame, since a rubbed drawing is always vague in part and resonant with the footprint of what was there before the eraser, in the manner of a musical chord carrying the overtones of the one before it. Kentridge works like a musician, intuitively and harmonically. In this, chorded visual opacity seems to reside the aura of the past, of memory, remembrance, the haunted nature of things gone before but remaining in the mind, the blurred intensity of old stories powerfully haunting. Again, in the manner of overtone or aura.

At the moment of democratic transition, Kentridge's work not only bespoke narratives of the old days of big capital and racial exploitation—the days of silent film—it resonated with mourning, nostalgia, and the suffusion of memory. Soho, like Felix, is *of* Kentridge, a fictional character

Figure 3.2 William Kentridge, untitled drawing for *Mine*, 1991. Image courtesy of William Kentridge (see also https://www.youtube.com/watch?v=M8TpcdmCTHo).

not unlike his own forebears, part of his world, a rough edge of his present, and the discomfort and sadness of such intimacy comes through in the film. He is monstrous, but also human, the film says, and more than that: mine (Kentridge's). He lives, as it were, in me. And Felix is directly modeled on Kentridge himself, his mirror image.

Kentridge's use of the silent film medium feels at once old/antique while, like all films, about a continuous present. This is a general aesthetic feature of film. One always feels, watching a movie, that it seems to be happening right now, even if a history drama one knows is set in the past, or a sci-fi set in the future. This is why film is such a unique bearer of memory. It is of the past and projects in the present as if the past were a continuous state of presence. Which is the structure of memory. Especially in Kentridge's case, he can control duration—the speed at which the narrative takes place—by slowing or speeding up the change in the drawing, frame by frame. Time is sometimes rapid, other times stilled. There is a musical function to this (balance of phrasing) but also an emotional one. Equally important is his use of montage, of cutting between moments in time, space, and narrative that suddenly shift perspective, and at the most dramatic, stilling time into tableaux. There is a love of old technology in his work, of silent film with its simplicity of message, its profound lighting and visual effect of character, its love of body and landscape. The days of the randlords were days when good was good and bad, bad, and it was penchant for simplicity of story that he resurrected from silent film.

More recently, the mining of the diamond has been given a brilliant inversion in an installation by Standard Bank 2016 Young Artist Award winner Mohau Modisakeng called *Lefa La Ntate* (roughly translated "inheritance father"). At the Iziko Museum in Cape Town in 2017, Modisakeng painted a long room dark gray and black so that no light could enter without being dampened as in a mine shaft. In this dark room with grayish-black slate on the floor, he placed a long table, empty except for a small number of mining tools at one end. There sat a miner cast in what appeared to be dark bronze (probably a substitute material), one hand resting on the table. Kentridge's miners tend to appear deflated, subdued, with bowed heads and tired bodies. They endure. Modisakeng's miner is rather a powerful if subdued figure, paternal, and dignified. A life in the mines has not destroyed him.

The rock on the floor of this installation resembled the kind of slate one might chip away deep inside a mine. The walls were painted a deep and luscious gray and covered by large photographs of the powerful, naked bodies of miners (actually the artist) whose bodies are lit so that they glisten in a brown, diamantine brilliance as if covered in diamonds. It is as if the radiant power of the diamond is fused with the beauty of their bodies. The men themselves glisten and become beautiful.

By highlighting their bodies, the artist not only acknowledges but celebrates the sepulchral power of labor, as if the real beauty in the mine is the person doing the mining rather than the thing mined to be bought by others. This restitution of beauty and dignity to the miner is a way of inverting the aesthetic values of extraction, which as a norm make the laborer invisible and the product all-consuming. To dignify the body and being of the miner is a form of recognition, indeed idealization. The recognition does not challenge the system of economic inequality and human degradation central to the history of mining and colonial extraction. Rather, it refuses the *denial* of recognition that was part and parcel of that system. Soho Eckstein, had he bothered to consider who his laborers were, would have believed them to be limited and destined to labor on the colonial model of the *Untermensch*. Crucial to his ability to own, to play the role of the master would have been his denial of recognition to those who scraped from the earth what he profited from. Modisakeng seeks to return dignity, decency, and aesthetic beauty to the miner. He seeks to show how the miner remains a person even in degraded conditions. This acknowledgment is both real and idealized. It is a gift to the miner of a form of beauty the miner may himself not notice in himself, given his exhaustion, depletion, and the limited conditions of his life.

[I am unable to acquire a high-resolution image of this installation, so I invite the reader to view it as a video clip: https://www.youtube.com/watch?v=kin2tzlcrCo; https://vimeo.com/191418355.]

Part IV

There is something right about Hegel's notion that history is about the struggle for recognition, not simply the struggle for goods and opportunities.[6] At the core of that struggle is the master–slave dialectic. This dialectic is by now widely adopted, pried apart from Hegel's systematic thought, to become a creatively adopted and freestanding way of reading the structure of historical oppression, from Alexandre Kojève's Marxist reading of European history to Frantz Fanon's reading of colonial degradation.[7] The power of the dialectic consists in this flexibility. The general terms are well known enough. In the struggle for recognition, the master comes out on top (Hegel says this is because he risks his life, but we can leave that aside). And this means there is an asymmetry of recognition. The slave recognizes the self-consciousness of the master, meaning the master's ability to formulate plans for his life and enjoyment. But the slave has no recognition of himself as also having life plans and aspirations. Hegel's original way of putting this is that the slave lacks self-consciousness. It is better and more truthful to say the slave's sense of self is degraded, given the conditions of his life. Degraded but crucially intact. He wants more for himself than this life but has no language or situation to articulate and achieve his desire. And half the time, he is too exhausted to even think on the matter. Which suits the master fine, since all he wants from the slave, all he recognizes in worth of the slave, is brute labor. Hegel's way of putting this is that while the master possesses self-consciousness, the slave is pure consciousness, pure locomotion, and skill.

The drama is resolved only when, in the course of fortuitous, happy history, a reversal takes place. The master comes to recognize he is slave to the slave, utterly dependent on him for everything the master needs and wants. He owes the slave a debt because he is incomplete without him. Similarly, the slave comes to realize he is master to the master, because the master is nothing without him. This empowers him. Each is now in a position to realize he needs something from the other. The master needs the slave's skill, his "consciousness." He has to learn the art of laboring himself to achieve his ends in order to be fully free/human. The slave needs the master's ability to reflect on what he wants from life and act on this, meaning the master's self-consciousness. Each realizes—and this is the important thing—that he must assimilate something from the other. At which point they become alike, because each interpolates from the other what he lacks, and in a way that makes them now metaphysically "the same." At this point, according to the Hegelian tradition, the concept of equality (and of human rights) can arise in the world. Not before. For at this point, each recognizes their sameness with the other. And so democratic law can enter the scene of history.

One might think of this democratic law as the South African Constitution of 1996, and before it the Interim Constitution of 1994 and the Promotion of National Unity Act of 1995 mandating elections, the Truth and Reconciliation Commission, and so on. But the story is idealized, meaning oversimplified for various reasons. Of relevance here is that inequality remains on the mines, untouched by the most advanced constitutions in the world, and with it the denial of recognition. The conditions of production remain invisible; the laborer is not to be seen. An elite class has arisen, thanks to GEAR and black empowerment, which now plays the role of the master, having once played the role of a historical slave.

The aesthetics of the diamond depend on the failure to recognize this inequality, or to put it to one side when dazzled by the jewel. Which is why, taken together, these artists are a good start as an ensemble speaking to South Africa's conditions of extraction.

Kentridge's film is a story focusing on the owner, who is the only real character in *Mine*, and whose voracious terms of ownership refuse recognition to those he employs, thinking them to be mere packhorses—colonials fit for menial tasks whose day begins in the film when he rings the bell used at the white dinner table to call the servants. Modisakeng's is a story that returns the recognition of personhood to the miner, through idealizing him, including aestheticizing his body. Each makes art about what he knows and feels most deeply. That the one artist is white and the other black is not uninteresting in this regard. It takes art that *crosses racial lines* to picture a situation adequately of this kind. One might call that the joint project of democracy.

Part V

This kind of recognition or lamp is not exactly political, if by politics one means the power to effect social change, that is, if by politics one means the *agency* to change the world. By painting a miner, you are unlikely to change corporate or state policy. This is a commonplace that everyone knows. But if by politics one means making a system of brutality visible, acknowledging its relationship to ownership of the means of production (Soho's empire), then one can say the work is political.

Political *agency* always goes beyond the work of art itself. This should be a commonplace as well, except that sometimes art is fetishized to the point where representation is confused with resistance. I think the pages of history have shown that art takes on *political agency* when institutions like the state, the court, political parties, or specific group solidarities give it force, as has happened in the past with monuments and memorials that proclaimed power and generated communalism in Germany, America, South Africa, and so on. Or when the artist is some kind of celebrity with the media at his or her fingertips. In other words, political force is a matter of fit between the art object and the context that empowers it.

This particularly applies to disturbational art—art aiming to disrupt the system, disruption being sometimes identified with resistance. It is a widely held belief in the artworld today that disturbational art is almost automatically political in the sense of having mysterious agency. This is a legacy of the avant-gardes, for whom disruption of ordinary habits of perception was a key to engineering and engendering political awareness. The avant-gardes aimed to structure the alienation of perception from its habits of taking in the world (see introduction on Rodchenko). Just as a goal of philosophy is to render the world uncertain, so the acute reader (and the reader must be acute) throws up her hands and asks, "Is this the world I anymore know?" So, the Constructivist photographer aimed to challenge perceptual habits to the point where the acute subject would ask, "Is this the world I ordinarily see, and if so, why does it now look like this?" The goal was to cause a reflection on the visual perspective one brings to perception, but also to enthrall the viewer with the sense that the world could be otherwise; that its shifting perception sublimes it, thus causing in that viewer a heightening of perception; that what formerly appeared stable is not, and could be seen differently; that the world is processive and capable of plasticity (change). And a utopian sense of historical possibility, indeed inevitability.

It takes more than the visual image to do this. It takes words. Even Eisenstein, the great poet of montage, which he believed to be inherently political, depended on plot, and inter-titles, and a huge background of theory, to get political force from his operatic/cinematic masterpieces. It is for this reason that Lenin believed the party needed to play a highly directive role in engendering worker consciousness. Because left to themselves, workers could derive from the conditions of their place and time a wide range of things, from a belief in virulent Nazi nationalism to a belief that the Third International was correct. What is true is that Eisenstein's work cannot help but show us the brutality of the police, and the slaughter of victims, and sailors who have had enough of bad meat and are ready to revolt. The film images do carry some immediate political freight apart from the inter-titles. Which a viewer may be free to ignore or willfully misread.

After the Second World War, the notion of disruption began to change, so that, by the time of Paris 1968, disruption was no longer controlled alienation from habits of seeing and knowing, it morphed into any challenge to "the system" in the name of revolutionary anarchy, as if an entire student movement—and many of these students became well-known French writers and thinkers—could take to the streets, man the barricades, take down the signs, paint in deep red on the walls of the university, "We have made love in your citadel," and thereby change the world. (This happened at the Parisian University Nanterre in 1968 to someone I knew, a dean who was thrown in the trashcan while these words were painted in his office.) The year 1968 relied on a more anarchic and less directed notion of disruption from the earlier versions of Russian Constructivists. And at this point, one has to ask: if disruption is undirected, why is it not merely entropic? Time and entropy are coexistent natural features, and entropy is simply disturbance in the system. If an art of disruption is not purely ceremonial, a pageant of simulated politics for the already converted, it *cannot be controlled* unless some further directive is in place. Will disruption lead to right-wing reaction, left-wing promise, or merely a shaky center? Disruption is now the darling ideology of the Ted Talks in right-wing and liberal America. Where the talk is meant to shake rattle and roll the audience out of the box. This is debatable.

Kentridge's work and Modisakeng's might plausibly be considered disruptive in the sense Jacques Rancière means it (see Chapter 2). Which is to provide new forms of visibility for a system run on invisibility (the dark world of the miner expelled from the aesthetics of the diamond and of gold). But their work does not specifically aim for the politics of avant-garde disruption, which is to challenge the viewer's perceptual system in the way Rodchenko seeks to do this, by creating an "antimony," if you will, between what the viewer knows they are seeing (ordinary reality) and how they are shown it (from what point of view), thereby causing reflection and, it is hoped, consciousness-raising.

If one means by politics something like what Hannah Arendt meant by it—namely the power to voice one's position in the agora, in public life—then, maybe, this art does do that, depending on what one means by the public in a society like South Africa, where the majority of people are impoverished, lack education, and have little to do with high culture and its institutions like the gallery and the museum. Until recently, Kentridge's work was more closely studied abroad than in his home country, although the pair of stunning exhibitions at Zeitz MOCAA and Norval Foundation in Cape

Town signal that that has changed. Modisakeng remains hardly known: I was the only person in the Iziko Museum in Cape Town the day I went to see his show. I fear one could count the number of people who saw it on the fingers of one hand.

More importantly, for an artwork to voice something in a public/political forum, it has to say something, and it is unclear exactly what these artworks "say," what "statement they make." Nor is it clear that the purpose of art is to "say something"—clearly and forcefully—in such fora, as opposed to showing, suggesting, or revealing. More on this below.

I think it is wrong to measure the power of this art purely or even primarily in terms of political agency, a criterion that would probably compromise it, make it look like a failure. Art is rather the lamp on the helmet of the miner— there to illuminate and reveal. The works by Kentridge and Modisakeng acknowledge the failure of recognition built into the culture by which labor is exploited, its manual power extracted for profit, its products turned into self-referential dazzle. It depends on the thought that the best hope for political action depends on the light of recognition. Let us hope that in the right circumstances these images play some role in the culture of political change. Put another way, let's hope that *recognition* has a political value.

Part VI

Now I want to speak specifically about William Kentridge. Kentridge's work is steeped in the recounting of colonialist and Apartheid violence, Truth and Reconciliation, the brutality of labor; the great political forces of the twentieth century are everywhere in his work, nearly omnipresent in it. His work is *about* politics, and *about* history, and *about* the role of history and the tremors of past violence in human memory. It raises moral questions about remembrance and its duties, about culpability, about acknowledgment of others. If it is a political refusal of colonial and Apartheid violence, its route is through rumination rather than any call to arms, storming of the ramparts, or measure of agency. We might call Kentridge's work a politics of rumination.

If one seeks a political statement, political rhetoric, an attempt to make art the efficient cause of some political statement, policy, or action, one will not find this in Kentridge's art. Rather, politics and history, time and memory are the *materials* from which he composes great art in the further hope of political change, which would demand a change in *thinking about the world, including the past*. Even his theatre piece of 1997 on the Truth and Reconciliation Commission, *Ubu and the Truth Commission*, based on a libretto by Jane Taylor, seeks more to capture the shattering intensities of the event than to make any political comment on it (for art that does critically engage the Truth Commission in a way that might be called political; see my Chapter 6). The purpose of this work is to respond to the intensities of the time in a way that creates something powerful and profound from them, to coax these events into form and medium, visual geometry, line and character, duration and plot, so as to produce a work of art that at once contains and vivifies the intensities of politics and history, and vivifies their poignancy, taking the audience on a journey of deep rumination. This is the world of Shakespeare, where the failures of kingship and the overthrow of the crown, the problems of ruler and servant, the anxieties of living in a religiously conflicted and nationally fragile state are transposed to the stage, where they may at once find an aesthetic form that transcends them, thanks to composition and prose, declamation and dramatic resolve, but only to deepen their nagging reality for us.

There is something deeply right about T. J. Clark's claim in *Farewell to an Idea*:

> Politics ... is the form ... of the contingency that makes modernism what it is ... in some strong sense modernist art is obliged to make form *out of* politics, but also to leave the accident and tendentiousness of politics in the form it makes—not to transmute it. [Earlier art's project] was to transmute the political, to clean it of the dross of contingency, to raise it up to the realm of allegory, or ... to make its very everydayness appear quietly miraculous ... Modernism turns on the impossibility of transcendence.[8]

This seems to me to fit Kentridge to a T. His work is drenched in the *problem* of politics, its ongoing catastrophe and strophes of liberation, which usually turn into disappointment, fury, or recalcitrance. The work is about living in this conundrum. One may say that the problems of life are not overcome in art but given room to be thought in all their contingency.

Art is a form of thinking, one that can and usually should stay away from a lucid propositional declamation and rather vivify the question of life, its existential predicament, in a way that is unresolved. This is what rumination is: the kind of thought that is not organized around an endpoint, a successful argument, a logical deduction, a clearly stated proposition, but which rather reviews the world from a number of angles, shifting in mood from hope to guilt, despair to resolve, resolve to comedy, comedy to the joy of making things up. Rumination is a kind of permanent state of skepticism. Kentridge's art is this kind of thinking. It is not art that seeks to "make a statement" as the great philosopher of art Arthur Danto would have had it.[9] Rather, it is full of one-liners that come and go in the manner of sound bites, propaganda posters, moral adages, homilies, ideological prompts, remarks from the history of assertion (meaning of politics), none adequate to the journey betwixt and between them that his art makes. Often layered against multiple images in the frame, they serve as part of a larger form of presentation in which they are subjected to reflection. You want propositions, the work asks, well there have been too many such certainties and look what they have wrought in the world. Let us rather be wrong for once, or uncertain, the proper existential condition. (That is as close to a statement as you will get from Kentridge.)

Beginning from history and politics, the events of South African and European trauma and power, but also from the history of ideas, Kentridge subjects these materials to reflection, the slow and deep process of rumination on the intensities through which he has lived, the footprint of his time, and that of his parents and grandparents—a footprint reaching across the history of racial capitalism, of colonialism, law and Apartheid, of Jewish immigration to South Africa and its various forms of life and remembrance, of the great themes of the 1920s and 1930s: fascism, communism, the shredding of democracy, impoverishment, collapse, violence, of guilt, pain, of degradation and the spirit of endurance, of the crippling and exuberance of living a life and empathizing the lives of others. Rumination usually finds its home in the *past*, even if it is motivated to understand what should happen next, and in a past that cannot easily be worked through or reconciled, but remains uncertain—a question, a nag, a form of regret and even horror. Where there is uncertainty, there is anxiety. "His anxiety flooded half the house"—the inter-title of his first film in the Soho series, *Johannesburg, Second City after Paris*—says Soho's rival Felix Teitelbaum, pining for his lover, Soho's wife. And Felix is modeled on Kentridge himself. In collaborations Kentridge took on with the South African artist Neo Muyanga, and again with the German baritone Matthias Goerne and pianist Markus Hinterhauser in a live video/theatre performance of Franz Schubert's great song cycle *Die Winterreise* (2014, Avignon Festival), this same figure, now twenty-two years older, appears walking, hands in pockets, head pointed down to the ground, across a landscape of newspapers (the news, the world) his thoughts internalized, his posture ruminative. Since the song cycle is complete in itself, not to mention a masterpiece of darkly ruminative journeying into the long winter of the soul, Kentridge is freed in his part of the collaboration to create complimentary work without a beginning or an end, loosely tied to the imagery and content of the story, but also very much an experiment in dialogue between music and image. In short, he is given license to riff and ruminate.

The future perfect tense often appears in Kentridge's work in the form of machines that bespeak modernity reeling toward its future while being treated as auratic, old, ruined, quaint, and lovely. En passant, if there is anything Jewish about Kentridge's work, it is the tendency toward deep and unresolved rumination, although Jews are not the only people in the world to ruminate, as one can easily see from Rembrandt's famous image of Aristotle contemplating the bust of Homer.

It was the avant-gardes who turned art into an activity of constant innovation informed by ideas, and who began to compose visual works that were not only sublime but also forms of processive thinking. Their interests were in biology, cognitive perception, the construction of a new world on higher (more scientific) principles, the relation between aesthetics and ideas, the way history might be shaped by the thinking mind, deduced from historical propositions and unfolded in the course of events. This side of the avant-gardes (the Bauhaus, constructivism, Le Corbusier) aimed for historical certainty. That is not Kentridge's side. The other side of the avant-gardes aimed for *uncertainty* of the kind that liberates the human being from habits of attention and perception, from institutional commitments, and from the social systems of modernity. This is where Kentridge lives. He no longer believes, as the constructivist did, that his work will change the world. Constructivism was a movement inaugurated in 1917, created in the wake of the Russian Revolution and meant as its conduit. That went out after the Second World War. Rather, Kentridge believes that the vast tapestry of history, when presented in the manner of theater or reframed as memory, is the revisiting of tumult and fragment in the manner of a question rather than an answer, an invitation to thought rather than an endpoint in knowledge, or worse, the illusion of mastery and historical inevitability.

Enough of the avant-garde thinking is preserved in Kentridge's work to allow him the hope than it might contribute to consciousness-raising. But then, much art carries this secret hope.

When art thinks, it does so largely apart from propositional content, logical argument, deductive reasoning, dialectical synthesis. Or should largely do. (This is why the avant-gardes introduced theory-driven art: to fill in the gap and allow art to "declare something.") An art that *in its essence* asserts, argues, deduces is philosophy, law, history, or even perhaps science masquerading as art. This would be the price of pushing the medium beyond its proper limits. Which can be interesting sometimes, even important, but cannot be the norm of art-making on pain of dissolving the difference between visual art and philosophy, to the point where one might as well read the book and dispense with the visual object. Visual art properly thinks from the inner, instinctive mind whose talent is to find ways of framing its inner, largely unconscious or intuitive thoughts in ways that allow them to appear. It works through training, and through intuition, like a writer composing a work of fiction. Ideas obviously enter, but the work is not the elaboration of an idea. Kentridge's ideas include such things as the critique of epistemological certainty; that absolute certainty is a central driver of colonial practice and the making of war.

Here again, Kentridge's sources are in the 1920s, which is in many ways where he lives as an artist. Think of the painting and drawing of Paul Klee, which is more musical in its line than strictly characterizing or delineating, and whose line and color takes one on a journey around figures and scenes, encircling them, exaggerating them in a way that is comical, thoughtful, strange, beautiful, disturbing, and unresolved. Klee's poetry is that of whimsy and wonder, his tonality obscure. He makes life seem peculiar, calling forth its existential nature in the form of thoughts found deep in the mind, of the kind Freud called archaic or childlike. Klee paints the world like an adult but also a child. Freud's idea, which can be easily separated from his psychoanalytic explanations, is that the artist retains an early childhood capacity to know the world through drawing it, to discover it by finding it in the medium of color and shape, to play at the world in a way that excites the mental capacity for rethinking, re-vision, reformulation in a way that is humane, poetic, and deeply felt. His or her genius consists in the ability to access and call forth feelings, desires, hopes, attachments with the resonance of the archaic and the subtlety of a brilliant observer. Genius is the ability to give these deep childlike thoughts shape or form.

Call shape or form play following a long aesthetic tradition. And play is a form of *thinking*, one that is not deductive or logical or written in the form of an argument for or against, but instinctive, abrupt, juxtaposing, full of shifts in mood or language and of ambivalence, deeply felt and deeply poetic— although ideas may be involved. This is I think why he loves early silent film, because it was early to invention and incomplete in its capacity to invent. Everything was new then, and magical, film in its childhood, its thinking was strange, funny, sad, its plots simple, its invention magical. (His most direct homage to early silent film is his take-off on *Journey to the Moon* by Georges Melies: *Seven Fragments for Melies*, 2003.)

Of the many kinds of drawing, there are three kinds of relevance to the work of William Kentridge. The first kind of drawing, derived from the Renaissance, delimits, shapes, frames in architectural space story and character, depicts. One might say very loosely that it is propositional, more strictly that it is iconographic. The second takes one on a journey in the manner of cinematic line. This is what Klee is about. His line is music. And third, drawing seeks to bring something into existence, as if by drawing it

Figure 3.3 William Kentridge, untitled drawing for *Felix in Exile*, 1994. Image courtesy of William Kentridge (see also https://www.youtube.com/watch?v=k5w_CkyPapY).

one can make it live. Here is the child's world—that of magic. Here is the Pygmalion fantasy. It is Kentridge's world in perhaps his most poignant film, *Felix in Exile* of 1994. Felix is separated from his black lover, and in the days of Apartheid, miscegenation was a crime. Alone in what seems to be a prison cell but isn't—since he has a mimeograph machine, which in the old days is what one used to print political pamphlets by cranking a drum round and round—he draws her shape and it magically appears before him.

Drawing is the act that brings her close to Felix, a fantasy of her presence literally drawn into existence. The unconscious does not recognize, Freud said, the gap between wanting a thing and having it. This kind of drawing satisfies that deep unconscious desire. In *Felix in Exile*, this kind of drawing is the work of longing, of desire, and of magical fulfillment, a fulfillment that will turn rancid as she is brutally shot, and abandoned to the empty liminality of the Veldt, to be covered by stray newspapers blowing aimlessly in the wind.

Kentridge lives in the tension between these three forms of drawing, perpetually unresolved. This is the tension between trauma, memory, fact, representation, knowledge, desire, and the magic of the unconscious to erase time and distance. It is pretty much how I think I live in this world, and perhaps also others do. Art in this way is an icon of (my) life. But mine is, I have to say, the life of a highly ruminative philosopher.

And so, in a deep sense, it is a wrong kind of question to ask: Does the work motivate agency, make a statement, generate solidarity, and so on? Is it a weapon? Rather, the question should be: What does the work make of politics? And how does that lead to reflection that might in turn lead to politics, if at all? How is the aesthetic created from the tumultuous materials of history, politics, and family? Politics is in Kentridge's work, along with the rest, the substance from which his aesthetic is formed. It is tempting to say Kentridge mines or extracts from politics their inner intensity. Except that there is no profit motive to the mining here—unlike in the history of mining. Rather, artistic "profit" comes from aesthetic power.

4

The Politics of the Witness: Georges Gittoes

Part I

The most ordinary and obvious notion of political art is about the power of a work to accomplish something in the world. Agency is crucial to this notion of politics. By agency one means the ability to change the world in some nontrivial way. The avant-gardes wanted to do exactly this: to change the world by raising consciousness, also by completely redesigning the built and cultural environment—from housing to typeface to clothing—believing that by giving us a new environment this would alter—and elevate—our relations to self, property, society, politics, and one another. The great modernist architect Le Corbusier wished to create uniform blocks of housing believing they would create a new perception of equality between those living in them, and that this would, could, should change social and political relations between persons, making them more emancipatory and democratic.

The avant-gardes largely failed to achieve either goal. They were not successful in changing mass perceptions of reality on account of their formidable abstraction, theory-driven innovation, and radical experimentalism, which were simply too complex, requiring too much background knowledge, for even the small number of people aware of their work. Nor did they, as a rule, change political reality itself (a claim that I think is empirically demonstrable). European and Soviet states at best tolerated the avant-gardes (Lenin) and at worst destroyed these movements (Stalin, Hitler). As to their claims of redesigning the built environment, their plans too often ended up in the hands of the real estate developer, out to make a buck on modernist office blocks, or in the hands of the city planner, whose urban renewal blocks of flats blight our inner cities with their drab uniformity, poor-quality concrete, and nonworking elevators today. Ironically, only Mussolini applauded the avant-gardes, seeing in Italian futurism a mirror of his own fascist goals.

Nowadays, political agency is no less difficult to achieve through art, but for different reasons. Let me mention two. The first has to do with the abstract nature of financial capital, against which it is hard to protest, given the way the system is shielded within global computer systems, investments, and trades. Art can cry out against this system, hoping to change minds and challenge institutions, but even mass mobilizations like Occupy Wall Street fail to touch the flow of financial capital in the way a worker's strike can affect factory production. Add to that the fact that the players in the financial system are also largely the art collectors who drive the market, acquiring with pleasure even and especially the very works that speak out against what they do for a living.

The second reason is more directly germane to this chapter. Art must complete with the media when it seeks purchase on the witnessing of humanitarian disaster or other political events. And the media is an all-encompassing force in shaping popular opinion, forming ideology, reducing the world to sound-image bites and political brands, exerting hegemonic control over how the conditions of visibility are drawn (how the world appears), confirming entrenched opinion on the right or the left, empowering policy as a result of these. The seductive force of the media is for many persons overwhelming, as can be seen in current American politics where apprentices become presidents, thanks to their TV shows.

To state the obvious: the media's ability to record facts is also its ability to slant them. This power comes from the camera's direct and immediate relationship to the reality it records, which gives what one sees on the TV screen or the internet the sense of unchallengeable *fact*. The camera has a unique ability to lie because it is also automatically connected to the reality of things in virtue of its mechanical function. It is easy to confuse the immediacy of the recording process, which is indexed to the reality it is of, with the way the camera *pictures* what it shows, which involves all kinds of choices: what to leave out, how long to linger over an event, how to frame that event (camera angles, etc.), the role of background commentary, choice of "witnesses," and more.

The authority of having-been-there proves all important, even if what one sees while there may be eminently challenged. My grandfather used to ask, "Vas you deah Charlie?" when one of his grandchildren claimed to know what happened in some distant place, or even down the street from his house. If you weren't a witness, you couldn't really know. If you were, you could. All of which is inevitably ideologically loaded.

The media has thus usurped the witness position.

In some cases (Fox TV), its slanting of fact is fact-killing, replacing fact with propaganda and disparaging truth claims as political lies perpetrated by enemies of the people. The political authority that derives from attention to truth disappears; viciousness replaces it, becoming its own form of authority. This is the strategy of despots, fascists, totalitarians, and all others who wish to abolish fact-based democratic challenges to their point of view by writing these challenges off as simply another kind of politically based lie. The false claims of the dictator cannot be challenged, because they are written off as politically degenerate. The dictator can do no wrong: it is always someone else's fault, which the media is there to confirm.

We know the stakes of this in America, Hungary, Russia, India, and many other places. Science disappears from view, no longer able to hold political debates to account. Corruption becomes rampant, since power can get away with anything, thanks to fake news.

There is also the point Susan Sontag makes in her still timely book *On Photography*. The overabundance of images drenching the world over the internet, over the TV, in magazines, books, on the walls of homes, museums, and galleries can paradoxically drain such images of their intensity, dulling our ability to react to them. The first time we see the pictures of emaciated survivors from the camps, we are overwhelmed. The ten thousandth time, we turn off, or vaguely notice. Traumatic images become mere flashes across the screen if hammered at us until we cease to notice.

Complacency or indifference are themselves political stances. I think the oversaturation of images in the media, on TV, on internet news sites, on social media, in the newsprint (for those who, like me, still read it) is not only an effect of market forces, which push the media towards an endless fixation on death and disaster, celebrity and the news flash, to keep audiences rapt and subscriptions or advertising content high. It is also that the culture of financial capital wants complacency and fixation rather than dissent. Its oversaturation of images paradoxically drains people of feeling, attention, recognition, and real politics. Media truly is the opiate of the people. It opiates them and is part of the global fentanyl crisis.

It is therefore a moral and political duty of art to counteract these ways of deadening fact.

Art is vivification. Here is where the aesthetic can play a role. The beauty of an image, its sublimity, are always memorable and can short-circuit the banality of photographic presentation, allowing things to remain potent to the imagination, indeed *awakening* the imagination to its depths of feeling and capacity to think otherwise (out of the box). Fact becomes again memorable. It becomes a task of photography to find new ways of making the image memorable/indelible. This is far from easy. We know some of the great photographers of our time proceed in this way. In Chapter 2 I discussed David Lurie's work in Cape Town in this light. His bringing to light of new forms of visibility is as it must be, always *based in fact*. (If new forms of visibility are not fact-based, they simply become the latest propaganda.)

Photography does have the capacity to record and witness and is, of course, standardly used by newspapers and circulated widely across the internet. What then of other visual arts, like painting? Painting would seem to be a medium that is miles from the ability to occupy the witness position—installation art also—since neither is privileged with a direct relationship to fact of the kind you get when you snap a photo or shoot film footage. This unless the witness is the artist herself, creating a painting or installation to reflect her own relation to the world, say in the manner of identity politics where *my work witnesses me, testifies to me*. But when identity politics are not at issue, as they so very much are in the contemporary artworld, and instead when the issue is an unfolding humanitarian disaster, painting and installation would seem to have at best a marginal ability to play the role of witness. A painting does not standardly carry the witness position because unlike a photo it could have been done, and probably was made, without the painter having seen what happened with her own eyes. This does not mean painting cannot be expressive in the extreme, that it cannot speak in the name of something, that it cannot picture the world in a deep and true way. A painting may speak against atrocity, as Picasso's *Guernica* of 1937 did against the bombing of Basque Spain by fascist Italian and German planes during the Spanish Civil War. But, it need not and usually isn't painted directly from the reality of being-there. Picasso's painting, a great political statement about violence and fascism, is a soul-cry, but not an act of witnessing. (Picasso was not there, which is why he survived to make the picture.) Painting as a medium simply does not have the automatic and direct relation to reality that a photo does. And so, it doesn't have the same authority to capture fact.

Put another way, a photo is tightly indexed to the world in a way a painting isn't. This point was made years ago by Kendall Walton,[1] who argued that in order for a photo to be a photo of X, X had to be what was photographed. For a photo to be a photo of Winston Churchill, it had to be Churchill who was in the camera's lens. A painting of Churchill, by contrast, can be made in the studio and be a picture of Churchill whether he was there, sitting for the artist, or not. The artist might rely on pictures in magazines or from a book cover—or simply paint from memory or from films of Churchill. Churchill could be deceased, and the painter can still make an excellent portrait of him. You cannot do this with a camera lens. The link between a painting and the world of facts is nonessential to the medium. Put another way: *painting is not a recording device.*

This means that for a painting to capture the intensity of fact, it cannot rely on a direct and immediate index to the event. The days before the invention of photography, when Goya's *Disasters of War* could stand as the most powerful record of the wars of his time, are gone. The difference is now between photographic and digital arts that record reality (photography, film) and visual arts that don't. Part of the reason visual art has gravitated to *identity politics* is because these are suited to the plastic medium, to painting and sculpture and installation with its representational capacities. Identity politics are largely about the critique of representations (representations that stereotype, disfigure, render invisible, diminish, and/or disdain particular human groups), not *delivery of events in the world*. Identity politics are about speaking from the self or in the name of group rights (see Chapter 7). A painting can, I suggested, give voice to the subjectivity of the person who makes it, as if a kind of self-witnessing. There is a long trend in modern and contemporary painting, beginning with geniuses like Frida Kahlo, which do this.

If plastic art wishes to break forth from identity politics into another kind of political stance, one demanding the witnessing of real events outside the self, in their brutality, how should it begin? What kind of innovation in the work of art is required for this to happen? How may visual art speak from the witness position, recruiting the moral and political force of that, when the issue is not voicing the experience of one's identity but what happens in the world outside?

Part II

Consider the Australian artist and filmmaker George Gittoes, winner of the Sydney Peace Prize in 2015. His trajectory is highly instructive.

Gittoes's art seeks to work from the witness position. How does he do it? Gittoes has lived a life in the trenches. He draws rapidly at the scene of devastation, scribbling notes in the manner of a journalist observer and taking photographs also, which he then brings back to his studio in Australia. There he makes huge, staggered oil or acrylic canvases from these materials, exhibiting the entire process. His work thus moves from the position of on-site witness (the drawings and scribblings) to that of artist-in-studio, and it is only because he starts from the position of witness that the power of his art can unfold as it does.

Over the course of a long career, Gittoes has worked in Afghanistan, Gaza, Chechnya, Rwanda, Somalia, Bosnia, Iraq, South Africa, and many other places. He sometimes travels with peace-keeping forces or nongovernmental organizations to ensure access to at-risk areas of the world. Other times he works alone. He is often in real danger. The map of global suffering has been his terrain. It is this position of witness, of journalist as well as artist, that partly allows him to break through the comfort zones of the art world, in line with the best war correspondents and other journalists.

Since the traces of immediacy are retained in his paintings, the work undercuts the comfort zone of autonomous studio productions to shock us, enveloping with something of the immediacy of suffering. We too become witnesses, confronting his victims as he does. We do not see his drawings in real time in the way we might a newsflash (usually with its seven-second delay), but when we see them, we know they were drawn at the scene. There is a clarity about this that is astonishing, as well as a feat of talent, for anyone who has actually witnessed human trauma knows that it is nearly impossible to capture the power of what one has seen without giving into weak stereotype or formulaic emotion. Events literally fall apart when one tries to represent them. Their formlessness defies pictorial shape. Drawing at the scene, speed is crucial. Artists of war must draw fast or paint fast—while the thing burns before the retina. They must commute it into drawing or painting before it turns to ash, fades into the haunting shadows of mourning, becoming spectral. Their finished product has to retain this sense of reactivity. His drawings capture the chaotic formlessness of actual events, while giving them just that: a shape. And so, they look finished and unfinished at the same time, as if caught in a moment of time itself.

Gittoes won't paint unless he saw what happened and recorded it and, by the way, tried to help whenever possible. And this is crucial to the unique moral urgency of his project, to its combination of journalism and subjectivity, to its capacity to take over from television something of the circulation of information, that he always is there, making drawings right in front of the victims, wandering the aimless trajectory of refugee camps and military operations, scribbling notes about victim and circumstance on the sides of drawn pages.

Figure 4.1 shows his work from Kibeho, that site of massacre during the Rwandan genocide of 1994.

As can be seen, Gittoes's drawings exist midway between the drawing and the *sketch*. They have the balance, complication, and refinement of drawing while retaining something of the quick, unfinished, spontaneity of the sketch. He executes them on the spot, right in front of the victims, the children in camps, the passersby. The people he draws often stare back at the artist as he works, talk to him, and this relationship of person to person becomes central to the drawing.

More amazing still is that an incessant quality of invention should pertain to each and every drawing. For this is, above all, what counts: The fact that each drawing seems *invented* on the spot, that no two should be "the same" or "repetitions of the type," as if the singularity of each person, each event, each horror should call for an attention achieved through the invention of a new variation on the idiom, or even a new idiom altogether. Gittoes never repeats himself because reality doesn't. And this is his way of highlighting

Figure 4.1 Gittoes, *The Preacher*, 1994. Photography by Silversalt, rights courtesy of the artist.

the individuality of each figure, each gross violation of human rights as a unique, irreducible event in history that happens to *someone* and not merely to an anonymous "victim." Gittoes's way of keeping the power of each figure and what happened to them *alive* is to render each as freshly to human consciousness as each person is—or should be—to the world. This is called, from the moral point of view, respect.

This also has to do with the words. Along with drawing, words are scribbled furiously across the page, describing, in the manner of a journalist or writer, where he is, who he is talking to or drawing, what is happening around him. In Figure 4.1, a preacher is reading, speaking out to the dying in Rwanda. This preacher, the words tell us, spontaneously stood up among the slaughter to read the bible, so as to try to give the people back their dignity at the moment of death, or at least solace. He was soon to be cut down himself. Gittoes told me that although he tried, he could do nothing to help other than draw and write. He then brings this drawing back to the studio and paints *Blood and Tears* (1995).

This work was done some time ago, in the 1990s. For the past twenty years, Gittoes has largely gravitated to film because of its power of recording and of

Figure 4.2 Gittoes, *Blood and Tears*, 1995. Photography by Silversalt, rights courtesy of the artist.

circulation. This is the other fault line of visual art when it seeks to witness. That it is often confined to the encomium of the art exhibit, preaching to the converted. Whereas film and video circulate widely, photos also. So Gittoes has turned to film, both documentary and docudramatic fiction based in actual situations where he is living and working. He makes films by taking up residence in a place, befriending those around him, documenting their stories, and also shaping their stories with them, following the often-truncated course of their lives as if those around him at the site of disaster were his family. This makes his work brave, bold, and humane. His generosity of spirit and irrepressible buoyancy are central to the humanitarian message. His empathy is central to portraying them as robust, living people who, in spite of daily trauma, manage, endure, feel, love, and seek to prevail.

His most recent film of 2019, *White Light*, was shot during the year he lived on the south side of Chicago, some ten blocks below the rarified and elegant brownstones of the University of Chicago in a world apart of ongoing warfare (gun-fare). Chicago is not composed of distinct precincts; it is composed of distinct universes. The one he lived in (and he still retains his apartment there) is so fraught with gun violence that he wrote to tell me on the fourth of July it was impossible to tell which were the blasts of firecrackers and which of gunfire. At least one of his neighbors is permanently disabled, thanks to bullets; others are no longer alive. Mothers are afraid to let their children outside to play; a stray bullet could happen anytime of day or night.

The neighborhood is invisible to an America that clings to weapons as a Second Amendment right and wishes to portray nothing of gun violence and its absolute degradation, unless the focus is on a veteran with PSTD, stylish gangster, or a psycho-killer (sometimes female).

White Light, the film he workshopped within this community, is documentary, but its texture and meaning are not of someone arriving from the outside determined to capture those within the prison halls of the south side below 63rd Street without any pretense of intimacy, gazing down at local residents in stern pity and terror. Because he lived and worked among these people for more than a year, his film becomes that of a friendly insider. He lives among them and is in some sense (however qualified) one of them. They are friends, neighbors, those you give a wave to as you get your shopping, people who you follow in the spirit of cousins or co-workers. This *filming-from-within* proves crucial to the take on gun violence that emerges, for his films show how ordinary persons negotiate extraordinary circumstances as if daily banalities—*because* daily banalities. And so, the banality of evil, of a system that has abandoned these people to foreshortened lives, becomes the larger frame for story. Story is written again from the witness position: and even more than that, from within since witnesses can be accidental outsiders as well as local inhabitants.

White Light is formally innovative because it introduces each of the main characters through a *painting* he did of them. These paintings are done in fierce and jagged dayglo, in the manner of graffiti. They blaze with color, light, and the spectral intensity of character. And so, visual art finds a new life inside documentary film. Because they are painted on-site, in the neighborhood, with the figure there, they too claim the position of witness, of I-was-there.

Figure 4.3 Gittoes, *P. Souljah, Love and Pain*, from *White Light*. Image courtesy of George Gittoes, photograph by Helen Rose.

There is always a question of exploitation when local communities are the source of documentary film. Street children, the poor and vulnerable, may at the worst be used then thrown back onto the streets while the filmmaker gains political credit (and maybe dollars) for using them. This is as far from Gittoes's work as can be imagined. His every project, whether in Afghanistan or Chicago, has built trust within the community and connections outside it, which Gittoes has then used to empower his retinue of locals. Some of those featured in *White Light* have gone on—thanks to him—to enroll in school, earn medical technology certificates, quit their gangs, and in one case turn from a gang member to a social worker for the gangs he used to "hang with." That too is political, and a kind of "art." The art of a community organizer.

5

Virulent Nationalism and the Politics of Offense: The NEA 4

Part I

The modern nation-state arose in the wake of the Treaty of Westphalia of 1648, which ended the catastrophic religious wars of the seventeenth century that devastated Europe, establishing terms of national sovereignty that remained in place until the end of the Second World War. These terms crucially limited the scope of international law by assigning total internal control to each and every nation-state. What happened in France or England belonged in France or England; it was no one else's business to interfere. In turn, the modern nation-state could no longer found itself primarily on transnational religious authority and had to find other ways to unite its populations—populations that often comprised multiple religious sects with a history of previous enmity.

This need to create new terms of belonging for a divisive citizenry led to the creation of the modern European form of heritage. The nation-state began the great game of scripting a shared past that became understood as the source of national unity, authority, and superiority. Courts of law, universities, concert halls, and museums became understood as the bearers of national patrimony and civility. Morals, norms, and habits were assigned national character, this to the point where, in a Europe that, thanks to colonialism and empire, relied on race as a central lens for the understanding of human reality, even national character began to be understood as *racial difference*, the English "race" differing from the "Italian" in the way pale-skinned English reserve, grace under fire, wit, and rationality were opposed (in the English imagination anyway) to dark-haired, Roman volubility, ebullience, liveliness, zest for life, and a tendency to murder rivals (which the English considered operatically "Italian"). This is the stuff of fiction, but also of actual cultural beliefs. At a certain point in the nineteenth century (with the writings of Matthew Arnold, Fredric Nietzsche, and others), heritage was declared the philosophical origin of the nation, from which modern life had strayed, demanding romantic return and fidelity to civilizing sources. These were inevitably to be found in ancient Greece.

Heritage was always a script under contestation. Fights about the character and importance of the national past were signs of deeper arguments around belonging. Who among the diverse citizenry of a nation-state should rightly be said to *belong*, and who should be considered marginal, an outsider, a threat to national character and culture.

Every nation has such contested notions about its proper or authentic identity, about who it is really *for*. A democracy thrives upon such differences, if they are not extreme and are nondiscriminatory/violent, but the nation-state, every nation-state, also has the permanent liability of descending into fundamentalist, puritanical visions of what it is and to whom it belongs—ideas that unify populations under the idea that others within and without are the source of national threat and malaise (usually minority populations). Virulent nationalism demands conformity, seeks a vice-hold on diversity through exclusionary practices. It is discriminatory, liable to be violent, and, at worst, genocidal, removing entire groups of people from the face of the earth in the name of national purity, strength, and force.

The United States has been an ongoing battleground between an open and a closed vision of its citizenry. It has welcomed immigrants who have been needed to build the workforce and who have offered new ideas to the national conversation. But America has also and simultaneously closed ranks into white nationalist heritage with all the ills of a settler society: xenophobia, small-mindedness, paranoia about the Indian or black or immigrant threat, small town prejudice, demands of religious and cultural conformity. And so, the Statue of Liberty with its open arms embraces the "tired and poor, the huddled masses yearning to breathe free," versus the Palmer Raids of 1919– 20 targeting immigrant populations believed to be bearers of disease, lice, and communism. Virulent nationalism rears its ugly head in the name of a closed, purified vision of the nation (and who rightly belongs to it). It can be found everywhere in the America of today, and in much of the rest of the world.

Part II

It would be easy to say that art, being an icon of liberty, inherently opposes such nationalist politics, except it isn't true. The role of propaganda has been a central one for art in modern times, blasting the message of the state in oversized, overwrought images, usually easily comprehensible, since propaganda art functions as a weapon aiming for clear and comprehensible damage to its target, and applause for what it lauds.

But art has equally opposed the virulent state. And whether actively opposing the state or not, art has often been picked out as a poster child for everything the state does not want to become. Universities have also suffered this fate. This is in part because the institutions of art and of research and thought are easy targets, weak enemies, usually unarmed. It is not easy to attack markets, or the law, or the police, which are powerful forces in many nation-states. So, an artist or intellectual is targeted in virtue of his or her incomprehensibility, far outness, edginess, identity, or creativity, all of which amount to the right to liberty abrogated through censorship, repression, and killing.

Cultural innovation and knowledge creation are, to state the obvious, enemies of authoritarianism because they are acts of liberty. Which is why the program of state control is so devastating when, as in India, the Bharatiya Janata Party (BJP) is systematically replacing top intellectuals with party lackeys, and Hungary has shut down the European University, forcing it to move to Vienna. The way the state attacks culture is often through attribution of offense. (It may then move on to treason as in the anticommunist McCarthy witch hunts of the 1950s.) Attributions of offense, often of *obscenity*, allow the law to be marshaled as a weapon by the army of majoritarian moralists against the chosen enemy of the state.

In the late 1980s and early 1990s, American art found itself at the center of such a contestation: the drama of the NEA 4. Performance artists John Fleck, Karen Finley, Tim Miller, and Holly Hughes had won grants from the National Endowment for the Arts (NEA), which were then vetoed by its then chief John Frohnmayer in June 1990. John Fleck's grant was revoked because of his performance comedy with a toilet prop; Findley's because of the raw nature of her performance songs (as in "Lick It"); Miller's for his explicitly gay lyrics (he was also a member of the HIV/AIDS activist group Act Up). My colleague Holly Hughes at the University of Michigan had her grant revoked because of the nature of her performance content that included sexuality, masturbation, and less than idealizing use of Jesus. These four artists, consigned to the outhouse, then sued and won their case in court in 1993. As a result, they were awarded amounts equal to the grant money in question, though their case would make its way to the US Supreme Court in *National Endowment for the Arts v. Finley*. The NEA, under pressure from Congress, responded by stopping the funding of individual artists, a practice that has continued to this day, leading to a standoff between the claims of artistic liberty and of national control in the name of public morals.

The charge against the four was obscenity, and there had been a prehistory to this. In 1989, two artists drew complaints from the NEA: Andres Serrano

Figure 5.1 Andres Serrano, *Piss Christ*, 1987. From the contemporary art collection of the Lambert Foundation, Avignon, southern France, after its partial destruction by two catholic activists. *Piss Christ* is a photograph representing a small plastic crucifix submerged in a glass of the artist's urine. Photograph Boris Horvat/AFP via Getty Images.

with his *Piss Christ* and Robert Mapplethorpe with *The Perfect Moment*. Their works were meant to be shown in the Corcoran Gallery, Washington, DC, but the exhibition was cancelled and led to right-wing scrutiny by Jesse Helms, a right-wing conservative senator par excellence at the time.

The best writing on the NEA 4 and its political ballyhoo was by the late Robert Hughes, who says in his *Culture of Complaint*:

> Senator Helms and his allies on the fundamentalist religious right had [before the NEA 4] gone after Mapplethorpe—and Andreas Serrano too, and others—for two basic reasons. The first was opportunistic: the need to establish themselves as defenders of the American Way, now that their original crusade against the Red Menace had been rendered null and void by the end of the Cold War and the general collapse of Communism. Having lost the barbarian at the gates, they went for the fairy at the bottom of the garden. But the second reason was that they felt art ought to be morally and spiritually uplifting, therapeutic, a bit like religion.[1]

This Hughes traces all the way back to Puritanism.

Of Serrano's work, he writes that it

> showed a cheap, plastic crucifix, of the kind sold everywhere in devotional stores and religious-kitsch shops, submerged in an amber-colored fluid streaked with bubbles. The title of the artwork, *Piss Christ*, made it clear what the liquid was. It was the artist's own. *Piss Christ* was in every way an autograph work.
>
> If Serrano had called his large and technically splendid Cibachrome print something else ... there would have been no way of knowing that it was pee. But Serrano wanted to make a sharp, jolting point about two things: first, the degradation of mass religious imagery into kitsch (inescapable in America as any thoughtful Christian is aware), and second, his resentment of the coercive morality of his own Hispanic-Catholic roots. Serrano is a highly conflicted lapsed Catholic, and his work ... is about these conflicts. No image is without a history, and Serrano's is a fairly old strain in modern art—Surrealist anticlerical Blasphemy ... Not all Serrano's work seeks its effects through blasphemy. But *Piss Christ* certainly did.[2]

We may add that an artist with a Catholic theme drenching a canvas in his own urine must recall the blood of Christ, as if he were replacing that with his own juice. This act has to offend certain Catholics where they live. It is of course a tactic with an avant-garde legacy in Marcel Duchamp with his *Fountain* of 1917, a urinal submitted for exhibition in the Armory Show of that year until it was removed. Serrano is carrying forward Duchamp's provocation, if not assault. In June 1989 Helms and fellow senator Alfonse D'Amato were joined by twenty-five members of the Senate who co-signed a letter written to the NEA requesting reforms to its grant-making policies. A month later, the House passed an amendment that no NEA funds may be regranted by other organizations; therefore, only work that the NEA sponsored itself will receive its funding. In March 1990, NEA grantees began receiving a new clause in their agreements that stated:

> Public Law 101–121 requires that none of the funds authorized to be appropriated for the National Endowment for the Arts ... may be used to promote, disseminate, or produce materials which in the judgement of the National Endowment for the Arts ... may be considered obscene, including but not limited to, depictions of sadomasochism, homoerotocism, the sexual exploitation of children, or individuals

engaged in sex acts and which, when taken as a whole, do not have serious literary, artistic, political or scientific value.

This was the political context that led to the removal of funding for the NEA 4.

Now the NEA 4 were themselves highly political. All stood for disturbational art in the name of the emancipation of identities. Not only that, their *intent was to offend*. This is what makes their case interesting. Otherwise, their case would have simply been another in a long line of bullying censorship by an overbearing, self-righteous, right-wing government. Offense offered and taken on both sides (the artists and the conservative members of the House and Senate) is what makes the case interesting.

Offense was in the hands of these artists a wake-up call, a gesture seeking attention in an indifferent, hostile political landscape, a gesture of exasperation, a way of saying: listen to me, I am unrecognized by your society, my lifestyle disdained, prosecuted, left out! Those like me (in sexual preference, gender, etc.) are subjected to the greatest indignity.

In the case of gay men, they were dying from a pandemic and then being blamed for it, as if their suffering were the wrath of god.

These voices were a refusal of the indignity of silence (of being silenced).

Now there is a big difference in moral heft between something discomforting and something offensive, even if the line may be unclear in practice in certain instances and to certain persons. Much of the avant-garde aimed to *discomfort* the viewer, alienate her from her received perceptual and intellectual habits, thereby forcing reflection. Discomfort is a central component of the learning process, of the self's confrontation with its limitations. Eliminate it from culture and you have the pure consumerist form, according to which all culture, from universities to biennales, should coddle the consumer like a first-class cruise with its dining, swimming, social activities, and high levels of service.

Here the point was to go further than discomfort. To offer work that actively relied on norms of indecency, pornography, religious lambaste, sexual shock. The legacy upon which the NEA 4 drew was earlier performance art: naked women writhing on stage, delivering shock in acts of felt resistance to a system of structural discrimination in the hope of creating vibrant/violent communities of solidarity. I refer to people like the late Carolee Schneemann, who let it all out on stage, full frontal vaginal nudity, in your face emotional intensity, raw erotic power, and earth-spinning rage. In a liberty-spinning gesture, the point was to say: This is what I am, and if you don't like it, then eff-off. I am free to be myself and I refuse to remain in the closet, thanks to your hypocritical norms where I am stifled and dying. Art has seldom been so radically in the service of the proclamation of liberty as with the NEA 4.

The proclamation of both individual liberty and communal liberation in the form of joyous narcissism.

In that sense the work was absolutely American. The use of offense was meant to say: Stop badgering us. Leave us alone. Stop seeking to control us, to silence us with your legal firepower, your church morals, your police. The pursuit of happiness is mine to have also. Their claim of a form of freedom of expression ample enough to include them was a demand for procedural justice, nondiscriminatory justice that would allow for their freedom as much as that of everyone else (the silent majority's). And it was a demand for public recognition within the nation-state.

Their target was what used to be called the "silent majority," except that it was hardly silent given the contempt of law, Congress, and the state for such persons and their claims of liberty. The idea was to meet disgust head on with disgust, an eye for an eye. To offer up a version of the self so potent to an America disgusted with anyone who didn't fill the bill that they would have to take notice. I refer to an America of white Christian nationalism, family values, and small-town golf, to an America at the time unwilling to entertain LGBT rights, equal rights for women.

The hatred of black people, uppity women, and religious minorities by certain quarters of America has been a perennial feature of American life. Of people like my great grandparents, off steerage from Riga, Eastern European Jews with nothing but burning in their hearts for what they or their progeny might become in this cornucopia of possibility called America as they traipsed their way around New York City, bones aching, pockets empty, scraping out a living from sewing and rolling cigars while making sure their children and children's children would inherit the American dream.

The children's children of these immigrants (i.e., me) are precisely those on the left who support the identity politics of the NEA, while less sanguine about quality or subtlety of the artistic vision involved and more than a little upset at the craven self-righteousness of those artists who believe their identities trump those of all others, conveying to them the special right to make foul things and expect the public to love them, or at least learn from them.

As Robert Hughes puts it, "The conservative mixture is tinged with paranoid exaggeration."[3] To which these artists responded with the force of exasperation. Such work as that of Serrano and the NEA 4 had to expect and probably explicitly courted ring-wing reaction, being of the currency of "blasphemy," and Senator D'Amato obliged. The point was to dramatize identity, thanks to a boxing match with government. Art became a weapon in the struggle.

Part III

D'Amato had a point. It went something like this: You want to do something offensive to the Americans who pay for your work with their taxes, do it in private, with your own money on your own time. Why make them pay for it? Is this reasonable? There is something to be said about the right of a paying populace to pay for what it wants, rather than paying for that which slaps it in the face. Why not agree with him and say: If you want to make something politically edgy, go ahead by all means, but don't expect the public taxpayer to fund you if your purpose is to insult him or her. The doors of public culture are not open to the likes of you. Including the doors of the publicly funded Corcoran Gallery.

Two questions follow.

First, whether material meant to offend should also have the right to demand government money to support the offense. Certain taxpayers will find it adds insult to injury that they are paying for material that they feel is deeply insulting. Why should a public pay for work it considers offensive? This cuts deep into the question of what the role of public culture should be in a democracy.

Second and related, what does the "rhetoric" of offense really amount to? I think of it as a declaration of war. But is it also public debate by other, alternative means? This gets to the discussion of Jacques Rancière in the previous chapter. Should the NEA 4 be considered dissent from within the ruling democracy in the name of inclusion, or instead anarchistic war declared on it from the outside? And how does one sort out the answer to this question? If offense is public debate (dissent from within), then a democracy is obliged to encourage it, or at least tolerate it, even if not also encouraging it by financial and other means. If it is disgust, indecency, or treason, then it should not. The problem is that the two sides will, as expected, differ about how this question is answered, with the likes of D'Amato claiming the work is un-American, and the likes of me claiming it is a soul cry of exasperation demanding inclusion from a marginalizing society. Rancière will say that, if genuinely emancipatory in intent, the work is dissent from the outside. But ironically, that is to agree with D'Amato about who speaks from inside a democracy and who speaks from outside it!

I would like to call the language of offense a kind of dissent from within, a refusal of the civilized game of democratic consensus-building because consensus-building within a democracy has always depended on tacit norms that exclude and disenfranchise, then render those disenfranchised invisible. (The other name for these norms of exclusion is ideology.) This kind of dissent refuses those tacit norms by calling attention to them and does so through performance. But, if its goal is inclusiveness, nondiscrimination, and recognition, then it is not a war on democracy but within it and in its name. Such dissent is also solidarity-building, since the art of provocation may dynamize a hidden and excluded community.

It seems to me that a democracy must allow for this kind of dissent if it is to remain emancipatory. Call it dissent from the edges, with all due edginess. And it seems to me, that is a good way to characterize the intentions of the NEA 4. Not the only way, but I think the best way, as opposed to branding it nihilist, anarchic, disturbational, narcissistic, or merely performative, which is classic right-wing exclusionary politics: find an enemy against whom you can motivate the base constituency. Or better, four of them.

The issue of public funding is obviously connected to this question of how to characterize the intent of the NEA 4, because if these artists were speaking within a democracy about its failure of inclusiveness, then they ought to have been funded by said democracy. Since inclusiveness, nondiscrimination, and recognition are fundamental democratic norms to which every democracy should aspire. Indeed, they are rights.

Of course, no society should be expected to fund every kind of offense: those by child molesters, fascists, or terrorists, for example, not to mention hate crimes, disparaging stereotypical remarks, and so on. So, the society must, on a case-by-case basis, be able to decide if the recipient is bending or challenging certain laws (like laws against pornography) in the name of democratic inclusiveness, and/or because those laws are what at least some reasonable people would consider bad, or whether they are merely off the legal charts in what they do, and with no redeeming value. To my mind, an artist *should* be offended if they are denied the right to liberty accorded to citizens of the "right stripe."

The right wing will claim that the NEA 4's work falls into the same category as that of pornographer. And who are we to disagree, except to say they are deluded, reactionary, and self-righteous bullies, which simply leads back to the original disagreement?

An alternative is to control the rhetoric of dissent, purge it of all offense, because someone is always hurt or feels hurt as a result. But this is a refusal of the great claim in America of freedom of speech. America may well have a concept of free speech (and related, freedom of expression) that is too broad, allowing for Nazis to march down the streets of a city full of Holocaust survivors chanting Heil Hitler, because the neo-Nazis know that's where these Jews live. This seems to me to cross the line from freedom of expression to violence in a way no rational person can argue the NEA 4 have done or meant to do. And yet civil liberties lawyers, some Jewish, defended the Nazi party when they did what they did in Skokie, Illinois, in 1978. However, freedom of speech should remain ample enough to include the active cultivation of dissent, including dissent on the edges of legal fault lines. Refusal of free speech (freedom of expression), even in its radical forms, inevitably curtails cultural innovation, university research, and a culture of free thinking that is central to the democratic culture, not to mention economic vitality. Curtailing free speech inevitably bolsters the worst of majoritarian politics. Cultural autonomy should include the right to edginess, the right to make mistakes, to go too far on occasion, to try and fail. These micro-failures are built into the larger creative process of artistic and intellectual gain, without which the creative process atrophies. The histories of knowledge-making, and of art, are largely histories of the slow conversion of mistakes into triumphs. This pertains to the histories of medicine, science, philosophy, and visual art.

I take this to be an empirical point, a lesson learned from the study of history.

But it doesn't resolve the disagreement. X feels the NEA 4 are tough, shocking, even on the edges of the unacceptable, but the cause is worthy and the tactics understandable. Theirs is a democratic cause. Y believes these artists are beyond the pale, gross, indecent, harmful, and hurtful. X believes we should fund such work; Y believes we shouldn't.

Whether freedom of speech, or artistic creation, demands public funding is a long and unresolved question and I won't seek to resolve it here. I myself believe with J.S. Mill that rights demand public infrastructure for their exercise, and so the right to freedom of speech or creation is not simply a right negatively stated, a way of protecting persons from arrest for what they say or create. But it comes with positive demands: we need to make the society one in which substantively, such freedoms may be taken up. But this is debatable and I won't pursue it further here.

What then were the possibilities for resolving this impasse between the NEA 4 and the right wing at the time? I suspect none, given the incendiary moment. So we might rather think subjunctively: Ideally what might have been different? What lesson can we learn about how a cycle of offense could, perhaps in more hospitable circumstances, be, if not reconciled, then brought to a civil and tolerable disagreement?

In a democracy, one has to accept that there are diverse points of view about what is perceived to be offensive across populations. What offends one party may not offend another even if some things should rightly offend all (we know what some of those things are even if the list quickly becomes uncertain). Various things follow from this. First, the democracy, recognizing diversity in such matters, has to be open to dissenting positions even if hurtful. This in the name of a populace larger than its own cabal. But second, those who do offer offensive work (to some, perhaps many) must also bear a certain responsibility. There is a *moral obligation on both parties*: the offending party and the party who takes themselves to be the recipient of offense. How?

I can offer a personal example about the problem of the diversity of offense, something offending one party and not another. I had a close friend in South Africa during the 1990s with whom I broke because he would not stop referring to the State of Israel as Nazi Germany. I told him: Call it an aggressor state, a state that brutalizes Palestinians, an occupying power, and I will agree, and even if I weren't to agree, yours are genuine political points around which rational argument should take place (about issues of national security versus colonial expansion, the multiplicity of claims on the same tuft of land, etc.). But, when you identify Israel as Nazi Germany, then given what happened to my forebears during the Second World War, I cannot bear to hear it. Whatever Israel has done and is doing, it does not include genocide. I cannot and will not tolerate it, I said.

Now I know that not all others feel the way I do. That my outrage is idiomatic to myself and probably other Jews (although not all). It is personal. Others might find my friend's remark wrong, cruel, naive, or provocative without taking offense. (Or they might agree with it.) The remark won't hit them like it hits me. This variability in the perception of offense is crucial to its moral negotiation.

One is obliged to take offense seriously wherever it may be found, certainly if one is the offended party, but also if one is the party giving the offense. It is something the NEA 4 had no place for in their work, or rather they wished to count those genuinely offended people out. Their work offended more than the government types who are completely hypocritical in their values, more even than those majoritarian nationalists who were already looking to find an excuse to prove to themselves that gays and artists and women are inferior. These types were their targets. But the offense also extended to genuinely moral people who were tolerant by nature but shocked and upset nonetheless. The work of the NEA 4 never accounted for the collateral damage it inflected beyond its target audience, the Jesse Helms, and company of this world.

The giving of offense is inevitably an act of hurt, even if also one of necessary dissent. There seems to me no way around this. It comes with the territory. Therefore, the offending party always incurs a moral debt, a responsibility. This seems to me a principle.

But the *offended* party also has a moral responsibility, which is to acknowledge that in some cases what offends them has to do with things peculiar to them and may not strike others in the same way (as happened to me). This is the second principle. The offended party must realize that, although personally offended, in many instances she cannot will her judgment universally, assuming that all others should be offended in the same way and that, therefore, the offending gesture offends absolutely (i.e., is absolutely wrong). She is offended yes. But she must acknowledge others are not.

How then to resolve such mismatches between persons? Sometimes you can't, I couldn't with my friend. Ideally what must happen is that each party finds a way to tolerate the other. To do this, each must do a job of work. This is the third principle. If the offended party feels humiliated, this must be acknowledged by the offending party. Conversely, if the offending party is acting out of humiliation (as at least some of the NEA 4 were), then the offended party must acknowledge that fact and seek to understand why. Both parties have to get beyond themselves and try to understand where the other is coming from, what the source of the other's sense of offense is. Each must endeavor to determine if they lack some kind of knowledge that, once gained, could change their position. Each must scrutinize their own attitude. Is it rooted in humiliation, in grandiosity, in the belief that all others must conform to their views? Just how idiosyncratic is it? And since both inevitably share a common ground, this too should come to light.

Moral reappraisal has to happen as an ensemble, or it fails. This is the fourth principle. Both parties have to engage with it. No one can take the risk without the expectation that the other also will. Otherwise, a power imbalance between them is produced or replicated. Will the result of moral action on the part of both parties resolve the difference in moral perception between them? Probably not. But it may lead to toleration. I can't abide by what you are doing, but at least I understand where you are coming from. I know I hurt you, but I have to in this instance; the collateral damage is very unfortunate, but I've got to act as I am anyway. Too much is at stake not to.

Of course, none of this was going to happen in the right-wing America of D'Amato. Which is why the case led to no good conclusion: ostracization then celebrity for the NEA 4, the abolition of single-artist grants, more vile right-wing rhetoric. More arrogance and entitlement on the part of edgy artists. And so on.

Sometimes people can learn to live with each other in spite of the dislike between them. After all they don't have to go on a two-week cruise together or get married. Just inhabit the same society gracefully. Then "political culture wars" are reasonably resolved into the happier currency of moral recognition.

This conundrum is why the art of giving offense is problematic in spite of what might be its necessity under desperate circumstances. Offense hurts; it divides even when the aim is inclusiveness. If moral negotiation does not intervene, offense breeds more offense, and then more, until an endgame is in place that no one can exit. The use of offense is often less win-win than lose-lose, with one offending party giving rise to a more severe reaction by the other, and so on, until dignity is lost on both sides. This closed circle of provocation versus provocation is what transpired at the time. And so, a grotesquely self-righteous Puritanical America was caught between right-wing fundamentalism and political correctness.

It seems to me the more a democracy is willing to fund dissent, the better its character. Taxpayers routinely pay for many things they don't personally like. This is what it means to live in a political society. Since I find D'Amato's point of view revolting, I am happy to live among the misfits. Oppositional artists in turn should be less self-righteous about their right to offend/censor in the name of identity politics. Democracy runs on generous toleration on the part of all citizens, without which it has the liability to descend into even worse forms of virulent nationalism.

Here is a final worry about the art of giving offense. Such art has the liability to run roughshod over aesthetic canons of subtlety, talent, beauty, sublimity, freedom of imagination, and the like—although not in the case of Mapplethorpe who was a fine photographer with deep feelings for his subjects. And this sets a very poor precedent for art. Therefore: as a general rule, the less offense, the better. Neither conformity to right-wing ideology nor to left-wing identity politics conveys the least bit of *aesthetic quality*. Serrrano's work is beautiful in its way, as is Mapplethorpe's. But on both sides of the NEA fight, *aesthetics was held hostage to politics* and that is something to worry about. The offense spoken by the NEA 4 was deserved by a nation that was then still homophobic, antiwomen, and prowhite, and which refused diversity of just about any kind other than in choice of guns or athletics. And where rampant disease was killing an entire gay population. But both positions are antithetical to aesthetic quality and possibly contemptuous of it. This point is central to Robert Hughes's critique of the NEA 4 in spite of his disgust with right-wing fundamentalist control over the liberties of others. Call it the aesthetic critique of politics.

Message should never (or only in extraordinary circumstances) dominate aesthetic quality, as if the fight justifies the art. When art is turned into a weapon in the struggle, in the words of the great anti-Apartheid intellectual Albie Sachs, the entire culture is degraded. Even if the weapon is meant to combat degradation. When art is viewed as a weapon, Sachs argued in his important paper to the African National Congress in 1988:

> Instead of getting real criticism, we get solidarity criticism. Our artists are not pushed to improve the quality of their work; it is enough that they are politically correct. The more fists and spears and guns, the better.

The range of themes is narrowed down so much that all that is funny or curious or genuinely tragic in the world is extruded. Ambiguity and contradiction are completely shut out, and the only conflict permitted is that between the old and the new.[4]

So: only in exceptional circumstances, and acknowledging ensuing problems, is the turn to offense justified. (People will disagree about what counts as an exceptional circumstance, of course.) All of this points to the principle that the art of offense should be considered a once-off tactic of dissent rather than an artistic norm. A gesture performed in situations of desperation, exasperation, indifference, repression, and the brutality of power. And always performed in a way that allows the society to perhaps understand (if it tries) that the gesture is meant in the name of inclusiveness rather than anarchic disruption of the system. Unless that is its true purpose, at which point we are in a different ball park from the one I have outlined here.

The real irony is this. The attack by Senate and Congress gave these artists a visibility they never would otherwise have had. Without the revoking of their NEA grants, no one would have likely heard of these artists outside of the artworld (with the possible exception of Mapplethorpe). Even the art of offense lacks agency until someone with power, or some institution, is offended. And equally ironic, by revoking their grants, the right wing managed to call attention to the cause of the NEA 4, thus empowering their work—at least for a while. Yet again, we have the lesson, that art depends on a context beyond itself for whatever agency it has. It is not in control of that context. The best it can do is try to prompt it, which the NEA 4 succeeded in doing with luck.

6

Literature and the Politics of the Truth Commission: Dorfman and Coetzee

Part I

J. M. Coetzee's masterpiece *Disgrace*,[1] published in 1999 and written during the tumult of the South African democratic transition, may seem beautifully oblique, hovering above political events without naming them directly. From one perspective, his novel may be understood as creating a strange, luminous, haunting story from the events of the South African transition (as Samuel Beckett, his literary mentor, did with *Waiting for Godot* for the French Resistance), rather than commenting directly on the tumult of his time and place. There is something to this. But I think not everything, for the book is closely written in relation to questions so crucial to the democratic character of that transition as to stand as a stern, brilliant moral commentary, with a story that closely parodies key moments of that history as it was being made.

I will spend a good deal of preparatory time in this chapter addressing those events, also comparing them with their Chilean predecessors and an equally powerful work of fiction addressing the Chilean democratic transition—Ariel Dorfman's play *Death and the Maiden* of 1990. Let me first introduce Coetzee's novel (Dorfman's work will come later).

Disgrace begins in the city of Cape Town and ends up in the rural Eastern Cape, where David Lurie, the book's protagonist, flees the university that has fired him, to visit his daughter Lucy, only to find himself—and more than himself his daughter—the victim of horrifying violence. Lucy is raped, David knocked unconscious, and the three toughs who do it shoot both of her dogs just for the sport of it. The effects of this violence catalyze the rest of the novel. The novel ends with Lucy pregnant by one of these boys, and deciding against all odds to have the child. The boys who raped her turn out to be related to her farmhand, Petrus. The price for staying on, she tells David, is to allow Petrus to become the symbolic father of her child, thus offering his protection. The price Petrus will extract (Lucy knows this although it is never explicitly bargained) is that he take over her farm, with Lucy, in a state of reversal, now becoming his vassal. The painful nature of this reversal of fortune is that Lucy is exquisitely conscious of what is happening to her; indeed she chooses it.

Some think of *Disgrace* as a monument to white anxiety: the anxiety of being swallowed by black culture at a moment when the white racist Apartheid state is giving way to a democratic South Africa with a black majority. What we did to them they will happily do to us, and far more, the thought goes. Fear of reversal, retribution, annihilation is part and parcel of racism, embodied in the Apartheid project of fending off the "Swart gevaar" (black terror, those who will devour us in revenge). What I think is inadequate about this racist attribution leveled at the book (by many prominent people in South Africa, including then State President Thabo Mbeki) is that the violence unleashed in rural South Africa during the 1990s was very real, not merely sprung from the anxious head of the white writer. And Coetzee sets the core of his book in rural South Africa. He is picturing very real things in picturing the excesses of violence.

Not entirely, however, and I will have more to say about this toward the chapter's end when I return to Coetzee. Let us, for starters, remember the opening beats of the book. "For a man of fifty-two, divorced, he has, to his mind, solved the problem of sex rather well. On Thursday afternoons he drives to Green Point. Punctually, at two p.m. he presses the buzzer at the entrance to Windsor Mansions, speaks his name, and enters. Waiting for him at the door of No. 113 is Soraya" (*Disgrace*, p. 1). This weekly exercise of coitus, purchased from a woman who turns out to be married with children, serves him well enough until, by chance, he notices her walking with two boys who are evidently her sons, taking them into a fish restaurant, and she also recognizes him. Soon she tells him she is going away on vacation, and he hires a detective agency to find her telephone number and address. When he calls her at her home, she is furious, demanding (Coetzee says "commanding") him never to contact her again. This is the first of a series of failed entitlements he will endure throughout this novel, a novel that represents his purgation. It is this sense of entitlement that matters, that he can blithely break the rules assumed by Soraya (my home is off limits) and, not incidentally, because she is a person of color, clearly a woman of Cape Malay origin, who would have been classified by the Apartheid state as "colored." Matters are made worse when—after a failed tryst with Dawn, a new secretary in his department—he seduces his student Melanie Issacs, who attends (in a somewhat indifferent way) one of the few classes he can anymore teach on literary work that interests him: the Romantics. David is "mildly smitten with her. It is no great matter: barely a term passes when he does not fall for one or another of his charges. Cape Town: a city prodigal of beauty, of beauties" (*Disgrace*, pp. 11– 12). Flirting with her after class in a vaguely amorous way; he invites her to supper and, after trying to engage her in conversational matters about which she is uninterested, he invites her to spend the night.

"Why?" she asks, no more bowled over by him than he by her.

"Why?" he answers. "Because a woman's beauty does not belong to her alone. It is part of the bounty she brings into the world. She has a duty to share it" (*Disgrace*, p. 16).

He is speaking from the pages of some ideal of women held by the Romantics, Byron in particular, a reference that will turn out central to the character of this book, to its hopelessly exalted, and finally failed, Eurocentrism.

His flirtation does sort of turn her on. She parries (about female beauty), "And what if I already share it?"

"Then you should share it more widely."

"Smooth words," Coetzee continues. "As old as seduction itself. Yet at this moment he believes in them. She does not own herself. Beauty does not own itself" (*Disgrace*, p. 16).

She will leave that night without copulation, but later he will pursue her again, stalking her to her flat and, once inside, carrying her to the bedroom. "She does not resist. All she does is avert herself: avert her lips, avert her eyes. She lets him lay her out on the bed and undress her ... Not rape, not quite that, but undesired nonetheless, undesired to the core" (*Disgrace*, p. 25).

And so the novel begins in the vein of Byronic obsession, but without any of the ecstatic joy Byron reputedly brought to seduction when he plowed his way through the Venetian upper classes until finally chased out of the city. David is no Byron, in spite of his inner fantasies. For me the crucial lesson of these opening pages is, however, something else, contained in the remark, made so casually by the writer, that "beauty does not own itself." Ostensibly about poetry or nature (its beauty is the joint property of humanity, a book open to all), in David's voice, this is rather the rallying cry of Don Giovanni, who believes in his gut that women belong to him, they are there for the conquest, their lives are finally not their own, that it is the proper role of men to extract their beauty (sex) at will. It is there for the taking.

There for the taking: This is the unspoken motto of colonialism, for it is what colonialism did with everything. Colonialism may be called a politics of extraction. It extracted labor from native populations for little or no compensation, sometimes enslaving whole villages, in the case of King Leopold and the Belgian Congo, in order to force men to work the rubber trees. It extracted gold, diamonds, and everything else it could tear out of the earth. It extracted artifacts. And here David is extracting beauty from women who do not themselves own it any more than the mine owns the diamond.

Melanie is also coded as "colored." "Issacs" is a colored name in the way "Lurie" is a Jewish one, or "Smith" English. Every South African reader of the book will know this. Indeed "Melanie" is a variant of "melanin," the word for color. David's casual omnipotence with these women is that of a white, privileged man. It is what happens to David in this novel that counts, what price he ends up paying for this casual claim on those whom he believes, without telling himself, do not quite own themselves any more than sheep do, a remark Coetzee will make much later in the novel of vast importance for it.

Part II

But why discuss this novel at all in a book on the political power of visual art?

This is my reason: While the book is primarily concerned with visual art and its political implications, it is useful to think about the power and limits of the visual medium (or media, in the plural) by comparison with language-driven arts, since a fair amount has been said about where words are needed to politically empower visual materials, that is about a certain deficit in the visual medium when it comes to propositionally asserting positions in the world, and related, speaking in a political voice. This chapter is concerned with literature and what it can do that probably visual art can't (there are no certainties here, just reasonable probabilities and norms). It focuses on the moment of political transition to democracy and where literature fits at such moments. Chapter 9 will consider opera, another language-driven art form.

Here I restrict myself to literature (Coetzee and Dorfman) in relation to a very specific instrument of democratic political transition—the Truth Commission: the way literature has been called forth to enter into a dialogue with the Truth Commission, revealing and challenging its range and power, exploring its relation to the stories of those individuals who may or may not be part of the Truth Commission yet who feel the shadow of its political force. Although Truth Commissions have taken place across Latin America, Africa, Europe, Asia, and North America, I will restrict myself to two examples of literature written in dialogue with this instrument: South African and Chilean literature and from the 1990s. South African and Chilean transitional events were not independent of each other, since South Africa—thinking about the kind of Truth Commission it might have at the moment of its democratic transition to investigate crimes against humanity during the Apartheid period—looked to and modified the Chilean example, which had taken place in the year South Africa ended the Apartheid state: 1990. I will be cautious in generalizing from these two examples. It is likely that each transition is so specific to place, people, economy, politics, that each transition has its own possibilities for human rights and social change, also its own demands on literature.

During anything as vast as a political transition from an authoritarian, totalitarian, or fascist regime to a democracy, there are the public events that mark the transitional process: trials, negotiations, the writing of a new constitution or destruction of the old, new economic policies, pressures on citizens and groups to break through encrusted stereotypes and create new relations to others, changes in the way culture and education are conceived and mandated. These events comprise the national story. The "big" story. Then there are the individual stories, the little stories of those under the national radar screen of the transition: persons left traumatized by the past, carrying private burdens, those who seek to profit in the interregnum, securing a place in the new regime if they can, those who choose to leave, those who remain, full of hope, those who remain with none, those who are skeptical, or who despise the shift in political dispensation, preferring the old, however just or unjust, and may stand ready to stage a coup.

Theirs are the little stories, which are the stories most of us have, stories certainly touched by what is happening in the nation but far from identical to the big story, even if the big, national story impinges on the little stories in all kinds of ways, adding or subtracting possibility. It is in the gaps and relationships between these kinds of stories (big and little) that literature and art may live at such moments. For what literature, and other arts, can do is weave the individual character in and around the larger-scale event. Or show how—whatever the good news (or bad) is—this news does not necessarily change what the victim continues to endure, that which remains locked inside their person. Literature takes on a specific set of tasks at these moments of political change.

In claiming democratic, uncensored, free speech at a moment of democratic transition, when the authoritarian clamp down on freedom of speech from the past regime must be forcefully overcome, the literary voice may be called political: an assertion of civil/political rights. In this way, literature can play an essential role in the making of democratic culture. And in its dialogue with the big events of political transition, the literary work may also be called political: an act of dissent. However crucial to justice a Truth Commission may be (and I will spend a lot of time exploring how), it inevitably interpolates victims and families into its procedures and narratives. While these procedures and narratives are critical to its national work at the moment of transition, they also may do a disservice to the very persons the commission wishes to acknowledge, encouraging such persons to perform acts of forgiveness, gestures of reconciliation, and the like, which may, from the victim's and family's points of view, feel hollow and false. The commission may set perpetrators free, to the consternation of those who have suffered under their vicious authority. From the sufferer's point of view, the commission reveals but also lies. Acknowledges but also distorts. Helps but also hurts them. There is where literature is demanded: To acknowledge this fact, this gap between what the national narrative demands and what a suffering individual requires. This focus on the individual story makes the literary work written at a moment of political transition an acknowledgment of the place where human privacy begins and politics at best half reaches.

Because a crucial role of literature at such moments is to propose counternarratives to the big national story, it is highly unlikely that visual art could fill this role. Film perhaps, theater certainly (and one of the works I will discuss is a play), multimedia installation maybe, but I think doubtful. Here is a task for an art dependent on linguistic expression and its resources.

A certain stage setting is required before returning to *Disgrace* and, before that, introducing *Death and the Maiden*. I ask the reader to bear with me in this. Without a sharp sense of each Truth Commission, the literary punch will be lost. Part of the purpose of this detailed segue into Truth Commissions is to show how much political stage setting is demanded in order to understand how the literary works speak to those instruments of transition.

In the course of outlining the terms, and limits of each Truth Commission, I also hope to provide a new perspective on the very idea of transitional justice.

Part III

In Chapter 3 I detailed the historical background to the South African transition, from the discovery of the diamonds through the Boer War and the disenfranchisement of the Boers, to their ascendency in creating the Apartheid state, to the miracle of the democratic transition, thanks to the collapse of the Soviet Union, to the Interim Constitution of 1994 mandating the first free and fair elections, the writing of the final constitution and the Truth and Reconciliation Committees. I will not go over that material again here and urge the reader to review Chapter 3 if that story wants refreshing.

Let me instead speak more generally about the nature of that democratic transition, and about such transitions in general.

Any historical project as vast as a sea change in the political dispensation of a nation-state emerging from authoritarian, fascist, or totalitarian control toward a freer, fairer, and more inclusive democratic dispensation must, of necessity, be tricky. For two groups of people—one having benefited from the former regime (in this case South African whites), even if not active participants in its security operations, the other having suffered its brutality and humiliation (persons of color), including denial of economic opportunity and basic freedoms—now have to learn to live together on new and better terms, without killing each other. This when some are calling for violence—in South Africa against whites—with twenty thousand right-wing members of the former military standing at the ready, in the early 1990s after Apartheid formally ended, to stage a regressive coup if only General Constant Viljoen were to give the order. Indeed, during the Kempton negotiations of 1991–4, the province of Kwa-Zulu Natal had been locked in battle between Zulu nationalists (the Inkatha Party) demanding provincial autonomy or even a separate state, and the African National Congress (ANC), with Inkatha secretly aided and abetted by the infamous Apartheid "third force"—this at the very moment the National Party was negotiating with the ANC. It is possible that more persons were killed at this time than during the Apartheid 1980s.

Any democratic transition is fragile. The terms of the new dispensation must be set quickly, since no state can exist over long periods of time without institutional structures in place: electoral procedures, laws, a constitution, courts, a bill of rights, not to mention mechanisms (or at least the prospect of mechanisms) to guide education, health, housing, jobs, and the rest. The question of who is empowered to negotiate these new institutional forms is itself a matter of greatest contestation. Should the military be given a place at table, the former members of the old state? Must an international presence be there to guarantee the success of negotiations? Who is to write the new constitution, supervise the first free and fair elections? What can bring dispossessed populations on board with the transition, believing that a better future might really happen for them? And what guarantees must be put in place to keep former perpetrators and representatives of the old regime from staging a coup, not to mention to prevent those who can (and whose skills are needed by the new regime) from emigrating to the UK, Australia, New Zealand, Canada, and the United States?

In the light of the unique conditions of democratic transition, a new scholarly approach has arisen over the past thirty years—during which time numerous democratic transitions have taken place, some now under serious threat. It goes under the name of transitional justice. Countries in transition have special needs. Among these are (1) the need to punish perpetrators from the past regime and related, thereby strengthen the rule of law against the forces of terror remaining in the society, (2) the need for the kind of social healing that comes from public punishment, (3) the need for the kind of social healing that comes not from punishment but instead from public images of reconciliation that allow citizens to reimagine themselves as at one with each other—this as a nation-building exercise, (4) the need for specific spectacles of transition, often in an international forum, which will build the moral capital of the new regime and garner support, and (5) the need to delicately appease those from the old regime, so that transition will not be derailed by a coup or other means. These needs are not exactly consistent, hence the dilemma of transition.[2]

Martha Minow argues that transitional justice has at least eight goals: (1) to overcome communal and official denial and gain public acknowledgment; (2) to obtain the facts in an account as full as possible in order to meet victims' needs to know, to build a record for history, and to ensure minimal accountability and visibility of perpetrators (the archive); (3) to forge the basis for a domestic democratic order that respects and enforces human rights; (4) to promote reconciliation across social divisions; (5) to reconstruct the moral and social systems devastated by violence; (6) to restore dignity to victims; (7) to punish, exclude, shame, and diminish offenders for their offenses; and (8) to accomplish these goals through ways that render them compatible rather than antagonistic with other goals.[3]

The key to transitional justice is that it cannot be measured by ordinary canons of constitutional/parliamentary law since there is no working constitution in place while such transitions are taking place—the writing of a new constitution being a central goal of the politics of transition. Nor is the system of governance (parliamentary, congressional, etc.) as yet established or confirmed. Transitional societies cannot rely on any previous constitution, or set of laws, to guide and evaluate the course of events, since any previous constitution, being of the old regime, will be unjust, the thing one wants to get away from. Such laws would have allowed for the violence employed by the security forces in controlling dissent. Apartheid South Africa, for example, allowed for detention without trial for up to ninety days, thanks to the Prevention of Terrorism Act, during which time persons were robbed of freedom, often put into solitary confinement without being charged. They were sometimes tortured, even thrown from the upper floors of buildings to their death. This was within the domain set by law.

In a working democracy where law is in principle responsive to rights, such acts of killing would (ideally) be prosecuted, with perpetrators arrested and tried. That is retributive justice. So how, it is often asked, can a society without a constitution, but wishing to inaugurate a moral and political regime based in rights, allow such killers from the past to walk free from a Truth Commission, which more often than not offers amnesty in exchange for testimony? How can a form of justice be applauded that is *not* retributive? What kind of fairness, what kind of justice is there in that? The deep and interesting fact about Truth Commissions is that this is what they often, indeed standardly do—offer amnesty from prosecution of some kind in exchange for testimony, raising the question of justification. In fact, the transitional society has done nothing less in the second half of the twentieth century than invent a new *form of justice*, believing it to be the best and most appropriate kind for this particular and fragile moment of being betwixt and between political regimes. This form of justice is both remarkable and problematic.

Part IV

Truth Commissions have come to occupy a central place in the politics of democratic transition. This on account of the systematic pattern of crimes committed against populations by authoritarian, fascist, or totalitarian regimes. There is something right about Jacques Derrida's remark, in his essay "On Forgiveness"[4] that what gave the South African Truth and Reconciliation Commission (TRC) its "ultimate justification … is the definition, by the international community in its UN representation, of Apartheid as a 'crime against humanity.'"[5] Even if, as Pius Langa, former chief justice of the Constitutional Court of South Africa, remarked, the real crime, that of the daily humiliation of the Apartheid state for persons of color, was never properly addressed by the TRC because of its emphasis on individual perpetrators and victims rather than on Apartheid as a daily reality. How one might have reprised the TRC to focus on daily humiliation is not obvious. It is (and Derrida understands this well) the saturation of authoritarian regimes in police violence, their daily violation of civil and political rights, the casualness with which such rights fail to be respected that motivates Truth Commissions at a time of transition. But it is the gross violation, not the daily humiliation, that is the Truth Commission's specific purview.

South Africa adopted the term "perpetrator" for those who committed "gross violations of human rights," the vast majority by the Apartheid state, but also in the ANC training camps. "Gross violations of human rights" was a tweak on the more generic "crimes against humanity," a moral, legal, and political concept invented by Hersh Lauterpacht, the Eastern European legal mind who responded to the violence perpetrated across multiple national borders during the Second World War by the Nazis. "Crimes against humanity" was the charge leveled at the Nazis in the dock during the Nuremberg Trials at the close of the Second World War, the idea being that the millions of extrajudicial killings of civilians, the systematic project of removal of Jews and gypsies from the face of the earth: these demanded new moral, legal, and political concepts adequate to their grotesque size and international scope. The Nazi crime, Lauterpacht believed, was of a scale and international caliber that appropriately branded it as an offense against humanity. It was therefore the duty of *humanity* to respond, leading to a sea change in the character of international law, a revoking of the terms of the Treaty of Westphalia that had secured the peace of European nations in 1648. That treaty, the foundation stone of European politics for nearly three hundred years, established the modern European nation-state by gifting each nation complete internal sovereignty, a gift of sovereignty that vastly empowered the nation-state, demanding and creating nationalism, and refused international legal oversight, much less trials brought by one nation or group of nations against another. The result was that what happened in country X stayed in country X and was its own business, not that of any other country.

At the end of the Second World War, the Nazi crime was believed to require an international legal trial, presided over by judges of the four allied powers—England, France, the United States, and the Soviet Union (presided over uneasily)—for the crime was, in the words of Associate Chief Judge Robert Jackson from the United States, an offense against humanity as such. There was no question at the time that the trials should be based on the principle of retributive justice, and all but two of the Nazi leaders on trial were condemned to death in its course. The purpose of these trials was not simply to impose stiff penalties of punishment for crimes committed, but to demonstrate to the world that the Nazi record of atrocity would be known (thanks to victim testimony and legal investigation) and therefore could not be erased from history, and that victims would be given the right to speak, acknowledged as legitimate human beings after enduring a level of political violence almost incomprehensible in its intensity. Finally, the purpose of these trials was to demonstrate to the world the authority of this new thing called international law, claiming for itself the status of guarantor of a culture of global rights capable of publicly and irrevocably disciplining perpetrators, and through them the Nazi regime.

Nuremberg was the first Truth Commission.

The turn toward the Truth Commission represented the need for law to face front and center the moral and political abyss that the Nazi crime had opened up between the nearly impenetrable trauma of the victim, the scorn of the perpetrator, and the need to create humane political authority/ security across Europe. The inability of judicial procedure to reach and heal traumatic victims in spite of its best intentions is a story that has plagued the post–Second World War landscape since the Nuremberg Trials, and also the Eichmann Trial of 1961 in Jerusalem, in which one of the chief orchestrators of the Final Solution was condemned to death. These trials opened up the problem of witness testimony. They depended on witness testimony to secure convictions, yet such testimony can be precarious given the habit of the mind to block or shield traumatic fact from consciousness. Moreover, after decades, witness memory may be faulty. The last thing judicial procedure wanted was for victims to endure the humiliation of tough cross-examination that might trip them up—and trip up the case for the prosecution. Add to that the pain victims must endure when they rehearse their most horrendous memories in a contentious public setting where they too are under threat (by the prosecution). And so retributive justice, facing the horrific, met with the problem of being an added burden for the victim, even if sometimes liberating since the victim could now participate in enacting a greater force of justice.

That is hardly a recipe for reconciliation across the abyss.

Those who attended the Eichmann Trial included the philosopher Hannah Arendt and the journalists/fiction writers Martha Gellhorn and Muriel Spark, all of whom wrote trenchantly as it proceeded and published books thereafter. Lyndsey Stonebridge says of their various projects that the problem was neither to subsume justice "under an incalculable trauma, nor [calculate it entirely from] within the law, but [instead imagine justice as] the just city ... through a politics which makes both law and ethics meaningful."[6] The key is Stonebridge's use of the word "imagination." Reaching out to both acknowledge and repair the Nazi abyss demanded a new form of justice, but also wider innovations in political reasoning, moral thought, and trauma recognition. I think the Truth Commission responded to this need. But also nonfiction (philosophy, Hannah Arendt) and fiction (literature, Martha Gellhorn and Muriel Spark). It is not going too far to say that literature was a central part of the new thinking demanded by the Second World War.

Since Nuremberg, there have been at least thirty Truth Commissions, which have taken place as a result of gross violations of human rights, mostly within nations.[7] By any set of measures, these have wildly differed in terms of success.

Most commissions have not followed the Nuremberg formula. Nor have they been international. Rather, the Truth Commission has found its home since the Second World War in the lives of nations. And there has been a vast change in the project of the Truth Commission, which has, as a rule, not been organized around principles of retributive justice (punishment for crimes committed) but rather amnesty for perpetrators in exchange for their testimony, often testimony given *in-camera*, in closed quarters secluded from public gaze. This was the Chilean model of the Rettig Commission established in 1990, one year after the shocking rule of Augusto Pinochet ended, thanks in large part to the prosecutorial talents of Phillipe Sands, the British QC who argued successfully that universal jurisdiction allowed this dictator to be tried outside of Chile. (Complications in Thatcher's government prevented this and he was returned to Chile.)

At the close of the Pinochet regime, and as part of the transition to Chilean democracy, it was decided that a Truth Commission was necessary to bring out the facts about the violence that had taken place during that regime: the arrests without trial; torture, rape, and killing in prison; the sadistic pleasure taken by military involved; the dumping of persons from airplanes; the sending of them into forced exile. A record of atrocity was demanded for the historical archive, a line drawn in front of the old regime. But, given the power still vested in the Chilean military, and their right-wing allegiances, the Chilean Truth Commission could only offer full amnesty to perpetrators in exchange for testimony.

Geoffrey Robertson, among the first to write on transitional justice, is respectful but uneasy about the prospect of amnesty:

> The starkness of the dilemma—whether to pardon or to punish gross violations of human rights by former government and military officials—has been temporarily resolved in many South African and African countries by the intermediate device of the truth commission … That is because truth commissions have reported enough of the truth to discomfort the perpetrators of crimes against humanity who still hold rank in the military and the police: their continued influence frightens politicians, who in consequence invoke the "interests of national reconciliation" as an excuse for granting them amnesties and pardons, despite emerging evidence of their guilt.[8]

Robertson is skeptical while agreeing that given the power of the military, Truth Commissions organized around the principle of amnesty may be the best "intermediate" choice, for they do build an archive for history and challenge past power by requiring perpetrators to give testimony before the commission. Still there was something grotesque about people who casually threw young people from airplanes and raped others going scot-free because they bothered to show up and speak to the commission in closed session, knowing well that their names would not even be made public. It is hardly the kind of justice their victims and families might have wanted or needed in order to feel justice had been done and thus (it is hoped) to heal. Even if there is some compensation to be taken in what Albie Sachs—himself the victim of a Mozambique car bombing in 1987 that cost him an arm and an eye and nearly his life—calls "soft vengeance," the kind that comes not from seeing perpetrators locked up or hanged but from seeing their political regime decompose into nothingness to be replaced by what he was fighting for. And taking soft pleasure in the fact that those who believed themselves to be omnipotent were forced to appear before a democratic commission and state for the record their crimes. Sachs's vengeance was, he wrote in *The Soft Vengeance of a Freedom Fighter*, the triumph of his aspirations for the future, rather than his desire for personal vendetta.[9]

Paraphrasing Robertson's language, transitional justice is problematic because it has to defer to the cross-current of reactionary and emancipatory forces, which it must, by necessity, balance. The theory of transitional justice understands that best possible justice in such particular and fraught circumstances demands subtle and precise forms of evaluation, ones that pay close attention to the fraught nature of the transition, its delicate balance of forces, its goals of setting to the terms for a new political dispensation while prompting populations to learn to live together according to those terms.

This "second best idea" of nonretributive justice is in a way right but also, I think, insufficient in grasping the *gain* that can come from a set of trials *not organized around punishment*. Sachs, a lawyer appointed by Mandela to the Constitutional Court in 1995, pioneered the concept of "restorative justice," at the core of the South African TRC. The idea is that by designing a Truth Commission around something other than punishment, all kind of gain can be achieved in the bringing about of a democratic transition that goes beyond preventing a backlash (military coup). The inability to prosecute on the Nuremberg model may lead to unexpected and profound compensatory gains for the transitional process.

This brings us to the TRC.

The South African TRC came about, thanks to serendipity. As part of the Kempton Park negotiations from 1991 to 1994 between the ANC and the National Party, which led to the Interim Constitution of 1994, it was decided that South Africa needed to adopt a procedure for investigating past crimes. Bishop Tutu, who would chair the TRC, argued that human rights abuses in the ANC training camps also needed to be included in the TRC's purview but that would come after the terms for the TRC were set by the Interim Constitution of 1994 and confirmed in the Promotion of National Unity and Reconciliation Act of 1995, adopted by parliament. This is important because a parliamentary mandate is more compelling than, as in the case of the Chilean TRC, a presidential directive.

In thinking about what kind of investigation into past crimes should take place, Chilean and Argentinian models were closely studied. Naturally, the National Party wanted to adopt the Chilean model: full amnesty in exchange for testimony, and proceedings shielded from public view, leading to a report with no names of perpetrators given. The ANC wanted a retributive set of trials leading to punishment (the Nuremberg model). The two parties were forced to compromise. And the compromise they hit on was that of *qualified amnesty*, a concept so contested that it was added to the Interim Constitution only as a last-minute codicil. The terms of qualified amnesty were utterly new to the history of Truth Commissions, offering perpetrators a chance to apply for amnesty, which they would get if two conditions were satisfied. First, full disclosure of their gross violations of human rights. And second, what the commission called "proportionality."

"Full disclosure" is hard enough to evaluate. A suspected "terrorist" (usually a black youth from the townships) is killed, with no witnesses. How then does the commission know if the perpetrator is fully disclosing what happened or not, since there are no witnesses? Well, in some cases, there were witnesses, police reports, independent pathological investigations, paper trails. And the commission did have a research division that managed to unearth vast amounts of hidden records from the police, in itself a victory of democracy because it was a way of disciplining the authorities (who would never have given up such information in the past, much less to persons of color who might be among the research teams).[10] Moreover, the pressure of cross-examination in a public forum stocked with reporters and broadcast over the television also had its effect. So, the demand for full disclosure was not untenable.

It is the second criterion for amnesty that is more problematical, namely the criterion of proportionality. This criterion stated that the crime had to be rationalizable (although not rendered less otiose) in relation to its political goal. In the abstract, such a criterion is neither very clear nor palatable (insofar as it is clear). If it means a crime is worthy of amnesty if it is committed in the name of a clear political aspiration, this hardly gets us very far, since the Nazis justified genocide in terms of their political goals: a world without Jewish virus, where Aryan blood flowed purely. In the South African case, throwing a young man incarcerated without charges from a seventh-story window to his death could be argued as essential to the goal of sustaining the Apartheid state, since that person (call him Ahmed Timol) was judged a danger to it by the relevant authorities (the security forces).

The best way to interpret this criterion is counterfactually. Proportionality is meant to exclude killings and the like for which no real political motivation could have been offered, even given the political goals of the Apartheid state. Acts like the killing of young children, the raping of old women, the bombing of schools for which an Apartheid perpetrator could not offer justification in terms of the "war against those who resist." Such acts would preclude amnesty because no one member of the Apartheid state could argue that killing a baby was politically essential to the regime.

This criterion sometimes led to major conflicts between the perpetrators testifying before the commission. Imagine the following scenario: three members of the security forces go into a house where a suspected member of Umkonto-i-Sizwe, the armed wing of the ANC, is believed to be hiding. He is shot, but so are two old women, neither of whom can plausibly be described as a suspect. The killer of the suspected member of Umkonto may get amnesty, but whoever killed the women may not. So each one among the three might say the others killed the women. All the policemen who applied for amnesty in the Craddock Four killing—where three members of an anti-Apartheid youth league were killed but also a bystander/friend who had nothing to do with that youth league—failed to get amnesty because it could not be decided who had killed the bystander. So, this criterion carried weight.

Of the 7,000 people who applied for amnesty, only 1,700 got it. However, and here is the scandal, those who failed to get amnesty were meant to be prosecuted in the courts (delivered over to retributive justice). But parliament revoked the law that required such prosecutions, claiming lack of resources to pay for all those trials, the result being that most who did not get amnesty went free. And some of the most egregious Apartheid torturers did get amnesty, in virtue of a full disclosure of their crimes and successfully arguing that what they had done was entirely for political purposes. These include Jeffrey Benzien, the waterboarder. Unlike the Bush administration that justified waterboarding in Guantanamo after 911, renaming it "enhanced interrogation" in the usual American double-speak, the TRC had no doubt that waterboarding constitutes torture. Yet, Benzien got amnesty, in part because he went through the motions of repentance, even claiming that he visited a psychiatrist (once) to find out what was wrong with him.

Qualified amnesty, while a distinct improvement over full amnesty, also had its problems. A number of key families of victims—such as the family of Steve Biko, the head of the Black Consciousness movement brutally killed by the Apartheid authorities in 1977—refused to participate in the proceedings.

The real virtue of qualified amnesty was that it allowed the TRC to be formulated around the idea of restorative justice, the justice that comes from forgiveness and reconciliation. This was the public gain when the public required new images of reconciliation to help them believe in the transition and, more importantly, believe in each other. What required change was *recognition*: the way persons viewed each other and understood their relation to the state. Every day from 1996 to 1999 when the commission met in Johannesburg, Durban, Port Elizabeth, Cape Town, along the Wild Coast, in the free state, across the country, their banner boldly draped the proceedings in the words "Truth: The Road to Reconciliation," people watched. Three members of the commission were members of the cloth: Desmond Tutu,

Archbishop of Cape Town, popularly known as "Arch"; Alec Boraine; and Bongani Finca. Tutu often broke into tears upon hearing victims bespeak their stories, weeping with them as they too broke down and were led out of the proceedings to gather themselves together. Women hugged each other, held hands, to buoy victims and families up. Tutu often prayed, asking God for help. These proceedings were the cold stuff of prosecutorial cross-examination (Prosecutor George Bezos addressing an Afrikaans member of the police: "I put it to you sir that your entire testimony is a pack of lies"). But also of a shared experience of purgation and redemption.

Importantly, the challenges faced by witnesses giving testimony before the TRC were quite different from those of Holocaust survivors in the Nazi trials. Since the Nazi trials were prosecutorial, witnesses could be fiercely challenged and shredded by attorneys for the defense cross-examining them for inconsistencies of memory, lapses, and so on, compounding their anxiety. The TRC did not cross-examine witnesses in this way. The point was to care for them, acknowledge them, applaud their courage, help them. If a witness stumbled before the TRC, he or she was treated kindly. Witnesses were given breaks to find composure and get their thoughts together. The proceedings frequently paused for this reason. None of which would have been possible in anything like the same way in a context of retributive justice, where there is far more burden placed on the witness given cross-examination.

Did a form of justice in which there was no witness cross-examination lead to uncorrected mistakes and inconsistencies, obscuring truth? Perhaps, although I cannot answer this definitively since we cannot know what might have been corrected if witness cross-examination had taken place. (And remember, there were other means of correction, including the researchers for the TRC and the data they came up with, and the testimony of other witnesses.) But here is the point. These were not trials seeking conviction and sentencing. Most of the perpetrators who came before the commission *had already acknowledged guilt* and were applying for amnesty. They were cross-examined, which became a key source of truth for the record. So there was not the same urgency placed on the absolute correctness of witness testimony as there would have been in an ordinary trial, where the witness is there to help convict someone who claims innocence.

None of this culture of witness care and of reconciliation would have been possible without the deeply forgiving nature of southern African Christianity, with its apostolic rituals and faith, its communal choirs, its fusion with earlier African spirit cultures where, in the words of David Bunn, what the victims wanted was to know where their loved ones were killed or buried, because of the belief that their spirits linger nearby, seeking comfort.[11]

The TRC became a public brand, thanks to the media that had also branded South Africa as the rainbow nation with Mandela at the helm in his multicolored biblical shirts: David's coat of many colors from the book of Exodus, symbolically enacted with South Africans crossing the red sea from slavery to the new state.[12] All of this cast the proceedings as offering South Africa a new moral culture, based in togetherness, equality, the overcoming of the divisions of the past, as if through a process of crucifixion and transfiguration. The currency of morals was, throughout the TRC, religion.

This is why the idea of amnesty as "second best" is inadequate. Because what a procedure or instrument based in amnesty could offer in the South African example was the dazzling culture of moral purgation and reconciliation with a religious cast. This may also be what made the TRC not exportable (easily anyway). Not every nation around the world is capable nor wishes to cloak its transitional events in this ecclesiastical garb.

And so, under Tutu's moral and spiritual leadership, a perpetrator's *performance of repentance* came to matter for how he might be evaluated. And forgiven.

Jacques Derrida argues:

> In order to approach … the very concept of forgiveness, logic and common sense agree for once with the paradox: it is necessary, it seems to me, to begin from the fact that … in truth there is the unforgivable. Is this not, in truth, the only thing to forgive? The only thing that calls for forgiveness? If one is only prepared to forgive what is forgivable … then the very idea of forgiveness would disappear.[13]

Adding:

> That is to say forgiveness must announce itself as impossibility.[14]

Is this not what the TRC was about really? Forgiveness was tough, unpleasant, distasteful, an object of serious ambivalence. After Winnie Madikizela-Mandela testified before the commission about the murders by "necklacing" of her football (soccer) team cum personal security force, Bishop Tutu literally butted her head together with the mother of one of the boys who was killed (Stompie), forcing the pair into an awkward embrace of "forgiveness" before the cameras. Mostly the public face of the proceedings deleted or rendered invisible the stiff, unyielding hostility that accompanied so many gestures of "forgiveness."

An astonishing moment of realism occurred during the documentary film *Between Joyce and Remembrance* of 2004, directed by Mark Kaplan.

A notorious Afrikaans member of the police, Gideon Nieuwoudt, who had been involved in the killing of black consciousnesses activist Steve Biko, visits the house of a woman whose family member had been summarily killed by him, seeking forgiveness and reconciliation (before the camera). The woman's son enters the room and smashes the Afrikaner on the head with a vase, breaking his skull (although not killing him). This becomes part of the documentary film. In another documentary film, *The Gugulethu Seven* of 2000, Thapelo Mbelo, an askari (black African member of the Apartheid security forces used to infiltrate potential resistance groups), seeks forgiveness from the mothers of the young men whom Mbelo had armed specifically so that they could be gunned down by the security forces. These seven youths were set up and brutally killed for the sole purpose of a photo shoot in which members of the security forces proudly posed before the camera as if hunters in front of their bagged lions, in order to prove to the Apartheid state how effective they had been in doing their "job." This so that more money would flow to the Third Force, that secret security force summarily exposed by the TRC researchers assigned to the case. Seven young men set up to die for a photo shoot, and the askari asks the mothers for forgiveness. They seethe with fury, knowing they will never recover, knowing that Mbelo simply wants to feel better about himself. Remarks are made like "I don't want to forgive you but I see no reason not to," or "I need to forgive you so I can move on," or "I will not forgive you," or "God will punish me if I don't forgive you." This is not exactly the stuff of Christian paradise. Nor exactly of reconciliation, if reconciliation is meant to mean a situation in which all parties to the state feel that they can belong not only to it but also in solidarity with each other. It is the stuff of grudging half-acknowledgment, again before the camera, when everybody knows these women detest this man for the pain he has wrought.

And so, the TRC exhibited a real disjuncture between its brand (forgiveness) and the steely reality of "reconciliation" as it actually took place between perpetrators and victims. Some forgave publicly and meant it; others went along grudgingly; others bristled or refused. But while the reality of forgiveness was tough, the *forgiveness-brand* had a genuine political purpose in helping to bring about new forms of recognition and trust across South Africans, even in spirit if not entirely in substance. This required that the events of the TRC were public and much publicized by the media.

Thabo Mbeki, a fierce critic of the TRC, argued that substantive reconciliation demands economic justice, the elimination of the vast racial inequality that remains largely unchanged to this day, in part because of the complete failure of his own state presidency to change things. Others agreed with Mbeki's criticisms of the TRC. But then, was the TRC meant to solve such vast economic and social problems or simply help steer a course into the new democracy where they might begin to be addressed?

Mbeki is surely right that genuine reconciliation must be the work of generations. Which the TRC could not possibly have been responsible for. However, what did happen during the 1990s was a neoliberal turn in the ANC's thinking, which, when hooked to the prominence of the TRC, did sideline conversations about inequality that perhaps should have taken place front and center then. In other words, it is not the fault of the TRC per se for taking up all the oxygen in the room; other conversations about inequality should have also been taking place, and these were swept under the rug of neoliberal trust in foreign investment, which mostly failed to take place (see Chapter 3).

Perhaps the moral culture prophesied as religion by the TRC would have had a better chance of taking root in the new South Africa if inequality had been addressed early on. I think this likely. But I also think that the later failure of the ANC to work toward the kind of economic emancipation that would have deepened reconciliation is largely at fault, not the TRC itself. It is the twenty-five years that came after the TRC that are at fault in their absolute failure to address socioeconomic ills.

How might one measure the good that the TRC did overall, given the disjunction between its limited mandate and its inflated utopian language of reconciliation? The TRC notoriously failed to capture any of the big guys, the state presidents who licensed the Third Force, the ministers, generals, businessmen, and church deacons who aided and abetted the pattern of human rights abuses that were its focus. It failed to address the systemic and daily degradation of Apartheid itself, something both Pius Langa, later chief justice of the Constitutional Court, and Mahmood Mamdani, then professor at the University of Cape Town, argued forcefully. That retributive justice did not follow for most of those who applied for amnesty—and didn't get it—was nothing short of a disgrace, imploding the very terms that drove "qualified amnesty." That reparations, intended by the Interim Constitution that mandated the three committees, were never given was no less shameful.

Here is my own take on the TRC: I think the very dissonance between the limited mission of the TRC and its inflated rhetoric of forgiveness and reconciliation proved crucial in changing the way South Africans thought of each other, preparing them for a new democracy at a moment when optimism was all important. This disjuncture was its point and crucial to its project of *recognitional changes* at a moment of transition. South Africa needed something morally grand to publicly steer it forward. In addition, as I said, the security forces were disciplined, the archive was built, victims and families were acknowledged, wrested from invisibility.

And the vivid dissent generated publicly around the TRC was itself a democratic good, the inauguration of a culture of free conversation that unabashedly took place in public. Including the literature to which I will shortly turn.

As to the question of what South Africa's transition to democracy would have been like had there been no TRC, we do not really know. Counterfactual explanations of history are seldom more than speculative (what would the world have been like if there had been no First World War, that sort of counterfactual question).

As to the export value of the South African TRC: Because the TRC depended on factors quite specific to South Africa, its singular process of negotiation, the nature of its Christian culture, it is not clear that the South African model is exportable, in spite of its role as a moral exemplar for future transitional projects. Toward the end of the TRC proceedings, Martin McGuinness came to South Africa from northern Ireland in the hope that a South African–style TRC might take place there, about northern Ireland's twenty-year history of violence that they now call "the Troubles." It didn't happen; conditions clearly were not right. Perhaps it should have, perhaps northern Ireland would be better off if it too had had a TRC, but who knows, it might have made things worse. A Truth Commission sets a moral and political example for others. Whether the unique South African formula (qualified amnesty) will work elsewhere cannot be known until tried. Political transition is always an experiment.

Part V

The Chilean TRC took place in 1991, at a particularly fragile political moment in Chilean history. Patricio Aylwin, a prodemocracy candidate, had won the elections, staging the prelude to the fall of the Augusto Pinochet regime and the transition to democracy. However, Pinochet—who had gunned his way into dictatorship in 1973, overthrowing the left-wing populist Chilean government of Salvador Allende, thanks to the Chilean military in consort with the United States—remained head of the military. The Pinochet regime had caused the deaths and torture of thousands. Twenty-two thousand persons remain unaccounted for and were/are presumed "disappeared," tossed from planes, killed in confinement, shot on the streets, or otherwise eliminated. With Pinochet still in control of the military, a coup against Alwyn's government was a live possibility. Moreover, the majority of the Chilean middle classes had been pro-Pinochet, a more substantial percentage of the total Chilean population than the minority white population of South

Africa that had ambivalently endured, sometimes tolerated, often benefited from, and, in some cases, embraced the Apartheid state.

Mindful of the military backlash and general unrest that had ensued when Argentina had pursued trials against the military responsible for torture and killing during the 1970s, complete amnesty in exchange for testimony was offered by the Chilean Truth Commission as a way of placating the Chilean military.

Still, the Chilean Truth Commission did accomplish important things. As a result of the testimony of perpetrators and the research done by the commission, it was established that of the 3,400 cases investigated, the military had been responsible for 95 percent of them, giving the lie to the military's claim that their killings had been quid pro quo (that they had been engaged in a war where violence was equally perpetrated on both sides). And so, fact was established against the lies of the past regime. Moreover, during the course of the proceedings, the Chilean court ruled that no amnesty could be offered to those who committed human rights violations against *disappeared persons*, since their cases were still unresolved (the bodies had not been found, proof of their deaths remained unconfirmed). This paved the way for the prosecution of some members of the military. Finally, as a result of the commission's work, Chile enacted new human rights laws.

Ariel Dorfman wrote in an afterword to his play *Death and the Maiden*, to which we will turn presently, "Aylwin was steering a prudent but valiant course between those who wanted past terror totally buried and those who wanted it totally revealed."[15]

Crucial to what compromised the Chilean commission, in spite of its important results, was the failure of a public face, which could have cut decisively into the unbridled authority of the military (but might have unsettled the military to the point of counterreaction). A public face for the commission and its proceedings might have helped victims heal. First, victims were never allowed to confront perpetrators during the proceedings. Second, since perpetrators were allowed to walk free and in anonymity, victims could only imagine the creepy situation where they might encounter their torturers in a shopping plaza, on the street, at a cafe, in daily life. If you were a victim, this scenario might have seriously compromised your ability to heal and move on.

It is well known that victims of torture or extreme degradation (life in the camps) chronically remain silent about what happened, finding themselves unable to share the intensity of their experiences—experiences that set them apart from others. This partly because even the most sympathetic of others with the best intentions had to find it nearly impossible to enter into their shoes and imagine what victims had gone through. This difficulty in communicating traumatic experience compounded victim pain, isolating victims from even the empathetic, if partly uncomprehending, gaze of others, condemning victims to a solitary confinement of the soul, and in perpetuity. Victims often bury their pain deep inside in a safe place, under lock and key in order to dull unendurable pain. Which makes pain all the more intractable. This has proved true of Holocaust survivors, victims of war at its most degraded, and to the victims and families of gross violations of human rights in regimes like Apartheid South Africa and Pinochet's fascist Chile. Even if a Truth Commission specifically designs itself to acknowledge victims and families—allowing them, as in the South African TRC, to testify in public and before the media—in their hidden recesses of the soul, trauma remains insistent and unrevealed. By a mechanism of self-safety, these secret spaces of the soul are sealed off, and not only because of the inability of others to really understand but also because this is a survival mechanism: the price of survival at a cost.

A public forum can alleviate that in part, if only in part.

If only in part: This means that a different kind of instrument is wanted to aid in the reaching of victims or, if this is too much to ask, to aid in public recognition of their plight, which includes recognition of the failure of transitional politics to really reach them. Acknowledgment is demanded. This is where literature is given purpose. Such writing will also be a way of critiquing the Truth Commission, whose emphasis on the creation of *national narratives*, utopian images, and an archive of what happened in the past can and does eclipse the very individuals—victims and families— it aims to acknowledge and support. These procedures and narratives are what that give the Truth Commission its value. But, they can and do fail to acknowledge the real details of victims' lives in ways that call for more fine-grained instruments like literature and art. Put another way, the Truth Commission can feel like a lie to a victim whose demands it cannot meet, whose suffering it may even increase. And literature can show this. I think a Truth Commission is wedded to literature because of this; one is deeply insufficient without the other. They form a *transitional dyad*. Perhaps this is why transitional justice is often met with new acts of literature and film, across the Americas, Eastern Europe, Australia, Germany, France, and many other places.

In what follows I turn to *Death and the Maiden* and then return to *Disgrace*, two extraordinary works of literature written in dialogue with the Truth Commissions I have discussed: one about the South African, the other about the Chilean. Here the point is to grasp what is called for in literature at such intense and exceptional moments in human history and society, when a society is unmoored from the past, with the future as yet unsolidified, when the prospect of human conflict may prove disastrous, and when the pain of the past remains secret and lethal.

Can visual art similarly respond? Much harder I think if not impossible. The story is too complex, demanding intricate verbal narrative. For visual art, the task is simply too daunting. Visual art can picture the victim, but cannot tell the story that needs telling.

Part VI

While the Rettig Commission was beginning its work, the playwright and novelist Ariel Dorfman began work on a play explicitly in dialogue with it. Dorfman, an Argentinian Jew, had been an advisor to Salvador Allende, whose leftist/populist regime had been overthrown by Pinochet. Dorfman had fled to the United States, where he wrote the play. One might say the play begins from the limitations of the commission, its blanket offering of amnesty, its in-camera proceedings, and unwillingness to name perpetrators, leaving them free to skulk happily about the streets of Chile, their freedom haunting victims in the way a rapist still on the loose causes anxiety and rage in his victims, preventing them from healing and moving on. Paulina, now the housewife of Gerardo and living in a comfortable house by the sea in what can only be called a state of limbo, is unable to move on and pursue her medical degree after being abducted and repeatedly tortured, including sexual violation. That her torturer, called "the doctor" (in a distinct reference to the Nazi Mengele, the Angel of Death), "worked" to the tune of *Death and the Maiden*—Schubert's haunting quartet based in an earlier song of his in which death comes to the maiden, beckoning her into the sweetness of oblivion, in a way that can only be called seductive (sexual)— meant that Paulina's channels of reception were permanently deranged. She can no longer attend the concerts she loved. Music frightens her, especially Schubert, who is among the most lovely and beautiful composers imaginable. No longer for her.

She inhabits the past like a shade, cared for by her husband the good Gerardo, who means well but is unable to reach her. No one is. Paulina is a victim whose trauma is secreted within, consigning her to a second disappearance. There is no child in the picture. She is bereft.

That Gerardo is a lawyer who has just been appointed to chair "the commission" (by which Dorfman means the Rettig Commission) is hardly incidental, for Gerardo is committed to democratic transition as a form of justice, however fragile and imperfect, given the terms of the commission we have discussed. He is optimistic about the potential limitations of the commission, believing it crucial for national progress. And he can be, because he was unscathed by the past regime. He says to his wife:

> Limited, let's say we're limited. But there is so much we can do ... We'll publish our conclusions. There will be an official report. What happened will be established objectively, so no one will ever be able to deny it, so that our country will never again live through the excesses.
>   Paulina: "And then?"
>   *Gerardo is silent.* (*Death and the Maiden*, p. 10)

This play (finished in 1990 and first performed in 1991) was written before the commission led to genuine changes in human rights constitutional law. As to the court's refusal to allow amnesty for disappeared persons, this too came after the writing of the play, and anyway would not have affected Paulina's case for she is not dead (permanently gone) but back in life, if a living ghost. *Her* torturer could not have been prosecuted for what he did to her, even after the supreme court's decision.

The anonymity of the perpetrators even when appearing before the commission proves central to the play, and more so because her torturer did his work when she was blindfolded, meaning she never saw him and could not visually pick him out even if she passed him in the street, making her life all the more disconcerting. But she remembers his touch, his voice, his smell, insinuating her very being like the music of evil or madness, making her mad.

So, what happens in this play? Gerardo breaks down on the highway while driving home late at night in the rain, and is helped by a passerby called Roberto who gives him a lift. Gerardo invites this helpful man inside for a drink and after tactful refusals he obliges. Paulina recognizes (believes she recognizes) his voice and takes him captive, intending to extract a confession from him. He refuses, claiming he is not the man she remembers, which may or may not be true and remains unresolved at the play's end.

> Paulina: We're going to put him on trial, Gerardo, this doctor. Right here. Today. You and me. Or is your famous commission going to do it?
> (*Death and the Maiden*, end of Act I, p. 26)

Paulina disdains the commission for its limitations. Her fury is unhinged by the presence of Roberto and all it triggers in her. At a certain point, Gerardo tries to convince Paulina—whom he fears has become unhinged—that murder (for that is what it will be, since there has been no proper trial of this man) will wreck not only his reputation (and ability to serve on the commission) but also lead to her incarceration.

> Paulina: You can call them fascists ...
> Gerardo: Don't interrupt. If something revolted me about them it was that they accused so many men and women, that they forged evidence and ignored evidence and did not give the accused any chance of defending themselves, so even if this man committed genocide on a daily basis, he has the right to defend himself.
> Paulina: But I have no intention of denying him that right. (*Death and the Maiden*, Act II, p. 31)

She will put him on trial. No one will know; the kidnapping and interrogation is happening in privacy of her home. Which is exactly how the Rettig Commission set up its terms. Since testimony took place in-camera, shielded from the public, no one really knows who was under oath, therefore who was guilty. She is simply repeating this failure of the Chilean Truth Commission to demonstrate transparency in its articles of justice, which to her is a failure of justice so dramatic as to inviolate it.

But it is not going to be a canonical trial, since she demands confession in exchange for his life, which is the way regimes of the past used to do it (Stalin's Soviet purge trials, Chile, etc.). She "knows" he's guilty, so she believes, and refuses anything less.

> Gerardo: He confesses and you let him go.
> Paulina: I let him go.
> Gerardo: And you need nothing more from him?
> Paulina: Not a thing. (*Death and the Maiden*, Act II, p. 41)

She demands acknowledgment. Face to face, which is what the South African TRC did provide, but not the Chilean. We could take this to be a criticism of the Chilean situation. But she is forcing Roberto's hand, since the only other option is death, meaning this confession is being extracted under threat to life. Which no court of law would allow.

Meanwhile, the sudden rush of power she has over Roberto has made her delirious with compensatory revenge. She is strangely lightheaded.

> Paulina: I'm in no hurry. Tell him I can wait months for him to confess.
> Gerardo: Paulina, you're not listening to me. What can he confess if he's innocent?

Paulina: If he's innocent? Then he's really screwed. (*Death and the Maiden*, Act II, p. 41)

Gerardo, appalled at Paulina's rush to vengeance, agrees to act as Roberto's lawyer. A trial of sorts ensues, with Roberto tied to a chair. She gloats over him waving her gun, seeking to terrorize and humiliate him in the name of punishment, an eye for an eye, the old biblical canon. Gerardo urges him to write out a confession, for she has made clear this is the only way his life will be spared. He does this, claiming responsibility, asking forgiveness. And while Roberto then says it was trumped up (he never did these things), Paulina believes, perhaps rightly, he has given away secret details that only the man who really was her torturer could know.

At the end of the play, we are left hanging. Will she let him go? Shoot him? Can she do it? It is one thing to wave a gun in threat, another to take a life in cold-blooded murder, even if one ardently believes the person deserves it. The relation of victim to perpetrator remains unresolved as the new democracy inches forward.

At stake therefore is the question of whose perspective on this instrument of democratic transition counts. For Gerardo the commission is all to the good, a democratic way forward, conforming to law. For Paulina it is a cruel farce, allowing the country to believe its past has been dealt with when she and those like her remain stultified, invisible, their torturers unknown, unnamed, and unpunished. Here we arrive at the deepest conflict internal to transitional justice, between the absolute demand for naming names and punishing acts, for acknowledgment and retribution, and the demands of a kind of justice that is not retributive but aims to be forward-looking, reconciling, restorative. How, one might ask, do you really restore human relations between perpetrators and victims or even victims and themselves, when the perpetrator is not even named, never has to confront the victim, ask forgiveness, appear before the public? Perhaps reconciliation in the end excludes both parties—the perpetrators and the victims—from its domain, relating mainly to those Chilean middle classes who were profascist and are now happily prodemocratic so long as the market works and the money flows. Which is a reconciliation of the willing, not of the nation, even if it takes place in national forums and in the nation's name.

These are the big issues raised by the play, once the depth of its dialogue with the instrument of the Truth Commission is understood. Perhaps the best case for literature at such moments is offered by Ariel Dorfman himself in his afterthought to the play:

It was then [at the time of writing *Death and the Maiden*] and now more than ever my belief that a fragile democracy is strengthened by expressing for all to see the deep dramas and sorrows and hopes that underlie its existence and that it is not by hiding the damage we have inflicted on ourselves that we will avoid its repetition. (*Death and the Maiden*, p. 73).

Dorfman goes on:

How to heal a country that has been traumatized by repression if the fear to speak out is still omnipresent everywhere? And how do you reach the truth if lying has become a habit? How do we keep the past alive without becoming its prisoner? How do we forget it without risking its repetition in the future? Is it legitimate to sacrifice the truth to insure peace? And what are the consequences of suppressing the past and the truth it is whispering or howling to us … And how guilty are we all of what happened to those who suffered most? (*Death and the Maiden*, pp. 73–4)

A democracy demands an intellectual class, which is dedicated to ruminating about from whence the nation has come, what its limits are, where it is going, whom or what it can or cannot heal. And ruminating in the name of the incipient democracy rather than against it or outside it. An intellectual class is as important to a democratic form of politics as an expert, professional class. It is the sign of populist leaders today from Victor Orban in Hungary to Donald Trump in America, who are antidemocratic and authoritarian to the core, that they attack *both* classes in order to expand their own unbridled grip through cronyism, oaths of loyalty, and fake news justified as "free speech."

Part VII

Crucial to the South African TRC was a public image of utopian reconciliation belied by the real tensions between perpetrators and victims. Was the image of utopian reconciliation then a lie? South Africa needed to create images of reconciliation at the national level. This brings up the role of utopia in history, a topic I can at best touch on. Utopianism is always a form of seduction, a crest of wave inviting persons to ride it like surfers toward glistening, faraway, historical shores. If utopianism is justified, it is justified by what it aspires to bring about, but also by its pragmatic role in the quagmire of the moment. By preaching an idealized historical future as inevitable, utopianism may inspire confidence and general enthusiasm, create excitement, and bring people together in its wake. *This is what justifies it: its role in the now, not the truth it preaches about an idealized future.*

And yet the utopian falsehood can also hurt. Clarity is also needed about the real problems of victims and perpetrators. Individual healing demands individual acknowledgment, while national reconciliation demands the lie or, more accurately, the luminously fictional, utopian image for all. Both truth and lying are required in some interestingly Nietzschean sense.[16] (Or, if one prefers another kind of language, more than one variety of truth is needed.)

I think this is a needed addition to the literature on transitional justice. That the transitional moment may demand both truth and lying. Lying in the form of righteous images and procedures performed for the public, procedures that also aim for truth (the archive, etc.) but which run roughshod over both victim and perpetrator. Here is where literature and other kinds of truth-telling than those of the Truth Commission are called on to play their role. To acknowledge the lives of individuals when the national story of necessity preaches an idealized version. While also perhaps acknowledging the importance of the ideal for the present and for the future.

As to proclamations about reconciliation by the TRC: The very idea of reconciliation in South Africa, of reconciliation as process and as goal or ideal, is *itself a fiction*.[17] For reconciliation implies that beings were once one, then torn asunder, and are now back together again. This is hardly, from a historical point of view, the case. From the moment the Portuguese settler set foot in Algoa Bay, there has been constant conflict. Through the Xhosa Wars, the Zulu empire, the great Trek, the Boer War to the Apartheid state, there has been little oneness between peoples. So, the very image of reconciliation is already a way of picturing a deep unity that was never there. This is of course part of the nation-building exercise.

Crucial to understanding the nation-building exercise are the religious terms through which reconciliation was originally conceived. The reunion of Father, Son, and Holy Spirit at the end of days, thanks to the work of Christ, has been for Millenia a divine image of final union. This inherited myth or ideal proved central, although unspoken, to the religious character of the TRC, with its emphasis on forgiveness and restorative justice. Restorative justice is tailor-made for religious elevation, which certainly happened in South Africa, given the religious character of both the members of the TRC commission (although not all) and the nature of African apostolic religion. And so, the guiding ideal of a people (the South African people) which has fallen out of relationship with God during the dark periods of history and is then brought back into relationship with God through the process of hard purgation, that is, through the difficult and painful work of the TRC. And in being returned to God, the entirety of the South African people reunited under the umbrella of God's spiritual grace. It is in terms of this drama that the script of reconciliation can be written as a script of reconciliation.

The concept of reconciliation entered into the stream of secular modern European life through the work of the German philosopher G. W. F. Hegel (1770–1831), who thought of history as a process through which European people (for Hegel the only people capable of producing history) came to achieve a relationship of unity or oneness each with their own self, each with the others, all with nature, and all with the state. This from a position of alienation on all counts. The work of history is, for Hegel, work toward one goal: the knowledge that makes such overcoming of alienation possible. Indeed, by "knowledge" Hegel means a state in which the claims and aspirations of self, other, spirit, nature, and the state all cohere without contradiction or alienation. At this moment the self's stamp upon the world is such that the world is now one with it. This state of "identity" nonalienation, or coherence (three names for the same thing) is only achieved at the end of history, prompting and defining its endpoint. This endpoint Hegel happily believed had landed in his lap, thanks to the French Revolution. In other words, Hegel wrote at the moment he believed history had achieved its goal and come to finality in the European nation-state. The nation-state became the goal of historical evolution. Reconciliation in its modern, secular formulation is about achieving a nation-state under whose auspices individuals may find and inhabit a nonalienated relation to the collective, to morals, culture and religion, to each other. Reconciliation carries the freight of nation-building.

This end to history arrives through a series of stages through which human life must pass through in order to reach it. These stages are the script of history. In each stage, human agency posits a new relation to self, other, and nature. Each stage gives way to the next because it fails to sync the knowledge of the world that is therein achieved with the conduct and aspirations of the age. Life remains alienated from nature; individuals from themselves and from the collective; the collective from culture and the state. Thus, does history move on, staking new forms of knowledge out of the old in a way that betters the old. Hegel's technical term for this dialectical process through which a stage is bettered is "Aufhebung," or "sublation," with each stage leading to the next through Hegel's well-known pattern of thesis–antithesis–synthesis until finally knowledge is achieved of self, other, equality, national belonging, culture, and the purpose of history which is coherent that does not alienate them but rather generates if not happiness, at least the consolation that this is the best there is—and is moreover good enough. Reconciliation does not come easily, Hegel is at pains to show in the *Philosophy of Right*, but it is there for the asking at the end of days. The *Philosophy of Right* is meant to show the world that, in spite of objections to the contrary on the part of many individuals, it is a world that—thanks to the nation-state founded on law, offering equality, build on a foundation of lived morality, culturally deep thanks to art, religion, and philosophy—is in fact a *reconciled* world.

This intrinsic connection between *the rise of the nation-state* and *a reconciled society* plays a critical role in the nation-building exercise of the TRC (1996–9), which took place at the same moment as the introduction of free and fair elections (1994) and the writing of the Bill of Rights and the Final Constitution of 1996. For the TRC could announce itself as the instrument that allowed pilgrim's progress from violence, racial domination, and the police, to a culture of morals based in forgiveness, truth, and victim-centeredness, a culture embodying both the Christian spirit of reconciliation and the modern Hegelian one, rooted in the nation-state. A culture in which all South Africans would be elevated, and together, under the auspices of restorative justice. They would become one: that is, reconciled. This ideal of nation-building as oneness was reflected in many of the advertisements and logos of the day, for example, the logo of the South African Broadcasting Corporations: *One nation one station*. Also, in the figure of Mandela, who stood in for all, as if capable of transfiguring the nation through the cross of his own suffering, only to emerge like Lazarus from twenty-seven years of prison like a radiant archangel in shirts whose dazzling multicolors were those of the new, dazzling nation, at once African to the core and multicolored/cultural.

Now crucial to the process of evolution through which history comes to achieve the goal of coherence, nonalienation, and identity is the historical stage where history is divided—better, torn apart—into relations of master and slave. This is perhaps the most well-known part of Hegel's writing, the master–slave dialectic. It has a specific philosophical form in his masterwork, *The Phenomenology of Spirit* (1807) but has become popularized as a way of describing relations of nearly total inequality, which certainly included those of earlier South African history. I discussed this broad reception of Hegel's master–slave dialectic in Chapter 3, but let me take the liberty of doing so again here. They are terms critical for the reading of J. M. Coetzee's *Disgrace* of 1999.

The terms of the master–slave dialectic are these. In the struggle for recognition, the master comes out on top (Hegel says this is because he risks his life, but we should rather say it is because the master is a force capable of domination). This domination by the master over the slave involves an asymmetry of recognition. The slave is pure labor; the master pure enjoyment.

The slave recognizes the self-consciousness of the master, meaning his ability to formulate plans for his life, plans for what will give him satisfaction and happiness. But the slave has no recognition of himself as also having life plans and similar aspirations. Hegel's way of putting this is that the slave lacks self-consciousness. It is better and more truthful to say the slave's sense of self is so degraded, abject, given the degraded conditions of his life, that he or she cannot imagine their own freedom except as a spiritual hope or dream. The slave wants more for himself than this life but has no language or situation to articulate, test, and achieve his desire. And half the time he or she is too exhausted to even think on the matter. Which suits the master fine, since all the master wants from the slave, all he recognizes in the slave, is brute labor. You will make everything for me, the master says, and the slave does. Hegel's way of putting this is that while the master possesses self-consciousness, the slave is pure consciousness, pure locomotion, and skill.

The drama is resolved only when, in the course of fortuitous, happy history, a reversal takes place. The master comes to recognize he is slave to the slave, utterly dependent on him or her for everything the master needs and wants. He owes the slave a debt because he is incomplete without him. He begins to *recognize* the slave for what he is worth. And this recognition turns back on himself: He realizes he is little or nothing without the slave. At the same time the slave comes to realize he is *master to the master*, because the master is nothing without the slave's work, his skill. This empowers the slave with a new form of self-recognition or self-worth. Each is now in a position to *realize the other needs something from him, but also that he needs something from the other*. The master needs the slave's skill, or what Hegel calls his or her consciousness. The slave needs the master's ability to reflect on what he wants from life and act on this, meaning the master's self-consciousness. Each realizes—and this is the important thing—that he must learn something from the other. At which point they become alike, because each interpolates from the other what he or she lacks, and in a way that makes them metaphysically "the same." And their mutual recognition of their sameness allows for the concept of *equality* to arise in history, not before.

The brilliance of Hegel's work is to show that in order for human rights to become law (human rights being equal and universal in conception), historical preparation has first to happen. Human rights, the concept of equality before law, are not simply dreamed up in the abstract by some philosopher's imagination or present in ideas innate in the mind. It takes the work of history to get human thinking to the point where rights by law become imaginable. People have to become the same (let's say, sufficiently alike) in order for them to discover or invent the concept of *equality*. John Locke, the first to formulate the idea of liberty as a natural right, could only have arrived at this dramatically new idea because the historical struggle against the monarchy by parliament took place in 1688—the Glorious Revolution that overthrew King James II and replaced him with William of Orange (who took the name King William III)—so that the idea of the divine right of kings could be, by Locke, challenged in his *First Treatise on Government* of 1689. Democratic law could enter the realm of philosophical ideas because it had already played an implicit role in history. Philosophy follows history and encapsulates its spirit, Hegel believed. Here the spirit was that of equal rights before government, rather than monarch–subject, which had been rather like master–slave.

In order for South Africa to arrive at the point when the Apartheid state was disbanded (1990–1), it took profound and painful struggle. One might think of this as the overcoming of the master–slave relationship, although it did not take place through a reversal of recognition, with the master coming to realize that he is slave to the slave and vice versa. Rather through intensive fighting, considerable violence, and determination, with the blessing of history in 1989 (the collapse of the Soviet state) that led to the possibility of a negotiated transition for both sides (again see Chapter 3 for more on this). The crucial point about South Africa was that changes in recognition did not precede the democratic transition, which came about as a mutually negotiated settlement because both parties realized they had no choice but to do so. The ANC had lost its chief funder (the USSR), the National Party was governing a failing state, and each realized the alternative to settlement was catastrophe.

And so crucial to the democratic transition was that formal democracy preceded the changes in recognition necessary for a democracy to function. I think this is the critical point for transitional justice. Indeed the fragility of transitional justice may be sourced to this fact. Had South Africans changed recognition about each other across racial lines, and about their relations to the state, prior to or at the moment of the abolition of Apartheid, there would have been no hitch to the transition, no worry about reactionary coup, no violence in Kwa-Zulu Natal, and so on. *Transitional justice is all about the time lag between the formal investiture of the transitional state and the new and better kinds of recognition required for it by its citizens.* Recognition inclusive of trust. Hence, the importance of changing the way South Africans recognized each other, to break out of the racial stereotypes, to create a situation in which the perception of equality and the recognition of shared dignity could begin to arise.

This goal of recognitional change was, I said earlier, a crucial result of the TRC; here I am saying it was a crucial *motivation* for it. The TRC was all about changing the *language* through which South Africans could understand each other, hear each other, believe in each other. And crucial to this was what Jacques Rancière rightly calls the need for new forms of public *visibility*.[18] The TRC made visible victim centeredness, perpetrator cross-examination, the performance of contrition, confession, purgation, and forgiveness. Every day on the TV, through the radio, in the newspapers. This is why the Chilean commission was so much less effective in steering the new democracy into being. It happened apart from public gaze, and could not play the same role in changing (reshaping) public recognition.

Now if achieving new terms of recognition requires the overcoming of the master–slave relation, this can only mean (and Marx harped on this) changing the labor relations between persons as well. And yet miners still suffer degraded conditions on the mines; the country has the highest levels of inequality in the world, hardly a sign of nonalienated relations between individuals, or between individuals and the state. With severe inequality comes distrust, crime (mostly poor against poor but extending to all), and the failure of better human relations that depend on people becoming more economically and socially alike. It has to be said that in South Africa, even today, the poor remain "slaves" of the rich, who exploit their labor for the pleasures of swimming pools, al fresco meals, and consumerist enjoyment, while taking the servant for granted in the usual paternalist way. This is a failure of recognition that can only be corrected when labor relations begin to change.

In the 1990s when South African national unity was being promoted in cities and on the media, rural South Africa remained mired in the past, which is still true to this day. Land reform is yet to take place, although endlessly discussed. Farmworkers are, for all intents and purposes, vassals of their owners (there are progressivist exceptions, enlightened farmers, just as in olden times there were enlightened kings, but never enough). The violence against farmers and others in rural South Africa is gruesome to this day, with weird satanic killings, rapes of small children, and bloody incinerations. The master–slave dialectic remains in place in rural South Africa.

This is crucial to J. M. Coetzee's *Disgrace* to which we now finally return. Written while the TRC was hearing its cases, I now want to explore what the novel might say, show, or intimate about the TRC.

That reversal rather than reconciliation structures this book is intimated in the opening pages, where the narrator writes: "Reversals: the stuff of bourgeois comedy" (*Disgrace*, p. 14). Suggesting that the book will have a dramatic or operatic form, since that is where such comedy tends to live. In fact, opera will be a central player in this book, since David's Eurocentric imagination gravitates toward an opera he is writing in his head about Lord Byron in Venice and Byron's lover Teresa who, spurned, lived an alcoholic, lonely overweight middle age. As David's life changes (deteriorates), so does the theme of the opera, which begins with the glory of the notorious poet-seducer of Venice, Byron, who was finally chased out as David was from Cape Town (more on that below), and ends with Teresa alone dispirited, alcoholic, and doughty in middle age as David ends up in the country, sleeping with a woman called Bev Shaw, herself doughty, with little enjoyment on either side, as if they're copulating like dogs.

I earlier said that some think of *Disgrace* as a monument to white anxiety—the anxiety of being swallowed by black culture. I also said that the book responds to real things—the horrifying untransformed violence of the rural areas. More problematic in the novel is Lucy's belief that the price of staying on in the new black South Africa, with its lawlessness, is total relinquishment of power. That corresponds to no historical reality in the 1990s, neither in rural areas nor elsewhere. It is a fear of reversal both unsubstantiated and, I think, not believable in terms of her character, given that she is a highly educated woman who has lived in the Netherlands and has the alternative of emigration. Or at least relocation to a South African city where she can live a middle-class life. I don't think she would choose to stay on. Both the starkness of her choice (the only way to remain in rural South Africa is to become the servant of the servant) and the actual choice she makes (to remain in servitude) cast a shadow over the book, raising the question of whether this set-up *is* partly driven by white anxiety rather than social reality. Lucy is after all not a farmer who chooses to remain because her family has worked the farm for generations and she can imagine, or want, no other life. She has grown up with alternatives. Her choice is quite frankly strange. On the other hand, Coetzee does describe her as a throwback, like David, an anachronism.

Lucy says to David about the alliance she must make with Petrus: "It is humiliating. But perhaps ... that is what I must learn to accept. To start at ground level. With nothing ... No cards, no weapons, not property, not rights, not dignity ... Like a dog. Yes, like a dog" (*Disgrace*, p. 205). In this nightmare of power reversal, she will have little or none. Anxiety? Reality? Believable? An image of a possible future?

This is another central theme of the book: the way human beings are shown to be like (other) animals. It runs throughout and finds its source in an earlier book Coetzee had written, in the form of a lecture delivered by a fictional character, called *The Lives of Animals*.[19] Most of the human action that takes place in *Disgrace* feels unmotivated, deliberation and reflection being characteristics that separate humans from animals, who lack the capacity to reflect on motivation. They simply act. Motivation is replaced by temperament: "His [David's] temperament is not going to change, he is too old for that. His temperament is fixed, set. The skull, followed by the temperament: the two hardest parts of the body" (*Disgrace*, p. 2). On trial for his job at the university (clearly the University of Cape Town, where Coetzee taught for many years), for sexual impropriety and more, David defends himself by claiming "the rights of desire" (*Disgrace*, p. 89). And, "One can punish a dog, it seems to me, for an offence like chewing a slipper. A dog will accept the justice of that: a beating for a chewing. But desire is another story. No animal will accept the justice of being punished for following its instincts" (*Disgrace*, p. 90). When students surround David after his hearing: "They circle around him like hunters who have cornered a strange beast and do not know how to finish it off" (*Disgrace*, p. 56). Lucy says to David: "You don't approve of friends like Bev and Bill Shaw because they are not going to lead me to a higher life, and the reason is, there is no higher life. There is only the life there is. Which we share with animals. That's the example I follow. To share some of our human privilege with the beasts" (*Disgrace*, p. 74). David too gradually relinquishes his claim on the higher life; his opera is never finished and hardly begins. He ends up assisting Bev in her clinic where dogs unclaimed are put to sleep. About the rapists Lucy says, "They spur each other on. That's probably why they do it together. Like dogs in a pack" (*Disgrace*, p. 259).

Central to the theme of animals is Coetzee's belief that what we do to animals mirrors the atrocities of human history, genocide, and colonialism. "Twins, in all likelihood," the narrator writes of the sheep that Petrus is preparing to slaughter for his party, "destined since birth for the butcher's knife … When did a sheep last die of old age? Sheep do not own themselves, own their own lives. They exist to be used" (*Disgrace*, p. 123). As Melanie's beauty apparently was. These are beings there for the extracting: one kind of flesh or another. The sheep is in fact a workable icon of Hegel's slave, who exists to be used by the master, in this case roasted, devoured, cannibalized.

The possibility of reconciliation makes no sense in the animal kingdom. And in the animal kingdom, reversal is a matter of domination, often violent. Change is rather prompted by external pressure, if not catastrophe.

Coetzee gives animals a given depth of feeling rarely found in literature. The book ends with David bringing a dog to the table where it will be put to death:

> Sunday has come again. He and Bev Shaw are engaged in one of their sessions of *Losung*. One by one he brings in the cats, then the dogs: the old, the blind, the halt, the crippled, the maimed, but also the young, the sound—all those whose term has come. One by one Bev touches them,

speaks to them, comforts them, and puts them away, then stands back and watches while he seals up the remains in a black plastic shroud.

He and Bev do not speak. He has learned by now, from her, to concentrate all his attention on the animal they are killing, giving it what he no longer has difficulty in calling by its proper name: love.

He ties the last bag and takes it to the door, Twenty-three. There is only the young dog left, the one who likes music, the one who, given half a chance, would already have lolloped after his comrades into the clinic building, into the theatre with its zinc-topped table where the rich, mixed smells still linger, including one he will not yet have met with in his life: the smell of expiration, the soft short smell of the released soul.

What the dog will not be able to work out (*not in a month of Sundays!* he thinks), what his nose will not tell him, is how one can enter what seems to be an ordinary room and never come out again. Something happens in this room, something unmentionable: here the soul is yanked out of the body; briefly it hangs about in the air, twisting and contorting; then it is sucked away and is gone. It will be beyond him, this room that is not a room but a hole where one leaks out of existence.

… He can save the young dog, if he wishes, for another week. But a time must come, it cannot be evaded, when he will have to bring him to Bev Shaw in her operating room (perhaps he will carry him in his arms, perhaps he will do that for him) and caress him and brush back the fur so that the needle can find the vein, and whisper to him and support him in the moment when, bewilderingly, his legs buckle; and then, when the soul is out, fold him up and pack him away in his bag, and the next day wheel the bag into the flames and see that it is burnt, burnt up. He will do all that for him when his time comes. It will be little enough, less than little: nothing. (*Disgrace*, pp. 219–20)

David has perhaps learned the Christian art of humility, even if he is also less than he was, deflated and without a future. This sudden achievement of Christian humility has expressed itself toward the end of the novel in his strange, unplanned visit to the parents of Melanie, the undergraduate he raped and whose grade he fraudulently changed, compounding the fault and leading to the procedure he endures at the university. In this visit to her parents, he kneels down in a gesture of penance, seeking forgiveness. He cannot have planned this; it happens spontaneously, yet was surely unconsciously prepared by all he endured as victim. He has become a Christian, this man with the Jewish name. He who, as we shall see, refused the charade, as he saw it, of penance before the university commission that relieved him of his post. Perhaps Coetzee is saying or suggesting, Christian penance cannot be artificially forced in a public show trial like the TRC, but must truly come from the heart, whose contingencies cannot be formatted by an institutional procedure (the hearings of the commission), a heart David now has doing the work of mercy.

Coetzee is also raising the question of whether David's mercy killing is not otherwise describable (like colonialism) as a form of atrocity. Otherwise why the odd word choice of the German word *Losung* (solution) in describing David's Sunday work (and Sunday is the Christian day of prayer)? To my ears the word *Losung* calls forth one of its compound noun forms, *Endlösung*, the Nazi code word for the Final Solution, raising the question of whether what Bev and David are doing is merciful or part of a larger genocide against animals. David feels love for these animals, identifies with them, given the way his life has unraveled, which has taught him humility and the need to be forgiven. And yet he may be participating in a monstrous crime. This is the fate of white settlers in South Africa, whose paternalism and capacity for love of the native cannot exonerate them from the colonial crime, even though colonialism was not (mostly not) about genocide but rather slavery or servitude.

That the book is in dialogue with the TRC and its religious images of reconciliation is clear from the procedure at the university David truculently endures, leading to his dismissal. He is a man of white privilege who, we have seen, thinks of himself as Byronic and bristles at the idea of public repentance. The undergraduate he has raped (recall that Coetzee calls it not quite rape but wholly undesired on the girl's part, which seems to me splitting hairs) is named Melanie—melanin, I earlier said, being the element of skin that gives skin its color. Her name is a direct metaphor for race. David's casual claiming of her is the very essence of blasé, white privilege, which he refuses to relinquish. More than once in the novel, both he and his daughter Lucy are described as throwbacks, anachronisms (of which the catalog of South African whites has many). When he is brought up by the university commission, consisting of persons of varying races, he refuses their request for a gesture of repentance from the heart, saying his heart is his own business, not for public display, then mockingly goes through the motions of seeking forgiveness, something that will come naturally to him only after all that subsequently happens. "Frankly what you want," he says to the faculty commission, "is not a response but a confession. Well I make no confession, I put forward my plea. That is as far as I am prepared to go" (*Disgrace*, p. 51). Moses Mathabane, one of its faculty members, says:

> Mr. Chair, I protest. The issue goes beyond mere technicalities. Professor Lurie pleads guilty, but I ask myself, does he accept his guilt or is he

simply going through the motions in the hope that the case will be buried under paper and forgotten? If he is simply going through the motions, I urge that we impose the severest penalty. (*Disgrace*, p. 51)

Farodia Rassool, another commission member, adds, "the confession must come from the heart" (*Disgrace*, p. 54). And "he must accept a statement— issued by him—admitting to serious violation of human rights" (*Disgrace*, p. 57).

Now this arcane way of speaking on Rassool's part is a direct transcription of the language of the TRC, with its inquiry into *gross violations of human rights* and its demand for, in addition to full disclosure of, the Christian gesture of penance. This was tacit but central to the way the TRC became understood as the work of forgiveness, restorative justice, and reconciliation in their Christian as well as nation-building aspects. Indeed, one of the horrors of the commission was the way even the most vicious torturers managed amnesty in virtue of their performance of repentance before the TRC. We have seen that going through the motions of penance helped some of Apartheid's most notorious killers get amnesty. This is what Coetzee is parodying in David's interrogation by the commission, which, in fairness, only wants to help him keep his job if he will cooperate and repent seriously from the heart. He says the heart has no place in a commission, rejecting the entire Christian overlay of the TRC in one fell swoop. Perhaps because he is throwback refusing to relinquish his easy and unconscionable privilege, perhaps because he is Jewish and far from the culture of repentance, something that will change as he learns suffering and lack of power in rural South Africa. Where the police play no role, and it is dog-eat-dog.

Speaking to Lucy after he has fled Cape Town to the Eastern Cape and is staying with her on the farm, he says, "No animal will accept the justice of being punished for following its instincts" (*Disgrace*, p. 90). And yet, Coetzee also makes clear from the proceedings of the commission that this may not simply be a question of instinct, temperament, but rather of historical privilege masquerading as such. Like so much in this book, the question remains unresolved.

At no point does Coetzee explicitly reject the TRC. Indeed, *nothing* is propositionally explicit in this book; the book makes no "statement." It is rather a deep rumination on human character, white privilege, reversal in a world that has not changed, and shows no prospect for reconciliation, and on the true meaning of forgiveness, repentance, and suffering, not to mention the love that may emerge from the experience of these things and whose name may well be Christian love. And yet the book's dialogue with the TRC is clear enough. Its representation of the public mandates of amnesty, forgiveness, restorative justice, and reconciliation are more than a little parodic. "These are puritanical times," David says to Lucy when he first arrives at her farm. "Private life is public business … They wanted a spectacle: breast beating, remorse, tears if possible. A TV show, in fact. I wouldn't oblige" (*Disgrace*, p. 66). Self-serving no doubt, bitter and recalcitrant are his remarks, yet also with a modicum of truth, since the very power of the TRC depended on its TV and radio presence.

David is, of course, correct: the claim to regulate the goings-on of the human heart, indeed the hearts of perpetrators, by the TRC, bringing them to the portals of repentance and forgiveness may be demanded as a utopian gesture for the national transition. But it is hardly believable about ordinary humans, whose hearts are as strangely foreign to them as David's is to himself. He does become something of a Christian, seeking forgiveness (from the Issacs family) and acting out of pity and love (with the dogs). But this happens only when he is stripped of arrogance in a story of disenfranchisement and reversal.

Here is the moral for the TRC: The big events of transition cannot plan and orchestrate such matters of the heart. In spite of their political necessity to be seeming to do so.

The lives of David and Paulina remain uncertain at the ends of this pair of books. We do not know what will happen. And this too is of the nature of the beast, the beast within and without (self or perpetrator). But also the "beast" of political transition that, at the time of writing, is in process without a clear conclusion.

The purpose of both Coetzee's and Dorfman's writing is to call into question the relationship between a public instrument of transition and the world of people and human relations it is bespeaking—the world of people whose lives may be far from the public/national trumpet call, and totally out of sync with it. Literature is about the private life of the soul, and what happens to it in those cases when private life is brought into the dramatic and glaring light of the big public story of transition. That is what requires acknowledgment. It is where literature, written at such moments, begins.

7

Identity Politics in a Consumerist World

Part I

Identity politics are among the political conundrums of our time. Identity politics are a key to political emancipation on the part of underrepresented and negatively stereotyped groups. In an America still battling to emerge from slavery and racism in accord with the Thirteenth and Fourteenth Amendments, identity politics are critical to justice.

They are also an antidemocratic reaction to the inclusive politics of diversity on the part of virulent (white, right-wing) nationalists who seek to gain or regain a stronghold on national politics in the wake of immigration, diversity, and globalization. Battle ensues between emancipatory and reactionary identity politics.

That is not all. Identity politics have become market-driven as markets encroach on more and more aspects of human life and thinking. Identity politics are liable to descend from the high church of voices achieved through the hard work of representation to self-capitalizing narcissism. Since identity politics have subsumed the arts and humanities in broad parts of the world, a careful and judicious discussion of their strengths and ills is wanted, and in the name of a better, more judicious, more emancipatory form of identity politics. Put another way, if I focus on certain potential degradations in this form of culture and politics today, please do not construe this as meaning I am not in support of the critical role identity politics play in helping to combat a racist society with huge ambivalence about women and other minority groups.

Now, in the field of art, identity politics are derived from the avant-gardes and their changes in the 1960s and 1970s, especially in America. The avant-garde strategy was really a paradigm shift in art-making, according to which plastic experimentation became linked to the goals of consciousness-raising and revolutionary political change. The avant-garde was about solidarity, not individual liberty and pleasure. It was about recruiting theory, science, experimentalism to the task of turning the work of art into an icon of the future. And in a way that would alienate the viewer from her habits of taking in the world so as to raise her consciousness and deliver her to the barricades of history. But the avant-gardes were also deeply aesthetic because their project of consciousness-raising was one of enthrallment. They aimed to give birth to a new form of perception through which the world became fresh, ecstatic, even sublime. Not all the avant-gardes were like this (Dada was more disruptive), but the core of avant-garde practice was aesthetic in this way (see Chapter 1).

Continuing that story, after the Second World War, the idea of radical social and economic change began to weaken as the terror of totalitarianism on the right and the left could not be swept under the rug. The failure of post–Second World War revolutions, Cold War imperialism, and the failure of left liberalism in Eastern Europe all led to increasing disbelief in the prospects for global, utopian political change. That and the sedimentation of the global financial system. The avant-gardes fell into disarray although their utopian spirit continued well into the 1960s with the work of Josef Beuys, Fluxus, John Cage, and others.

This work was important for what followed because Cage and Duchamp before him opened the field of artistic productions to seemingly include anything. "Permission granted," Cage used to quip, following Jasper Johns, "but not to do anything you want." Meaning, while the field of art production is totally open, rigor, seriousness, vision, integrity, and clarity are therefore all the more required. Indeed, *because* the field is without external constraint, there is all the more difficulty in achieving clarity and beauty. Which is why Cage was always keen to adopt instruments for the control of chance operations, computational or otherwise. You change the world by changing the aesthetic, which demands formal control. The lesson that complete freedom in the making of art demands all the more internal control is one which has not been taken sufficiently seriously, I think, by the artworld today.

The political movements of the 1960s—first-generation feminism, black consciousness, the student left, the Vietnam War and its protests against US imperialism, the emergence of gay rights activism—led to the remaking of the avant-gardes along new lines: those of identity politics and the critique of representation. The *locus classicus* is perhaps Judy Chicago's signature installation, *Dinner Party* of 1979. Consisting of thirty-nine place settings around a triangular table, each setting has a hand-painted china plate, cutlery, and napkin etched in gold and is dedicated to a woman of historical importance, from Eleanor of Aquitaine to Emily Dickenson, Virginia Woolf, and Susan B. Anthony (a suffragette who played a crucial role in getting American women the vote in 1924), or to a mythical goddess like Ishtar or Kali. The place setting reflects the personage. Georgia O'Keefe's is an icon of her abstract work from the Southwest, where she lived alone and painted into old age. Dickenson's individual table cloth has her name hand-sewn onto

Figure 7.1 Judy Chicago@ARS, NY. Installation view of Wing Two, featuring Elizabeth R. Artemisia Gentileschi and Anna van Schurman place settings from *The Dinner Party*, 1979. © 2020 Judy Chicago/Artists Rights Society (ARS), New York.

it in the manner of Puritan stitching, the sewing she daily did, like writing. Her place napkin is of soft pinkish brown, circular, with a glorious center and lace border feminine enough to stand in for the vaginal. Indeed, the entire triangle of worthy women's place settings is itself vaginal, explicitly so and in celebration of. This is a women's room for women, assembling singular geniuses and women of action and mythic consequence into a single solidarity, which is the aim of the work.

To the victor goes the story. And the stories of life that comprise history, myth, and religion are almost entirely written in a male hand, featuring men only or primarily, for men only or primarily. The talented female has always been isolated, marginalized as idiomatic, strange or unsociable, her genius or ardor or independence treated as a lone exception, she herself sometimes turned into the famous mad women in the attic. Lesbian relationships have largely been unmentionable. The vagina has been claimed by, owned by, taken by, worshipped by, and believed to be for men. The ancient Greeks thought of it as a passive receptacle for the man's sperm, which alone created

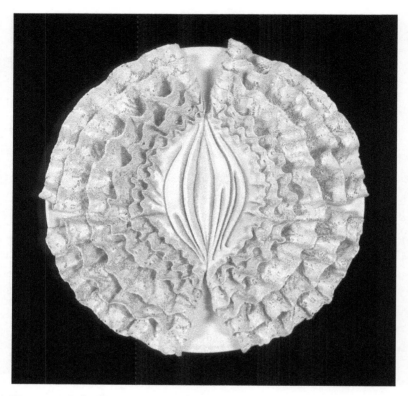

Figure 7.2 Judy Chicago@ARS, NY. *The Dinner Party*, Emily Dickenson plate, 1979. Mixed media. Photograph by Donald Woodman, Brooklyn Museum. © 2020 Judy Chicago/Artists Rights Society (ARS), New York.

life. The woman was simply a rental home while the baby grew to maturity. This to the point where genealogies of the bible inevitably run: *Abraham* begat Isaac, who begat Jacob, when the entire role of the man in the long haul of conception probably took between three and ten minutes, while for the women it lasted through gestation into birth into childcare of a lifetime. This theft of agency from women by men is a kind of symbolic castration, the less violent equivalent of real female castration, which men have also licensed in the name of religion. This bereavement of female agency and identity was during the 1970s challenged by the rallying cry of solidarity, women for and among themselves, apart from men in their own safe spaces, in what Virginia Woolf called "a room of one's own." The safe space of the dinner party is not the writer's individual room of safety and liberty where she may think, reflect, and write apart from the world of getting and spending and of men, but the room of the many brought into history as a *solidarity*, a force majeure, a gender of consequence whose stories must no longer be destined to atrophy, thanks to their willed isolation by men, but should be collected together to prove consequence and generate a sense of group identity and pride. For a key strategy—it is well known—of disempowering women from history was to separate each from the others, as if they were nothing more than a collection of individual freaks and odd balls, exceptions to their sex.

The artwork is handcrafted relying on traditionally female arts, sewing, cooking, lace-making, domestic design, now elevated into the realm of a political aesthetic, beautiful, erotic, loving, bonds of love and power. Chicago's party is dedicated to the critique and rewriting of representation (of how women have been historically represented). Here they are given new terms of representation: together. The avant-garde idea of solidarity is here reconvened as gender identity, female identity, the "instrument" of formal unity being that which all women and no men have.

Let Chicago's work stand for a number of innovative artists working along feminist lines at that time: Cindy Sherman, Barbara Kruger, Jenny Holzer, Nancy Spero, and many more. These artists shifted avant-garde practice from utopian politics to the critique of representation in the name of identities.

Part II

Identity politics overlap with what Charles Taylor calls the politics of recognition.[1] On Taylor's fine idea, there are certain situations where individual liberty is tied to group recognition. It is not simply that one's individual liberty is truncated by more general group stereotyping. It is also that a member of an identity-based group may come to depend on group recognition and group sustainability for her own pursuit of happiness. An individual is not an island; her own sense of plenitude in life is dependent, as often as not, on her sense of living within the group to which she finds herself in solidarity. If most Jews are treated like garbage, it makes me feel bad, cramps my own sense of liberty, makes me feel a traitor if I am doing well. If I were the last Jew in the world, I would feel unmoored.

Taylor argues for *group rights* in the light of his dialogic notion of individual freedom, dependent on group flourishing. When group identity is in danger of atrophy and unsustainability, or in need of redress, Taylor argues that special legal rights should be put in place to ensure group flourishing. His example is French Canada, where the Quebecois required education in the French language, their argument being that French is a minority language in Canada, in danger of being swept under the tide of English, and Quebecois need it to remain vital in order to pursue their individual happiness. If speaking French is crucial to one's individual liberty, then one needs the language to remain intact. One cannot be the only speaker. Individual liberty is so intertwined with group vitality, here around language, that it cannot be fully achieved apart from that. And so French instruction became a Canadian law in that province—a right cashed out as legal requirement.

One may reject all attachment and solidarity with those in the world who have formed one, or one may choose to live alone on an island. Both usually come at the price of emotional exile.

Identity politics need not make the claim that special legal rights (group rights) are demanded for group flourishing. The Quebecois have put laws in place in Quebec province requiring (with certain exceptions) that all children be educated in the French language. English schools are unavailable for many. This comes with obvious problems since the liberty of some is cramped at the expense of the majority. It is a response to anxiety about loss of group integrity. But identity politics may simply be about the aim of changing the way a group is represented in a society so that its individual members may have better, nondiscriminatory access to the social good. Which is the liberal idea of procedural justice.

These are key motivations for identity politics. But these politics around inclusiveness and rights are all too often subject to one ill often noted today, and another less so. The cure for these ills is not to drop identity politics, which would be to dispense with the goals of group rights and/or democratic inclusiveness. The cure is to create a better form of identity politics, freed from consumerist consciousness, coddled narcissism, and properly linked to the recognition of class-based inequality.

As to the first ill, which is, I think, well known: Identity politics tend to brush issues of class inequality under the table. However, the marginalization of racial and ethnic groups is inevitably connected to class inequality. The critique of stereotypes can only go so far until the class inferiority to which marginalized persons have been consigned also changes. This is a dialectical process. Without a notion of class, identity politics are condemned to backfire. When a nation-state like America has liberals equating emancipation with identity politics, this can only offend the dominant, white working class—a class that feels itself both under economic threat and also no longer able to voice its own concerns in the democracy. The situation has recently led to a virulent form of white working-class reaction in the United States, which furthers the interests of the 1 percent by providing the working class with the ideology that it is the power center of America, if only "enemies" from within and without are shoved to one side. This ideology, castigating others in the name of white America, does no good to either white America or its victims (black people, women, gays, etc.). Since it sets the white working class against excluded persons of color, the project is divide-and-rule. Whereas both parties should be in solidarity against the ruling class that is busy cutting wages for all (black, white, gay, straight) and giving themselves tax breaks. A total class reorganization of America must take place, demonstrating to white nationalists (or at least the white working class) that their interests and those of negatively stereotyped populations should be in solidarity. The point has been made many times, and I have little new to offer. Identity politics, without related changes in class structure, benefit no one beyond a certain point except the ruling class. (Whether this will happen in a racist society like America is another story.)

I will rather focus on the second ill that is, I think, less understood than the first. This is the way the market has expanded in America (and elsewhere) to subsume more and more spheres of life that were earlier on considered immune from it. In this case, identity politics, in contemporary America and in a number of other places across the world, fused with a consumerist form. The market (capitalism) has now expanded to encompass the very way persons see themselves. The market has done a fairly good job of colonizing identity politics. Persons begin to believe their identity is a form of capital, a bankable currency that earns them the right to any kind of expenditure they want, as if being a person from a disadvantaged group paradoxically earns the members of the group a special kind of spending power, which is *they themselves*. This emphasis on "me" becomes a "financial" guarantee that whatever you say will have value, earning cultural profit, in virtue of your identity. To be clear, many persons speak as responsibly as ever, but the whole culture pushes people in the direction of this kind of self-aggrandizing narcissism.

And leads to white counterreaction: You guys have no right to steal the America that rightfully belongs to me and my tribe. We are the ones destined for privilege in virtue of our identity, not you. We always have had our white skins to rely on in getting ahead in life. Long may this continue. It is our capital gains.

When identity politics are subsumed by the market place, and identities become forms of capital, the hard labor of craft, creative innovation, clarity, and purpose tends to fall away as unnecessary or irrelevant, for the real power behind my work is my *identity*. Talent need no longer be centrally part of the picture, nor hard work, nor the long battle with failure so many artists and writers go through before things work out. Talent, because noninclusive (most people don't have it) can and does become despised as an elitist throwback.

This is a corruption of the avant-gardes, which—although naively utopian in their belief that their experiments would solicit utopian change—understood well that many experiments would have to take place before results bore fruit. They understood that while an artist might be fiercely committed to emancipatory change, but if the work was insipid, it failed. The avant-gardes never thought politics were enough to allow them to disregard the power of the work of art to compel absorption. It was because the work was *aesthetically* compelling that it was believed to be consciousness-raising. Rodchenko (see Chapter 1) makes the ordinary transcend its banality until it becomes ebullient, shockingly dynamic, intensely new, as if reality were offered to the viewer for the first time. Aesthetic vibrancy is central to the photograph's work of disruption. This is a change in the nature of aesthetic practice from the eighteenth century as it substitutes solidarity for individual taste and liberty, but it is an aesthetic practice all the same.

It is useful to follow the course of photography from its avant-garde practice through Cindy Sherman to the present. Sherman virtually invents the genre of performance photography or is, at any rate, one of its first major practitioners. She features herself, but, by disappearing into the roles she plays, makes the photo less about her than about the fate of women in general, and in the gendered world of her time, a world that persists today. However, in the forty years since she began to make this work, the genre has significantly debased into a photographic equivalent of what the writer Nicholas Delbanco calls the *me-moir*,[2] becoming almost the equivalent of those endless selfies people take arriving at airports, driving in cars, walking on mountains, sitting in restaurants, playing with dogs, then share on Instagram or Facebook. Performance photography features *me* dressing up like a flapper, *me* in the half nude, *me* in a dark forest made dayglow courtesy of air-brushing, *me* everywhere. And the "me" is as often as not an identity that is simply proclaiming its value as such, presenting itself as a so-and-so in the belief that this guarantees aesthetic quality to the photo as well as political force. Performance photography becomes a form of hamming. Of course, not every performance photo is so debased, but many are and the image that follows must mirror me.

Me becomes the criterion of value (capital value) and the narcissistic pleasure point.

And with that, truth is sourced to identity. The truth of what I say and do is a matter of *me*, of who I am, from what position I am speaking, from where I am coming. That is what makes my voice true or false. I am suspicious of any larger and more abstract notion of truth, which is seen as an historical instrument of my oppression. This devaluation of truth is associated with the capital gains of identity politics because it overvalues *me*. What then happens when art or inquiry run up against the complex nature of the facts, the uncertainties, the many perspectives required to get at the way things are when these are disrespected as they inevitably will? These become the object of politically correct assault. *Truth*, in the larger and more abstract sense (bigger than me), is now the enemy. Whatever one might think of liberalism, its respect for the complexities of truth, the fact that truth is bigger than individuals, demanding as often as not dissenting voices from a chorus of others, requiring various other perspectives taken to best grasp it: These principles or norms are critical not only for inquiry but also for democracy. And so by a massive irony the very aims of democratic emancipation that originally drove identity politics—aims of inclusivity, respect, nondiscrimination, and equality of voice—are eviscerated in a power grab over truth conditions. Identity politics become the enemy of democratic respect for truth, and related, for the politics of dissent. Identity politics, forged in the name of democratic inclusion, become democracy's enemy.

To say this is not happening in America, or South Africa—places I know well, and in other places around the globe I know less well—would be a lie.

It is not that personal or group identity are irrelevant as conditions for truth. They can represent the truth in many ways: what happened to whom, in what way, what has to change, and so on. Individual voice has varying degrees of authority in various forms of inquiry. But, it is only one aspect among others, whose valence and validity has to be determined on a case-by-case basis. The relative weight of truth versus justice is always an open-ended question, not to mention a matter for dissent.

Part III

There is also a way in which identity politics intersect with celebrity culture to create celebrity identities for artists, in the manner of brands that then capitalize the artist and the work. Let's take the example of Damien Hirst. Throughout a long and tempestuous career assaulting the art world, and raking millions from it in the process, Hirst constantly assumed the posture of an avant-garde bad-boy, creating a series of installations featuring huge fish tanks with dead sharks, dayglow skeletons, sheep, and other animals—including human cadavers—embalmed in formaldehyde/water vitrines, installations about rape and murder using (and proclaiming the use of) actual human blood that Hirst painted onto the artwork. This succession of assaults might have seemed to presume avant-garde disruption of—if not a direct assault on—the artworld in the name of animal rights, abuse against women, and so forth. But the work's sheer obsession with corpses, blood, guts, and animal carcasses trumps all.

Bad choices? A serious artist gone too far? Charlatan? Snake oil salesman? There is a close resemblance between Hirst's work and Fox TV's *America's Most Wanted* show from the 1980s, in which unsolved crimes were re-enacted using live hand-held cameras after being introduced by an announcer whose TV "pedigree" was that he had lost a child to crime. Victims were encouraged to play themselves, making the docudrama all the more "real." But what kind of real was this? It was the reality of scopophilia, pleasure taken in the half-erotic buzz of sadism, the rough frisson of violence, the humiliation of victims now performing their fates for a ravenous TV public. The justification was meant, as it is in Hirst, to be political. Audiences were given a telephone number (this was in the days before the internet) to call the FBI if they'd seen any of these criminals-on-the-run in their school playgrounds, shopping malls, or perchance on an airplane flight to Las Vegas or Disneyland. In the first year of the TV show, a score of criminals were apprehended, and at least one turned himself in after being featured. So, this TV show became a political arm of the FBI. All Americans should be able to join the police, the FBI. The political purpose was to create a right-wing society bonded in surveillance (law and order) around a TV station that would and did make billions for the Murdoch family. A TV station that would push right-wing candidates who would support Murdoch's financial interests through tax cuts, government subsidies, and, if necessary, bail-outs. We have seen the propaganda value of this for the TV station since the 2016 presidential election, because Donald Trump seldom acts without first consulting Fox TV, which he is reputed to watch four hours a day. At one point (in December 2019), Trump called off an attack on Iran ten minutes before it was meant to take place, because a Fox commentator told him to.

By catching crooks, you become magically part of TV and its world; you are aesthetically elevated. By watching Fox's various rants, you are included in the solidarity of rage, made part of a bonded multitude for whom viciousness is its own self-authorization, indeed its own form of aesthetic pleasure. Trump's orchestrated rallies, his tweets, his endless furies are felt by his supporters to be power flowing right from the TV screen to them, as if by watching and listening they can literally receive and take on its power. And also, its financial force, as if rage were a currency, a form of capital gains. This is the very definition of propaganda, which vests the *image* with a power to transform you through identification with it, as if the image were a declaration of religious war and you part of its army. It is what Adorno and Horkheimer called the aestheticization of politics, referring to the Nazis and their vast propaganda machine, a machine so powerful that one could literally feel swept away and transported by it into communal ecstasy, a state of transfiguration that only petered out in the freezing winters of the Russian front.

Damien Hirst is not right wing; he aims to challenge violence within the system: violence perpetrated toward animals, violent attitudes inflamed by the media. Hirst is ostensibly, and probably in his heart, against all this. And yet, he too relies on celebrity tactics with his blood and gore art, to generate interest and market value. He is the bad-boy celebrity, the Marlon Brando Wild Bunch figure, what Jean Beaudrillard calls a pornographer of the real. And his feast of gore overwhelms his message in exactly the way *America's Most Wanted* turned violence into that which is most wanted. Art, like TV, becomes a staged event around which pleasure is taken in the gruesome, the humiliating, the monstrous. The art object like the TV screen is there to turn us on, under the pretense that it is combating violence.

Hirst became a doyen of the artworld, lending him the identity of a bad-boy celebrity, literally creating *identity-based capital* for him in terms of which his work is valued. And valued it is; one of his shark pieces (with a replacement shark as the original has by now decomposed or, as they say in the food industry, "gone off") recently sold for $12 million. Rather than actually motivating political change (about environmental issues or animal rights), Hirst's work has served the function of branding *him* for the market place. This celebrity form, pornographically based, is what has made millions for him. It is his identity politics.

Part IV

I have been speaking of producers (artists). The other side of this is the consumer of art. To consider consumer liabilities, please allow me to switch from the culture of art to the culture of universities where a similar point can be made. A new kind of consumerist attitude has encroached on American colleges and universities in the past twenty years or so. For many, university is a goal that is attained only through hardscrabble saving and struggle in the hope of access to a better life. People go into serious debt to finance a university education in the hope that it will put them in a better position to live life. Their initiative should be applauded. Many young people want a better future, not a consumerist opportunity from universities, although these goals are hardly mutually exclusive.

Colleges and universities are scrambling to hire the best sushi chefs, offer all-night "room service," and dormitories that resemble hotels in Dubai to satisfy students who have come to believe university is like being on a cruise. As tuitions skyrocket, the desire to attract the richest students has turned universities away from deploying money for scholarships in the name of equity and toward travel and beautification programs. Universities brand themselves as places where students can sail down the Amazon, visit museums in China, and spend semesters abroad in France or Cameroon while studying climate change or public health. These investments have put some of them in real financial jeopardy, thanks to debt incurred and the absolute need to have high tuition-paying students occupy their fancy premises each and every year. The term for this is "overspeculation."

Certain American universities have instituted a program of "triggers," requiring teachers to warn students of any materials that might prove offensive or discomforting. Offense is one thing; discomfort another. In any democracy consisting of diverse populations, there will be variability in offense: What offends one person will not offend another. One is obliged to take genuine offense seriously wherever it may be found, something I discussed in Chapter 5. However, too many students have lost the distinction between offense and discomfort, believing their rights or privileges, as student consumers ought to preclude anything in the classroom that makes them feel uncomfortable. This is a corruption of the idea of a safe space into a kind of I'm-on-a-cruise mentality-don't-bother-me. Don't teach me anything I don't like, after all I paid for this cruise.

This attitude is evidently destructive to the learning process. A core function of universities to teach students the art of discomfort: How hard it is to attain even the slightest degree of real knowledge about anything, how often one must fail to succeed even a little. Without incorporating the idea of failure, there is no way to develop self-critical mechanisms, learn the rigors of intellectual training, become expert at recognizing the multiperspectival, complex nature of reality, learn to respect the ineluctability of fact. The student must learn how to bear discomfort and turn it to their advantage in order to take knowledge seriously.

To illustrate how deep this consumerist attitude is in the lives of young people (not all, but more than a few), consider this personal anecdote. This morning I woke to an email from a student asking me if, when I teach *The Sopranos* during a class tomorrow on film and philosophy, I can avoid talking about the ending of the series. This student hadn't watched the series yet and did not want me to spoil the ending by speaking philosophically about it. Apparently, I am part of the entertainment industry, not a teacher. The student is actually a nice, smart, hardworking, well-meaning person. Which tells me the consumerist attitude (don't spoil my fun) is totally embedded in him/her, to the point of not being noticed.

Art should ideally be there to combat consumerism. And so, the importance of identity politics for emancipation has the liability of becoming another fixture in the marketing of the self and its consumerist pleasures. If the side of the producer says: my art has automatic value because it is about me and my identity, the side of the consumer says: art has value because it makes me comfortable, gives me pleasure, celebrates me, without challenge. This dyad is simply a degradation of the nature of aesthetic beauty and aesthetic pleasure. And is very bad politics.

Now, recent identity politics may be new in their market orientation but they also emerge from centuries of privilege. White privilege in the Ivy League, the Slaveholding South, Oxbridge England, the colonial settler world where one's identity as an upper-class male justified a Cambridge education and London job in the bank—similarly for the prep school youth of New England not to mention the white settler in the colonies. Nowadays, the privilege automatically earned by such birthrights (by identity) is simply generalized. Everyone deserves special treatment, thanks to their identity, which is meant to fast-track them to cultural and financial success. If you can have such privilege, then so can we. This in the name of equality. Centuries of exclusion have led marginalized persons (and indeed, everybody) to compensate through an identity politics that includes them in market gain, thanks to who they are. As if identity were a universal right-to-voice-and-success.

The cure for these ills is not the abolition of identity politics but a *better form of them* in the arts and humanities, as in public life. The project has to be to rescue identity politics from its consumerist ills, so as to discover again the genuinely emancipatory role of identity politics. And to do so while the market remains the dominant institutional form of culture. There are many artists and writers and intellectuals who are in fact taking this high road into identity politics. A long list of names could easily be offered/applauded. I do not wish to sound crude and one-dimensional about the many ways in which identity politics are playing themselves out today. By speaking of the worst, one hopes to encourage the best.

Art Market Politics: Manet to Banksy

Part I

It begins with Eduard Manet and his invention of critique in paint, a response to the modern artworld that developed in the middle of the nineteenth century, in the wake of the architect Georges-Eugène Haussmann's reconstruction of the city of Paris from 1853 to 1870, with Haussmann's creation of the system of boulevards and remaking of Parisian infrastructure. These events led to the birth of the department store or *Grands Magazins*, the culture of bourgeois promenading, the flaneur of the shop windows, the spectacle of Paris unfolded through the fans of women, the top hats of men, the splendor of self-presentation by a new class on the rise, call it the middle class with its newly minted consumer power, and desire to collect, own, and exhibit the splendor of self-profiling commodities, from fans and hats to paintings and an endless array of other bric-a-brac.[1] The rising middle or bourgeois class that became the denizens of the boulevards, the department stores, and the art galleries brought money, enthusiasm, and an endlessly consumerist optimism to the purchase of everything from dresses to paintings, all of which celebrated their newly found purchasing power and proclaimed their entrance into the world of consumer happiness and social prestige. The rising literacy rates of this class brought about the rise of newspapers, and with these the phenomenon of the art critic, who could make or break the galleries and private dealers who turned art into far more of a commodity than it had ever previously been. This artworld of galleries, critics, consumers, and, of course, makers (artists) was in effect the modern art market on the rise, where art was purchased in part because of its links to eternity and in part because of its pure commodity value.

The brutality of the market was captured by Eduard Manet in his *Jesus Mocked by the Soldiers* of 1865, in which a plangent Christ sits naked and vulnerable surrounded by soldiers, who are transparently based on the art critics of the day. Christ himself resembles Manet, whose treatment by these art-toughs wielding their unbridled social power is being compared to that of the one who would soon be crucified.

Manet responds to this system of market economy in which the work of art is splayed between the status of commodity and priceless museological object with brilliant insight. He grasps how the desire for art is fueled by a culture not only of display but of voyeuristic satisfaction and omnipotent self-confirmation, played out indifferently around the renting of women by men, the enjoyment of champagne at the theater, the purchase of goods, all of which compute to a culture in which pleasure is taken, in the first instance by men, since this world is gendered, in possession, visual, as well as financial possession. I spoke in Chapter 3 about how women, art, clothing, and property fuse in the imagination of the buyer, making the dripping gorgeousness of art a sign, and therefore article of excitement, of similar pleasures offered by women. The art market was one in which the desire for the art object was conditioned not only by the pleasure of ownership but by the symbolic whiff of sex, a kind of sex purchased for the eyes as well as the rest of the body, as if all things conspired to reinforce the pleasure of each by referral to the others.

Manet's critique of the art market is part of his larger critique of the *artworld*, given the way the market ran on these generalized and systematic interconnections between kinds of visual desire, which expressed themselves as a reinforced desire to purchase and exhibit art. Sometimes a work of art is more than a work of art, Freud might have said had he lived there then (his arrival in Paris was a bit later and to study with Charcot, not to buy things). The locus classicus of Manet's larger critique is his *Olympia* of 1863. The work is famously in dialogue with the most luscious paintings created for the male gaze, Titian's *Venus of Urbino* of 1538. In Titian's painting, a pliant nude reclines on a divan, her head turned toward the viewer in a welcoming gaze, her right hand holding flowers, her left resting softly on her sex, as if saying, I will remove this hand when you are ready, you are what I desire and I am yours. Titian's nude is passive, an overripe fruit that wants to be eaten before it expires. She waits to be activated by the predatory gazes of her viewers. Manet parodies Titian's painting by grotesquely foreshortening his Olympia, also nude and also reclining on a divan, turning Titian's pear-shaped Venus into the stunted body of a girl little older than a child. Olympia's expression is one of something between hostility and indifference, contempt and boredom, perhaps vacuity.

This is a Manet trademark. The more we seek to grasp her expression, the more we must conclude that it permanently eludes us. She is in a deep sense unknowable. This failure of the expectation that she is known and known as available, drooling if you will, is meant to challenge the bourgeois' expectation that the woman in the picture, like the world at large, is his oyster, that she will indubitably conform to his expectations, confirm his sense that the world is exactly what he wishes it to be, that he may expect to *know* her perfectly. Olympia is in effect blocking this possessive, all knowing gaze. Olympia's attitude seems to be: gaze at me if you will, rent me by the hour, but don't do so under the illusion that I am yours, that your pleasure is shared by me, that I enjoy it, that I am a mere figment of your world. If you rent me, you do so purely as a mechanical transaction, I allow you no voyeuristic pleasure. You do not know who I am, nor do you care and I know this. I don't care about you either. The flowers so softly held in Venus's right hand become in Manet's painting a strident image of Olympia's sex thrust forward into the face of the viewer by a black servant who stands behind her, black servants being a popular fixture in houses of prostitution of the time in virtue of widely held stereotypes about black African sexual prowess.[2] The religious element at the back of Titian's picture disappears.

The effect of Manet's picture is to crystallize and lambaste the entire tradition of the nude and its role in the texture of Parisian life. This attack on the artworld and its visual business, framed from within, is a central concern of this genius who almost single-handedly invented the critique of the artworld in paint.

In other Manet pictures, it is the art market with its malignant, conniving critics that is the subject of his lambaste. The important point being that the system as a whole, a market run on desire and satisfaction, owning and possessing, money and commodities, and this as part of the fabric of a rising middle class, that is his subject. The art historian T. J. Clark has written brilliantly on this.[3] To criticize art markets, Manet understood, was to bring out the wide sources of visual desire that fueled them, not merely their institutional parameters, those of critic, newsprint, gallery, and the like.

Part II

The avant-gardes, arising after the First World War, were even more dead set against the artworld and art markets. They detested both the eternalizing, ahistorical character of the museum and the bourgeois culture of price and possession. Their aspiration was to bring art out of the galleries and museums and collections and into the streets to build a future, to revolutionize consciousness and society, to stand as an icon for the utopian battles of history. The art theorist Peter Burger goes so far as to say the defining condition of the avant-gardes was their critique and attack on the artworld.[4] I am not sure how to evaluate the claim that this challenge to the artworld is *the* central avant-garde position, since it cannot be understood apart from the larger goals of consciousness-raising, solidarity, and revolutionary empowerment.

But it is true that at the birth of the Constructivist movement of 1917, formed in the year of the Russian Revolution, the poet Mayakovsky announced in the Constructivist journal *LEF* that the Constructivist program of destruction is complete, meaning what first and foremost had to happen in order for art to now turn to the future. By a program of destruction, he meant the eradication of the lingering aesthetic force of the art of the past and the institutions of the artworld that were its conduit.

It is that oddly apolitical artist, working at the fringes of the avant-gardes, Marcel Duchamp, who took the critique of the artworld one step further, including it as part of a wider critique—or prosecutorial investigation—into the various corruptions of visual culture. This with the double pleasure of comedy, and also a bit of nudity on the sly. One need only look to his masterpiece, on which he labored from 1946 to 1966: *Étant donnés: 1° la chute d'eau / 2° le gaz d'éclairage* (*Given: 1. The Waterfall, 2. The Illuminating Gas*). Duchamp's installation is situated behind a wooden door that looks old, with a hole in it through which the viewer is invited to spy in the manner of a voyeur. What the viewer sees through this peep hole is a young woman curled in a manger. Behind her is a completely artificial scene of nature painted as backdrop (in the Hollywood style). The scene is lit with the kind of brash internal light found in French Baroque painting (Georges de la Tour). This lighting is strident and dramatizing. The scene recalls images of the crime-ridden streets of Victorian London where Jack the Ripper did his nasty, miserable work. The color palette is that of a street seen through the artificial sheen of Victorian gaslight (the illuminating gas). The young woman may be asleep, she may be dead: murdered. Her genitals are directly exposed to the viewer, who is excited and shocked in the manner of a true peeping Tom. Her hairless sex may be a sign of her innocence (the virgin birth in the manger); it may be a sign of her violation; it may be that she is a mere doll tossed into the scene. Duchamp worked for two decades on this elaborate set-up, which speaks to everything from Victorian crime novels to the history of painting, from lurid thrillers to Hollywood films to the story of Christianity to penny arcades and film sets.

Duchamp plays the viewer like a musical instrument by placing him in the position of voyeur, a Norman Bates from Alfred Hitchcock's *Psycho* staring at Janet Leigh through a hole from his office found behind a painting into Cabin 1. Are we, like Bates, murderous, if only in the unconscious? Do we demand titillated violation in order to feel we've had a full day? This vitrine—this act of display—uses simulation (of these scenarios) to address a number of related forms of visual culture coldly and from the outside (watching, looking, excitement, voyeurism, killing) whose legacy remains wedded to the contemporary world, but which Duchamp's display treats as a strange, fascinating, bizarre thing.

Duchamp's position on visual culture and violence is—like Hitchcock's—ambivalent. Is he out to interrogate and condemn, to catch the viewer at his game of voyeurism, or is he inviting that game and (as I suggested) happily playing it on the sly? Does he manipulate the viewer because he is a sadist or because the viewer must be shown his complicity in the degraded trade of visual culture? Assiduously apolitical, a man who made sure he would never fight for any nation or cause and lived out the world wars in Argentina and New York, Duchamp turned critique into something drained of its political edges.

Art markets were a subdued part of Duchamp's attack. Unless one considers his *Fountain* of 1917, that readymade urinal passed off as an artwork in the Armory Show, until kicked out on its derriere. Much has been written about its uncanny likeness to sculpture, one feels in its gleaming surface the beckoning of touch, that is, the tactile values of sculpture, while being repulsed by the fact of what one would be touching. *Fountain*'s wide-open ovular front beckons like a female sex, while its pipe suggests the male counterpart. Pan sexual, all about visual surface and tactile stimulation, fountain is too close to sculpture to discount the conceptual link, while too far (it's not made by hand) to be called sculpture unproblematically. Its original purpose is ironically not unlike those many sculptures that happily urinate into gardens and pools, making it a window into what sculpture is, and the visual desire associated, a conceptual instrument for unmasking fine art and with it the desires of the viewer.

Of interest here is that this work is not simply about visual culture, because it is signed by Duchamp's proxy, R-Mutt, a character in a popular comic series of the time (and the work is a cartoon version of sculpture if there ever was one), but also suggesting in German, Armut—a word for the poor or poverty. Yes, this is poor man's sculpture, but it is also a way of raising the relationship between money and art, what is rich aesthetically and rich in terms of price wanted. At the time, no one would have paid out for this weird intruder, which is why Duchamp lived frugally and, when needed, would sell a Brancusi (whose gleaming surfaces resembled *Fountain*'s but whose price was far greater) from his collection to pay the bills. The rich buy art. The poor, well, they hardly have a pot to piss in.

And so, Duchamp's critique of the artworld and visual culture broadly is not unconnected to his interest in the relation between these and art markets. In this he is Manet's student.

Duchamp's apolitical/conceptual/fascinated stance on the artworld and on art markets is even more central to Andy Warhol's work, Warhol being, along with John Cage, perhaps Duchamp's most celebrated student. No one is more trenchant in his analysis of art in relation to money (market economy

Figure 8.1 Andy Warhol, *One Dollar Bills* (fronts), 1962. Silkscreen ink, acrylic and pencil on linen 24 × 30 inches (61 × 76.2 cm). © 2020 The Andy Warhol Foundation for the Visual Arts, Inc. Licensed by Artists Rights Society (ARS), New York.

and its valuations) than Warhol. Behind the pasty white skin, the white wig, and the dark glasses lived a mind minted not only of dollars but of genius. One can see this in Warhol's silk screen, *One Dollar Bills* of 1962.

The silk screen consists of images of one-dollar bills in various states of fadedness, as currencies tend to be. This variation of wear and tear makes for a visually pleasing picture, with aesthetic rhythms in green and gray running throughout. But it also serves a more analytical purpose. The George Washington stamped at the center of each bill also appears in various states of being worn down. This ought to cause a reflection on the place of the image of this American icon on the bill, as if Washington branded the bill not merely with national character but with his iconic "celebrity." Celebrity is a matter of being-in-circulation and Washington has been since the revolutionary war— his oversized head on the top of monument valley, his story (myth) in the children's history books I read as a child (all that bit about the cherry tree and never telling a lie), in countless paintings, sculptures, prayers and recitations, and on the one-dollar bill. The bill makes him a kind of celebrity after the fact, since in the late eighteenth century when he led the troops and then assumed the presidency, celebrity had not yet come into existence. He was famous, but not a celebrity. And gradually took on the stature of myth. And so, he brands the currency that also keeps him current.

There is a double life of the icon-image or celebrity when in this state. On the one hand, it is circulation (on the bills) that confirms Washington's celebrity (they circulate him), while his mythic status in America inflates the bill. And yet, the more he circulates, the more we take him for granted. This is the paradox of celebrity, which I discussed in my *Star as Icon*.[5] Being-in-circulation is the condition of celebrity, without which not. But circulation also flattens the celebrity image into something less and less meaningful over time, more and more ordinary, taken for granted and finally invisible. Celebrities around for too long become "old news." Even if it is the news that keeps them around for that amount of time.

This double condition of becoming famous, thanks to circulation and flattened in the process of being-in-circulation, is a central theme running through all of Warhol's work. It underscores his interest in his images of Marilyn, Jackie, Elvis, or Troy Donovan. Circulation enfranchises while deadening. These images are flat. As if worn down by excessive public circulation. And yet their dayglo colors vivify them, making them sparkle.

One Dollar Bills is a work not merely about Washington and the fate of his image, but also about money. It aims to raise the issue of art in relation to money. The question is whether the artwork itself is *like money*, a form of currency if you will, and if so how. It is now well known that art is a liquid form of capital, an investment that rises and falls like the value of currency, and is easily circulated like money, nowadays flipped from owner to owner in the manner of Wall Street trades. But there is more. *One Dollar Bills* prompts the thought that art is *valuated* in the same way as money or similar. If you ask what sets the value of a currency, the answer is the *system* through which each currency is valued in relation to the others. These currency valuations are, as a whole, set through politics, economic robustness, trust, global stability, and demand. If America looks like it is going to crash, then the value of the dollar goes down with respect to other currencies in the global financial system. If trust in the dollar declines for other reasons, financial players will be less keen to invest in dollars and again the tumble in value. If a global depression or pandemic occurs, currencies may devalue as a whole. The value of a currency is set within the system of players and through complex relationships of demand, risk, and investment potential as perceived by those players.

And how is the value of a painting set? Quite similarly. It too is a matter of demand (which changes depending on which Russian oligarch, Saudi

Arabian prince, or America billionaire is advised to invest where). This is also the matter of politics, economy, and trust across the system. And work is valued comparatively and systemically. Impressionism versus Old Masters versus contemporary Chinese art versus new trends. These are as a whole considered in the light of everything from national prominence (the value of Chinese contemporary art went up when the value of China went up on the global stage), to institutional commitment (on the part of museums, galleries, etc.), to questions of tax and the liquidity of capital, to scenarios run about raising or lowering of price over time. To who is collecting, what they are paying, who they are, and what they own (which gives them prestige in the art market).

Today art is increasingly flipped like real estate, literally turning it into a form of liquid capital. Art is money. This seems to me Warhol's genius. He got it, and got it visually. A work of art is a kind of one-dollar bill. One has to verbally riff on his visual achievement to make it "speak," but the germ of insight rests, I believe, within the work, understood in the light of Warhol's broader concerns. In this way the inarticulateness of visual work contains the germ of articulation, or what Hegel called "the idea" embodied "implicitly" in the work of art.[6] This is a way of saying that Warhol's work has genuine conceptual power. There has been no more trenchant understanding of art in relation to money and markets, branding and advertising in the history of art than Warhol's. He was the prophet of the postwar financial capital. But one cannot find politics in his analytical genius. He neither hates this system in the manner of an avant-garde leftist, nor applauds it. He neither despises dollars nor believes having them conveys moral authority in that greasy American way. He rather revels in the fact of money, is fascinated by it in relation to art. Warhol is the *flaneur* of American capital markets.

Nor is he interested in the question of what Antonio Gramsci called hegemony. Namely how a financial system presents itself as open, democratic, available to all, worthy of public trust, believed to be in the general public interest when, in fact, the system facilitates the interests of the ruling class, here the 1 percent of billionaires and the few critics who play the real role in setting price and value within the system. I may have my own ideas about what is good and bad in art, but these will play no role in the valuation of art as a currency because I am not an investor, lacking the means (and perhaps also the interest). And so, the system is a market controlled by its investors and advisors (critics, art advisors, museum curators, etc.) capable of absorbing any art object into its domain of valuation while also presenting the market as democratic, open to all. This system may indifferently claim art objects whose whole purpose is to challenge or reject the market as blithely as those that celebrate it or are indifferent to it.

This does not imply you cannot have your own taste and passion, collect what you will and can afford, enjoy what you enjoy whether condoned by market pricing or not. Such a situation would be preposterous. Most serious art persons are always at odds with the market to some degree. But the market can as easily assimilate their private and public preferences as anything else. This is what defines market hegemony.

Warhol was not alone in thinking about art in relation to markets during the 1960s when the culture of financial capital, aided by branding and advertising, was rising postwar. Others were taking a far more political stance toward some of the things Warhol blithely noted. Hans Haacke made a career in New York from the time of his Museum of Modern Art exhibition of 1970, by exposing art markets in relation to the growth of real estate. His fierce critique was of the way real estate and financial investment led to the frenzy of art buying and selling in the 1980s. Thanks to the dollar bills invested by those real estate magnates who gentrified lower Manhattan, a new crop of galleries came into being in Soho and Tribeca (they have since moved). The trading of art became closely linked to real estate, as if a work of art were like a new loft in Soho, ready to soar in price given the right investor at the right time. This soaring of the market depended on a new crop of persons with money to burn, especially given preferential tax treatment for the real estate industry. Hans Haacke's exhibits of real estate plans and New York property were a factual excoriation of the fate of contemporary art in such financial situations where art began to turn into liquid capital.

As the desire for the self-celebration of financial power, thanks to ownership of celebrity art, took hold in the Soho lofts of the real estate magnates, ownership fused with new ideas of art as *investment* along the lines of Wall Street and its trading rituals. This catapulted the darling bad-boy artists of the 1980s (David Salle, Julian Schnabel, and others) into mega-celebrities. In this rising market and celebrity climate, such artists were liable to have "retrospectives" at the age of 29 on account of their being "mega-geniuses," an inflationary term suitable to the inflationary market. If you wanted to buy a Schnabel, you would go to Mary Boone Gallery where you would be told they're on back order, with a six-month waiting list, please put your name on the list. Six months later, you would get a call: Your Schnabel has arrived. Now supposed you went over to Mary Boone and didn't like that particular painting, saying you wanted another. Well, depending on who you were (your "importance" for the art system), you might be sent to the back of the waiting list again. It all reminds me of living in Los Angeles during the late 1980s and showing up at a hot restaurant with my wife where the 18-year-old hostess with the slit dress asked in the most blasé possible voice: So, who are *you*?

Today, Haacke's documentation of 1970s real estate prices mostly excites envy on the part of those New York City viewers who may be heard to mutter: My god a building in Soho only cost eight million back then, I could have bought that building and become a billionaire, god I would be rich today. What a fool I am.

Part III

As examples of the hegemonic nature of art markets, we may turn to the way those artists, known for their edginess and assault on capital forces, become assimilated by the very thing they criticize, their criticisms turning into the latest market brand, there to titillate the 1 percent that is buying, so that that population may feel they own something really edgy and political, as if a hot potato or not entirely legal diamond or weapon that once belonged to some famous anarchist.

The topic is Banksy.

Banksy is an English, street-based artist. He is also a political activist, film director (who has won awards), and has been a part-time vandal. He is in his mid-forties and was born in Bristol. His real name remains hidden from the public. Banksy's career began with sardonic, politically motivated graffiti, images plastered on the walls of working-class England, about homelessness, job loss, pollution, and the like. David Lurie might have photographed this work (see Chapter 2). The work combines gallows humor with subversive epigrams and graffiti done in a fascinating and talented stenciling style. His aesthetic is taken from popular resistance art, from peoples' art rather than complex and theory-driven visual innovation in the manner of the Constructivists or surrealists. Until he hit international notoriety, it must be stressed he was a playful but also politically serious artist, something he endeavors to remain today with work in Israel/Palestine and elsewhere, but which becomes more difficult when every image he is invited to now make for the Venice Biennale, the gallery, collector, and is a celebrity bad-boy whom everyone wants around like James Dean.

Once deified as a celebrity-of-the-edge, the *value* of Banksy's interventions have changed dramatically, making him an object of desire simply because as a celebrity he gains capital in the artworld. Everyone wants a piece of the political action for their walls. This is Andy Warhol's universe. Also demonstrating a clear difference between the valuation of currency and of art: namely the role of celebrity and the brand in setting the value of art, something that plays no role in the valuation of the dollar or pound. The process is dialectical. Banksy becomes a celebrity, thanks to market interest, then his celebrity is part of what generates market price. Celebrity and value are mutually determined.

In response to his status as what the mafia would call a Made-man, Banksy pulled of his most dramatic and impressive stunt to date, and it is among the great acts of disruption that contemporary art has come across. A Banksy painting, *Girl with Balloon*, was put up for auction in 2017 at Sotheby's in London, and the bidding was steep. It sold for £1.4 million (about 1.8 million in US dollars at the time). At the moment, the gavel went down on the sale, a device was triggered inside the painting that shredded half of it (and only half of it), in front of a gasping audience. As if to say: stick that one in your pipe and smoke it. (Or: this is not a pipe, it's a smoking gun.) Contempt for the auction house was never more juicily delivered. Banksy turned the aesthetic pleasure of the smirk into a fine art. And shredded the system—if only symbolically. And only for a moment because quickly the work—now in its "completed," "half destroyed" state and understood to be a political gesture, not simply a painting—doubled in price, up to £2.8 million. The art market always wins, always rises to the occasion.

We will never be sure if Banksy staged this master-stunt in order to raise the price. Or whether it was rather an experiment to see what would happen

Figure 8.2 Banksy, *Girl with Balloon*, after shredding, London, October 12. Begun 2002, shredded at auction 2018. Photograph by Tristan Fewings/Getty Images for Sotheby's.

if the market were briefly shaken rather than stirred. We simply don't know Banksy's motives, which are probably various.

I want to say his work now lives a double life—as a political attack on the artworld and as the latest brand item, fetish, desirable quantity for those it attacks. No doubt Banksy will be dropped eventually, or turn into a curiosity.

This is artworld politics. The way genuine attacks on the system become incorporated into it and desired by it. Edginess has market value in the right circumstances.

Banksy has tried to remain political in spite of it all. The Walled-Off Hotel of 2017 he created, designed, decorated, and painted in Bethlehem is located at the Wall, that instrument of division and oppression, there to keep Palestinians out of Israel. They may wait for hours to cross into Israel even if ten minutes away by foot, thanks to this security apparatus and the military that operate it. Profits from the Banksy hotel go to the city of Bethlehem. The hotel is meant to stimulate the Bethlehem economy, providing jobs and cash flow into the city. The hotel does not have a fancy dining room, this so that its well-heeling patrons will utilize local restaurants. Banksy's gesture of the hotel is in its own way a matter of "good works." Many locals appreciate what it is doing for the community. As is his more recent help offered to refugees stranded in the ocean, thanks to a boat he purchased for the occasion. He is politically serious.

Figure 8.3 Banksy, *Walled-Off Hotel*. A general view shows the Walled-Off Hotel (L). Hotel opened 2017. Photograph by Hazem Bader/AFP via Getty Images.

Nevertheless, let's look more closely at the hotel. Here is Bianca Solonga writing about it for a popular magazine:

"We do not aim to pamper guests or to become a luxury destination. Our aim is to start a conversation and to get guests to think about the situation," explained Walled Off General Manager, Wisam Salsaa. The rooms range from the very basic budget rooms to the ultra premium Presidential suits. Budget rooms are dressed like very basic military quarters. For $60 dollars, a guest gets a key to lockers, personal safe a shared bathroom and complimentary earplugs. "We want to be accessible to all kinds of guests regardless of their budget." Other suites are customized art spaces created by contemporary artists like Banksy, Sami Musa and Dominique Petrin, to name a few. These rooms feature paintings, installation art and décor that merge opulence with political strife. Floor-to-ceiling windows frame what the hotel boasts as the "worst view in the world." Wisam reinforces, "Whereas other hotels are built to look out to beautiful landscapes, we give them an in-your-face view of the wall."[7]

...

The space was decorated as a reminder of British involvement in the Palestinian-Israeli situation. "The decision to serve afternoon tea in fine bone China is also reference to the Western world's involvement in this mess," declared Wisam. He adds, "We also chose not to serve meals in the hotel as a way of supporting other businesses in the city. We want to encourage our guests to step out of the comforts of their hotels and get to the know the city better."[8]

...

The Presidential Suite is an experience that stands out especially in a city where even a five-star hotel will most likely serve up cafeteria-style dinners. This suite which can go for up to $965 a night has "everything a corrupt head of state would need—a plunge bath able to accommodate up to four revelers, original artwork, library, home cinema, roof garden, Tiki bar and a water feature made from a bullet riddled water tank." Other amenities that come with the suite include a complete set of Dead Sea Bath Minerals an in-room dining service.[9]

At $225 a night and up, whom is this hotel really for? The evangelical Christian right that is the main tourist trade in Bethlehem, birthplace of Jesus? This side of Bethlehem is resolutely absent from the hotel, whose edgy decor and siting at the grit of the wall—symbol of Israeli oppression—will certainly not appeal to these generally right-wing groups. Aid workers who want to take advantage of the $60 slumming opportunity, staying in the hotel's low-rent rooms built from old Israeli army materials? A few maybe. The odd tourist with a human rights conscience? Maybe: these are the same kind of mostly European tourists who fly to Cape Town and visit Robben Island (where Nelson Mandela and his cohort of political prisoners were incarcerated during Apartheid South Africa), while also taking in a black township between glasses of wine at vineyards tucked beautifully under the umbrella of the mountain, and soft wind in their faces where the two oceans converge (Atlantic and Indian Ocean). There is nothing wrong and much right with that group; they probably support activist causes. But I think the hotel is essentially designed for the artworld, for those well-heeled curators, gallery owners, critics, artists, and collectors who want the adventure of a new, edgy, and fearful place, with art as yet undiscovered by the global art world. As if Bethlehem were the final pole to be discovered, after the North Pole and Antarctica, the source not of Jesus but of the Nile, that great colonial destination sought by the nineteenth century. Except that here the flag is planted, thanks to Banksy, in the form of a five-star luxury hotel crammed with political messages in the manner of overwrought and disturbational collage.

In short, what Banksy's hotel really does is extend art markets into a new and as yet uncharted terrain. This is also not a bad thing. It would be just for

Figure 8.4 Banksy, interior guests eat in the dining hall of Banksy's Walled-Off Hotel, December 21, 2019. Photograph by Musa Al Shaer/AFP via Getty Images.

Palestinian artists to have the same global access and opportunity as others. This hotel, while speaking the language of politics, is first and foremost a work of art, of total design by Banksy. It is—while preaching, and meaning, politics of justice—simply a conduit for the expansion of art markets. It is not simply, or perhaps even primarily, there as an outpost in the political malaise of Israel-Palestine for didactic purposes. Were it more dedicated to bringing Palestinian artists to art markets, it should have included a gallery, or at least Palestinian artists on the walls. Instead, the hotel is all Banksy. Although it does provide a pit stop for those who wish to find Palestinian art on their own.

Banksy is, in this sense, an ambassador for the 1 percent. And part of it. His hotel is am ambassadorial embassy for the art collector.

One need only turn to the matter of names to underscore this. Banksy is not the artist's real name. So why the choice. Think: BANK-sky. Of the bank. For the bank. About the bank, laughing all the way to the bank. And Walled-Off Hotel. Think Waldorf Hotel, that icon of the epicenter of the art world in New York City. Bethlehem is Walled-Off from New York City but also connected to New York City by the Banksy lifeline. The Banksy hotel is banking on providing a Waldorf Hotel for those who are heavily invested in banks.

Again: there are no Palestinian artists whose work is present in the hotel, which is frankly strange for a place that has not build a dining room so that patrons will be encouraged to venture out and visit local dining joints. One would have thought some of the work on the walls would have been theirs, or that at least a small gallery would have opened up to sell local work. Instead, patrons and locals are given art classes and license to paint on walls—in other words, to act like Banksy.

The Walled-Off Hotel is still young, and its career might take a different turn from what I have suggested. But my sense of it (at present) is that it is meant to serve the 1 percent with a political conscience—half-baked or fully risen—with their desire to occupy in a really edgy place in the Occupation, collecting really edgy art while remaining five-star. On the other hand, Palestinians approve of this hotel, saying it brings in tourists, money, work, and so on. The politics are unresolved, I think. As they usually are when it comes to the relation between art markets and politics.

Then, how to keep political critique alive given the opiating effect that turns the critical gesture into a pleasure drug for the market? How to keep politics from this aesthetic fate? I really want to say I have no idea apart from systemic, even radical change in the financial system, which is hard to see happening.

9

Autonomy as Negotiation: Mozart Reconsidered

Part I

Art is a beautiful instrument for thinking about politics because it spans the personal and the political, the private and the public, the transcendent and the engaged. Like studies of marriage, family, or friendship, art is a paradigm for studying politics in relation to human intimacy, privacy, and attachment. One need only recall Hegel's brilliant analysis of *Antigone* toward the conclusion of his *Phenomenology of Spirit*. Antigone is caught between her duties to state and her duties to family when it comes to the burial of her brother whom Creon, the king, has declared a traitor unworthy of proper burial. Hegel shows that at the moment in history when Antigone is brought into being in the Greek theater, these moral commitments are stratified, as yet incapable of reconciliation, and to tragic result. Hegel's is a beautiful example of philosophical analysis that understands family *dialogically*—in relation to love, society, law, and state power. It frames the Antigone story in a way that brings out these larger contradictions. Sophocles' drama demonstrates, according to the philosopher's story, how the personal and the political are inextricably fused or, in this case, sundered apart.

The experience of art affects each of us personally, drawing each of us in as if we entered the work courtesy of a sleight of hand, identifying with its emotional tenor, thrust, and parry. My teacher, the late great philosopher Ted Cohen, called this the cultivation of intimacy through art.[1] It requires sufficient autonomy for the personal transaction between subject and work of art to take place, as all free transactions do.

The eighteenth century had various notions of autonomy, which in diverse nation-states (England, Germany, France) were variously articulated in relation to citizenship, heritage, culture, and the state. Those notions all followed from a general acceptance of some kind of right to individual liberty, although the domain, range, and legal protections assigned to liberty were variously interpreted and matters of contestation. The right to liberty found its first bold assertion in the writings of John Locke, who stated that human beings are free in the state of nature, meaning prior to any government. Autonomy was quickly idealized, in England and elsewhere, as an ideal space free from the encroachments of the state and the church where freedom could be exercised, where a person could find and devise their own life script and seek to follow it. And where a person could live according to their own tastes and passions (financial wherewithal and racial/religious status being assumed).

The freedom to pursue taste and passion quickly became central markers of individual liberty. The discipline of aesthetics arose in relation to the connections between liberty, sense experience, and the pleasures of taste. Aesthetics understood the experience and judgment of beauty as an end in itself on the model of human lives, similarly treated. Taste, that marker of individual liberty (what I want, what I like, what I enjoy, what I find beautiful), found its purpose in the pleasure and intensity of the experience itself. Taste was also, both in England and in Germany, considered part of the way a Commons could be created: a community bonded together thanks to like experiences, and also shared ones. A community that would thereby train new members in their shared intimacies. This formation of a common bond of experience out of many individual ones—a bond that would then shape further individual experiences and so on—was crucial, it was believed, to the creation of national heritage. For those cosmopolitan philosophers like Kant, who distrusted nationalisms, the formation of a community of taste wanted instead to be universal, inclusive of all humanity. Some saw the common bond as a way of establishing the objectivity of taste; others not.[2] But all were interested in the power of individual experiences to shape the greater bonds of shared humanity (national or otherwise).

When taste (pleasure taken in the experience of an object) is taken to be the central marker of aesthetic experience, aesthetic experience is set apart from the rest of life, with such things as recognition, acknowledgment, proclamation, community devotion, and political agency becoming at best marginal and at worst totally excluded. Judgments about aesthetic matters (about what is beautiful, what is not) are understood to be affirmations of pleasure or pain (acts of sensibility) rather than propositions whose meaning and truth is undergirded by rational argument. For Kant, such judgments are reflective, turning the judger into an exemplar for all humanity. However, this universalizing claim is not rooted in fact or argument, but in the kind of pleasure the self takes in its objects and how that is referred to a "universal voice."[3]

Aesthetic experience, now thought of as a self-contained encomium of pleasure, becomes a space where each individual can exercise, enjoy, and celebrate their liberty *as its own end* (whether they stand as an exemplar for others or not). Aesthetic experience becomes an *icon* of liberty, a way for persons to recognize and take pleasure in their freedom of choice, indeed in their *capacity* for freedom as such. Liberty, understood an end in itself, could find its expression and symbol in aesthetic experience because aesthetic experience was similarly understood as an end in itself.

The historical creation of a sphere of autonomy was among the great inventions of modern Europe and America. And let's be clear about the obvious: Without some degree of autonomy, no one can be rightly said to be *free*: their freedom is always compromised and can be taken away at a moment's notice. And to state the obvious, there is a perfectly clear way to understand taste as freedom's correlate, where the exercise of taste is *for its own sake* without further consequence. I garden; you forage for mushrooms; someone else does yoga, tinkers in the woodworking room, or plays the guitar; another collects vinyl records or antiques. These are personal pleasures that we often treasure because they are a break from the rest of life. We do them for the love of it. The word "hobby" may be used to describe these *sui generis* pleasures. But they are important in making us the free people we are, the individuals we are, and allowing us to take pleasure in the recognition of that. And finally let's also be clear: the eighteenth century discovered something that is absolutely right. Whatever power art has does indeed centrally reside in its raptures of sensuous experience, even if, contra the eighteenth century, there is far more to art than that, even to the art of the eighteenth century, as I aim to show.

The question is which concept—or concepts—of autonomy is/are the best overall way(s) to think about autonomy in relation to art—back then or today. This is the question I pose in this chapter.

Now the institutions of the state that came into being in the eighteenth century were meant to facilitate autonomy: courts of law, museums, and concert halls along with universities, but they were also forms of state, nationalist, and colonial power and control. These institutions were under continual stress because they served two masters: First, to safeguard the autonomy of thought and culture. And second, to proclaim the heritage and authority of the nation-state over its citizens. It is well known that institutions both facilitate and constrain liberty, and these were no exception. There is no clearer example than the museum, itself an institution created by the eighteenth century to house and display what was understood to be national patrimony. The colonial artifact that had lived its original life in ritual, religion, on the street corner, or in the temple was stolen by the French or British conqueror, purchased at negligible prices, or otherwise heisted away from the site of its enmeshment with "native" life. Once relocated to the halls of the Louvre, British Museum, or Hermitage, the "native" object was given a second life as a mere sight, an object denuded of meaning and use, there for the contemplative gaze of the museum-goer. As such, it lost all social meaning and acquired a new one—that of *national heritage*. Napoleon went to Egypt and returned with pyramids that monumentalized his nation by becoming "French," a part of national patrimony.

The museum was a space of autonomy, where objects "freed" from their original social meanings (in which Europe was not interested) were now there simply to be contemplated. But contemplation as an aesthetic practice was also a way for citizens to grasp the power of the state that owned these objects and exhibited them as its heritage. Aesthetic autonomy and national politics fit together.

The question of how autonomous any or all of these institutions (the museum, the university, the court of law) could or should be from the state and/or church was highly contested. Their autonomy a matter of debate, and struggle. David Hume could never get a job teaching in university because his atheist beliefs flew in the face of religious authority. Mozart and Da Ponte's *Marriage of Figaro* was nearly shut down because its use of dancing contravened Hapsburg dictum. Beaumarchais, the writer of the play on which this masterpiece was based, was less lucky. His play was closed in Paris because of its revolutionary perfume, its political message.

And so, in the eighteenth century, autonomy was shaped in relation to political argument. Stepping back for a moment and taking the wide-angled view, it's worth pointing out that autonomy has always been an ideal as much as a reality, an aspiration as well as a fact, a thing to struggle for as well as to eschew, depending. It has always been both a safe space from the state and a form of state control. The question has therefore always been how best to formulate the ideal of autonomy while negotiating its reality. An institution such as the concert hall has never been entirely autonomous from the larger stream of life, sealed in its encomium. Nor has any individual life ever marched entirely to its own drummer. And this is as it should be. Too much autonomy isolates a person or work of art or institution from the networks of the world in relation to which these have meaning, identity, and purpose. Too much autonomy turns art or liberty into a thing of little consequence beyond a consumer item, opiate, or idle thing. Too little autonomy prevents the person or work of art from exercising any liberty at all. Autonomy is always a trade-off and a contested space.

Part II

Autonomy is as much about private as public life. The sphere of privacy expanded dramatically with the culture of liberty for the simple reason that liberty was understood, at least in England, primarily in terms of freedom of ownership—the right to private property. Privacy was a luxury of those who could afford it, meaning it expanded in relation to the rise of the bourgeois class with its free time, large houses, and money. All of which led to a kind of deepening of autonomy: freedom from external control, and self-governance or the ability of a person to devise and follow their own life script, aesthetically, morally, financially, in their own private space.

If Jurgen Habermas is right, the public/private debate was at the core of eighteenth-century politics.[4] This was the century when the public sphere came into being, a central component in the rise of democracy. In the pubs, cafes, and public institutions, the conversation of democracy, and with it of group solidarity, took shape, preparing and demanding political representation. Schiller's drinking song is of that time with its "all men become brothers" and raising-of-glass togetherness. Public and private are corollaries: One cannot have the one without the other. As public life became more highly articulated, and for a bourgeois class, so did the distinction between it and the private life of ownership, and life behind doors and curtains.

Both private life and public spaces such as the concert hall were *embattled spaces*, negotiated in the light of state control, church censorship, and the like. Some of the greatest visual art, music, theater, and literature of the time fought for the right to sufficient autonomy to pen incendiary social and political messages that the state, the monarchy, the church sought to disallow. Autonomy was idealized by these artists as the space to enter the political fray courtesy of aesthetic experience, and to do so freely. The struggle for autonomy thus expanded into a struggle for *freedom of speech*, in art as in philosophy, literature, and revolutionary politics.

But aesthetic theory retained its commitment to a form of experience (of the beautiful and the sublime) that made this goal (freedom of speech) secondary to the sheer transcendent power of art and nature, and to the pleasures of individual taste. Aesthetic theory valued the sensuous, nonconceptual encounter with art or nature. It focused on pleasure. But certain artists (like Mozart and his librettist, Da Ponte) valued sensuousness precisely so that freedom of speech might also flow from it. Mozart and Da Ponte not only pushed the boundaries of what was acceptable, allowable, producible in terms of *aesthetic form*; they did so that their operas could speak volumes about politics in relation to the daily commerce of life.

There was thus a tension between what aesthetic theory wanted of art and what artists wanted of it. More on that follows.

Art is well suited to adopt this struggle for autonomy in private as well as in public life because it awakens—in each person attuned to it—a sense of their own privacy, *a sense of the depth of their own self.* This is on account of its representation of human reality but also simply because the work causes the attuned spectator to engage in what Kant beautifully called the free play of the faculties—a play between sensuous experience, cognition, imagination, and emotion. For Kant, aesthetic judgment is reflective judgment, and traditions of a broadly Kantian cast, from Fredrich Schiller to Herbert Marcuse, have associated reflective judgment with imaginative self-awakening—awakening to one's own liberty to think, feel, and speak otherwise. There is nothing more private than this depth of self-awakening. Schiller believed the name for the feeling was freedom of conscience. For Marcuse, romantic that he was, aesthetic judgment is emancipatory in how it awakens the mind to liberation. Even if this must also be said: an awakened mind is not yet a political one, since one can awake to oppression or dumb constraint or other social ills with various political options available, from becoming a Nazi to a communist to a liberal.

The pages of history have unfortunately proved this, making the problem of how reflective judgment connects to political choice a contextual one. This aside, one may at least say that the arrival by Kant at the idea that aesthetic judgment is reflective has been part of the larger discovery of the interiority of the self that Charles Taylor identifies as crucial to the formation of modern life, a discovery that continued into the Romantic obsession with the wild, eroticized depths of genius, the role of memory in life, and on again into the projects of psychiatry and psychoanalysis in the latter half of the nineteenth century.[5] And that this discovery was not simply academic; art discovered it along with science, deepening its probing of interiority both in theme and in its capacity to awaken the spectator or listener.

Now the experience of art as awakening the private depth of the self in relation to liberty makes art the perfect instrument for exploring private life in a world where private life reflects and represents the political order. The arrangement of public with private life, in fact, underwent a significant transformation in the eighteenth century, as Jurgen Habermas has argued. First, Habermas denotes the arrangement of public and private life that came down through European history from the Greeks and Romans:

> The political order ... rested on a patrimonial slave economy. The citizens were thus set free from productive labor; it was however their private autonomy as masters of households on which their private autonomy as masters of households on which their participation in public life depended. The private sphere was attached to the house ... Movable wealth and control over labor power were no more substitutes for being the master of a household and of a family than, conversely,

poverty and a lack of slaves would in themselves prevent admission to the *polis* [public sphere] ... Status in the *polis* was therefore based upon status as the unlimited master of an *oikos* [household economy]. The reproduction of life, the labor of the slaves, and the service of the women went on under the aegis of the master's domination; birth and death took place in its shadow; and the realm of necessity and transitoriness remained immersed in the obscurity of the private sphere. In contrast to it stood, in Greek self-interpretation, the public sphere as the realm of freedom and permanence.[6]

By the eighteenth century, colonialism and the rise of markets had substantially changed the equation of public and private. Economy became less focused on the household and more on the firm, the state, the colonial market. With this the duties and authority of the head of household became less economic, and more tied into the encroachments of public life—the life of the market, the state, and, related, the rising nature of civil society. This placed pressure on the structure of the household: on its political authority and terms of lordship.

Part III

What kind of pressure? This household order remained in the late eighteenth century—one of class: count versus servant. However, households began to feel the ripple of these larger changes in the public/private spheres. While the count (head of household) still retained authority over his servants and his women, it was now a weakened form of power in relation to economy, state, and civil society. This challenge to private power led to political uncertainty about the terms of private life: the household, an uncertainty reflected in the question of who should be allowed autonomy to do what within this newly transformed private sphere. It is, I venture to suggest, exactly Mozart's and his librettist Da Ponte's question in *The Marriage of Figaro* of 1786, insofar as one can attribute to opera a guiding question. How should, within the household, those who lack rights to privacy (autonomy) because they own nothing and work for others also achieve private life (autonomy)? How can their marriage bed—a private place if there ever was one—be measured and protected?

The plot of the opera unfurls in the house of Count Almaviva, with his servant Figaro measuring the bed he will occupy with Suzanna, the maid, after marrying her later that day. The count has, in an emancipatory gesture, relinquished to the right of the master to claim first entry into that marriage bed, a relinquishment he perhaps believes in, but given his fornicating/ lecherous nature, also regrets. Suzanna understands this better than Figaro, being a woman accustomed to defending her autonomy from the usual male onslaughts, especially those of the count:

Susanna: Cosa stai misurando, caro il mio Figaro (what are you measuring, My dearest Figaro)?[7]

Figaro: Io guardo se quel letto Che ci destina il Conte Fara buona figura in questo loco (I'm seeing if this bed Which the Count has put aside for us Will go well just here).

Susanna: In questa stanza (In this room)?

Figaro: Certo, a noi la cede Generoso il padrone (Of course; his lordship's Generously giving it to us).

Susanna: Io per me te la dono (As far as I'm concerned you can keep it).

Figaro: E la ragione (What's the matter)?

...

Susanna: ... Cosi se il mattino Il caro Contino Din din e ti manda Tre miglia lontan. Din din, Don don, e a mia porta Il diavol lo porral, Ed ecco in tre salti ... (And supposing one morning The dear Count should ring. Ding ding, and send you Three miles away, Dong dong, and the devil Should lead him to my door— And here he is, in three bounds).

...

Susanna: Il signor Conte Stanco d'andar cacciando le straniere Bellezze forestiere. Vuole ancor nel castello Ritentar la sua sorte, Ne gia di sua consorte, bada bene, Appetito gli viene (The noble Count, tired of scouring the countryside For fresh beauties, Wants to try his luck again in his own palace, Though, let me tell you, it's not his wife Who whets his appetite).

(Act I, Scene I)

And so, the gift of autonomy, a bed, a bedroom, and the abjuring of the right of the lord are offered with an escape valve in mind by the count, since he's stuck them in a room with easy access for himself. Autonomy is fragile when offered paternalistically, until undergirded by law, and even then, insecurely established until rooted in shared cultural practices. And Suzanna is right: All hell breaks loose when the count conspires to take Suzanna on the sly, in spite of his relinquishment of the authority to do so by "right of the master." No longer able to claim her by entitlement, he must now insinuate himself through the usual wiles of seduction, in his case aided and abetted by his strength and his power of lordship, which remains in place in spite of the emancipatory refusal of the particular right he has refused. And so, the question of liberty plays itself in this opera around the question of marriage—marriage in relationship to class, autonomy, and privacy.

Then there is the issue of jealousy, apparently the flip side of passion. Everyone in the opera suffers this, but since the count is a brute lecher, he attributes the same to all others, erupting continually about the unfaithfulness of those around him when it is he who wears the dirty laundry. This leads to a number of locked doors, escapes through closets, subterfuges and intrigues throughout this comic masterpiece, among whose spectacular moments being when Marcellina, who has her eye on Figaro, turns out to be his long-lost mother (Su madre?, Su madre!!!!), and the lawyer Bartolo his father.

This furious free-for-all (or free-against-all) is punctuated by the loneliness of the Contessa, ignored and humiliated by her husband. Hers is autonomy unwanted, that of being cast aside, and it provides us with two of Mozart's greatest arias: *Porgi Amor* in Act II (grant me some solace) and *Dove Sono* in Act III (where did my happiness go?), both sung by the Contessa. Disappointment runs through the opera, the other side of unquenchable desire. It is voiced by women about men:

Marcellina: Il capro e la Capretta Son sempre in amista: L'agnello all'agnelletta La guerra mai non fa; Le piu feroci belve Per selve e per campagne Lascian le lor compagne In pace e Liberta. Sol noi, povere femine, Che tanto amiam questi uomini, Trattate siam dai perfidi Ognor con crudelta (The billy-goat and the she-goat Always live on friendly terms; The sheep never wages war on these ewe; The fiercest beasts Of the forest and the field Leave their mates In peace and freedom. But we, poor women, Who so love these men, Are treated by the traitors With constant perfidy).

(Act IV, Scene V)

Don Basilio adds in an aria soon following: L'accozzarla co'grandi Fu pericolo ognora: Dan novanta per cento, e han vinto ancora (It has always been dangerous to clash with important people: They can give away ninety percent and still win).

(Act IV, Scene VII)

Threats come from men, and especially powerful men, that is, the libidinous, well-off count. The count suspects everyone, including his wife, which is a sad joke considering that she is nothing but abandoned (by him). This pile-up of suspicion culminates in Act IV. The count has sent a pin back to Susanna, giving it to Barbarina. However, Barbarina has lost it. Figaro and Marcellina see Barbarina, and Figaro asks her what she is doing. When he hears the pin is Susanna's, he is overcome with jealousy, especially as he recognizes the pin to be the one that fastened the letter to the count. Figaro complains to his (newly found) mother. He vows to wreak vengeance on both Suzanna and the count, not to mention railing about all the other unfaithful wives at whom he'll get back. Marcellina tries to calm him, but he rushes off. This leads to said aria about wild beast by the fed-up Marcellina.

Two arias later, Susanna and the countess arrive, each wearing the other's clothes. (We know what will happen; this is classic preparation for comic misrecognition.) To infuriate Figaro, Suzanna sings an aria ostensibly to her lover, knowing Figaro can hear, and Figaro assumes it is the count. Now everyone is ready to have it out with everyone else over the wrong thing, all caused by the pile-up of passions, suspicions, jealousies.

They all assemble in the garden. It is night. The countess arrives in Susanna's dress. In one of the most painful ironies of the opera, the count begins making love to Suzanna, except it is his own wife dressed as the maid. He gives her a ring, and they depart. The Contessa (dressed as Suzanna) manages to elude him. Meanwhile, the real Suzanna, dressed as the Contessa, enters and is mistaken by Figaro as the genuine article. He begins to tell her what the count is after, when he recognizes that it is in fact his bride Suzanna. To toy with her, he offers love on the spot. She assumes he is offering it to the Contessa not herself, and beats him. Figaro finally lets on that he knows who he is really making love to: he has recognized her voice. They make up.

The opera is not yet over. The frustrated count, unable to find "Susanna," only now arrives. Figaro gets his attention by loudly declaring his love for "the countess" (really Susanna). The enraged count calls for his people and for weapons: he believes his servant is seducing his wife. In the game of love, war is between equals until firepower is commanded. This is crucial to the revolutionary character of the opera, which understands that real love, wild desire, overwhelming passion is classless and in antagonism to the social order. Private life has this defect or, rather, virtue.

The group now implore the count to forgive Figaro and the Contessa (still Suzanna in disguise). He refuses. Finally, the real countess enters and reveals herself to him. The count, seeing the ring he had given her, now understands that in attempting to seduce his maid, he was really making love to his wife. He is, for the first time in the opera, ashamed, singing *Contessa, perdono* ("Contessa forgive me"). More empathetic than he, she forgives him. And so, one couple is married, the other reunited.

This happy ending is somewhat idealized. We know that the count will remain the adoring, forgiven husband for about one second, until, once the final curtain is down, he returns to his inevitably lecherous self. As for Figaro and Suzanna, their prospects are better, since theirs is love as yet unquenched. They might just make it if they don't fall into an abyss of mutual suspicion.

Since the autonomy of the marriage bed and the question of rights to privacy and the pursuit of happiness are contested in the count's castle—this means for Mozart and Da Ponte, politics is worked out in private, not merely in public (the state, the court of law, the church, market economy). They are, I think, responding to the pressure on the public sphere in the eighteenth century to transform the *private sphere*. The wonderful feminist idea (first stated by Carol Hanisch in 1969) that "the personal is the political"[8] already found expression in this eighteenth-century opera (and is, I think, a running theme in the history of opera as such). The lesson of Mozart and Da Ponte was that autonomy is an achievement (of the right to one's own bedroom apart from the intrusion of the count) but always also a negotiation between various parties, a negotiation inevitably clouded and compounded by desire and its subterfuge. Class inequality cannot be resolved apart from sexual jealousy and satisfaction, at least not in private, and the erotic life will both reflect underlying inequality and challenge it.

What kind of autonomy did these Mozartian characters fight for? Was it of a piece with the extreme view of autonomy central to aesthetic theory? Aesthetic theory in its most radical version—a version that has come down to us from the eighteenth-century thought of autonomy as a regulative ideal, that of a space where aesthetic play could take place in complete separation from the wider social and political world. Where individual liberty could be realized. But there is no such thing as individual liberty apart from a social set-up like the house of the count, nor apart from a nation and its forms of power, nor apart from class and labor relations. The picture of autonomy—as the space where individual liberty takes place in and for itself—was at odds with the way individuals in fact exercise their freedom, which is together and in relation to each other, not apart. *Autonomy is established dialogically*. It is established through struggle, if not given as a gift, and is always in danger of being revoked. The terms of autonomy shift when the dialogic character of human relations change.

Part IV

Aesthetic autonomy, if presented in the extreme version, cannot serve as a regulative ideal, since the ideal is out of sync with the voice and experience of art, which preaches a different idea of it, less ideal and more in line with human life. Then, why did such a picture of autonomy ever come into being in the first place? Of course, one cannot address this vast question in toto. But here are a few thoughts. First, art really does have a transcendent side and this is crucial to its value. A work of art does seek to create a peculiar and glorious experience set apart from the world, in which much of the world drops out. Mozart's work may be about the struggle for freedom in situations of inequality, but it also soars above this story into a dazzling realm of sound where everything else seems incidental. It has a beginning, middle, and end that compute to a complete experience and a sensuous one for the listener/ audience. *Beauty of well-wrought form* really does matter, as the ear floats from the words into a feel for sound color and intonation, phrasing and melody, and what Roland Barthes calls "the grain of the voice."[9] The grain of the voice is nonconceptual, mysterious, convulsive for those who love it.

And so, a double experience is essential to art. On the one hand, art is a conduit for an experience of the beautiful and sublime. On the other, art is a way of speaking within and to the world about the world and how we live in it, urging us to take up a position on the world by acknowledging how things are.

Second, such an extreme view of aesthetic autonomy was demanded by the cult of individual liberty. I began with this thought but would like to amplify it here. The Lockean, empiricist picture of a self is a picture of the single person born "tabula rasa" (with a clean slate), which slowly learns to negotiate the world by itself, acquires beliefs through experience, learns to know and to cope on its own terms. This picture of each person as an *island* understands autonomy in purely individualistic terms. Autonomy is where each of us, alone with our minds, may be gifted space free from external constraint so that we may come to devise our own scripts for living. This notion of autonomy came to be understood as absolute because the individual who occupied it, who had it, was conceptualized apart from others.

Then the question became how a Commons, a community of taste and spirit, could arise from a string of individual lives with their self-made experiences and in a way that would inflect each individual. But the accretion of a Commons was always precariously theorized, given the emphasis on the epistemic individual and their liberty. Rather, one must start from what Hegel and, following him, Marx called the dialectical form of human life, that I am myself through others, and cannot imagine my being anything at all apart from my interpolation of them that becomes the core of who I am. Self-formation arises in the context of social engagement, is defined through social norms, and forms in the light of power relations—often unequal. We come to know ourselves through others. We come to know the self and the world through interpolating shared discursive practices of science, law, nationalism, religion, racism, gender, empire, and so on. These meaning-giving norms are what Hegel glossed as "*Sittlichkeit*," the currency of moral and epistemic truths through which the very possibility of knowledge is encoded within each of us. We may resist, seek to change these norms, but only through them. There is no perspective we can take outside of them as a whole, no "view from nowhere."

There can be no individual liberty apart from the networks that link the individual to others, to law, society, science, culture, class, and politics. In the light of this dialogic picture of the individual, autonomy must be thought *relationally*: in relation to the social order; to politics, economy, and history; and, above all, to other people. It is only *as an ensemble within a social order* that each character in *Figaro* seeks autonomy for the fulfillment of their ardent desire, wishing to exercise a modicum of liberty. Autonomy always comes into being in relation to others, which is why even the count is stymied throughout the opera in spite of his power. There is no autonomy apart from an ensemble. The ensemble qualifies the kind of autonomy each character has, while also allowing autonomy (the right to one's own marriage bed) to arise as a quest. A quest whose terms are happily resolved at the opera's end, but as I said in a somewhat fantastical way. The count will turn again to flirting soon after we exit the theater; the poor Contessa will again be consigned to neglect. Call the entire ensemble of characters a marriage writ large (for richer, for poorer, until death do us part). And, so it goes.[10]

The question is when autonomy may be called sufficient, and for whom. And that surely is a contextual question: it depends on circumstances.

A person alone on an island is not autonomous; he or she is simply alone. Autonomy only arises when persons are shaped by, and living within, a world of others. Call autonomy that space that each achieves for themselves in the midst. Autonomy is a way of living with others that is, it is hoped, tractable. It is always dialogical.

10

Film, the Individual, and the Collective

Part I

The previous chapter was about the way the history of aesthetics deriving from the eighteenth century organized itself around what I call the cult of individual liberty. The chapter was also about challenges to that by the very artists who seek to maximize liberty by expanding it into freedom of speech. Mozart and Da Ponte break the barriers of what is allowed in opera, almost getting theirs chucked out in the process. But they also *challenge* the idea of autonomy understood as an individual encomium, seeking to show that, especially in the sphere of *private life*, autonomy is dialogical and contested across lines of power, authority, and human attraction. In their opera, there is no sorting out passion, subterfuge, misrecognition, and jealousy from the politics of autonomy (the privacy of the marriage bed). Across the eighteenth century, one can find a mismatch between the kind of autonomy aesthetics demanded and the kind to which art (Mozart's anyway) aspired.

We should also remember that although aesthetic ideology focused on the value of *individual* experience, taste was also about building a larger social bond between individuals: a community unified in taste that would then serve to shape further aesthetic experiences others were to have along its lines, producing a cultivated and nationalized citizenry. This idea of how individual experiences accrete to a common bond was a key problem of the eighteenth century. In part because nationalism was reinventing itself, demanding new ways in which persons could imagine themselves part of what Benedict Anderson famously called an "imagined community." Taste became one way in which this perceived sense of oneness was cultivated across individuals. Although taste was about individual liberty, it was also about creating a national Commons from individual experience.[1]

The cult of the individual ran through the nineteenth century at the same time as quite contradictory ideas were formulated about art. As I said in the introduction, aesthetics and art practice today are a mix of eighteenth-century ideas with those of the centuries that followed, a mélange more rich than consistent. These new ideas, emerging from the aesthetics of the eighteenth century but transforming those in a considerable way, came from

Hegel and Marx, who stressed the social role of art in variously articulating the aspirations of the age (Hegel), issues of class, alienation, base and superstructure, ideology and power (Marx) that prepared the avant-gardes of the twentieth century. I will turn to the avant-gardes later in the chapter, but first I want to discuss those aesthetic and artistic traditions that retained the eighteenth century's aesthetic character.[2]

These took a number of different turns. First aestheticism, the cult of the individual aesthete, for whom life should resemble art. Life was meant to turn into style, even be completed by the writing of life, as if one could compose oneself into the right form of existence by turning (thanks to literature) one's life into the work of art one is writing. Writing or painting or poetry or music became thought of as acts of becoming—becoming oneself. As if in some magically Nietzschean way, the self could be remade and enhanced through its re-formation on the model of and through the making of art.[3] Oscar Wilde, Walter Pater, Joris-Karl Huysmans, Marcel Proust were dazzling examples.

Formalism was another legacy, deriving from Kant, wherein the aesthetic value of art is claimed to reside in purely formal properties, relying except peripherally on nothing outside the work, and where formal properties are taken to be thereby peculiar, indefinable, untranslatable, and, hence, glorious. Formalism comes from the pages of Kant and runs through the nineteenth century and on through the twentieth.

Finally, the legacy to which I will now turn: the cult of the aura and the World Tour. One cannot discuss the aesthetics of the aura without mention of Walter Benjamin's seminal essay, "The Work of Art in an Age of Mechanical Reproducibility,"[4] which begins with the thought that the aura emerges from religious and ritualistic cult practice. Think of the runes of Stonehenge, bespeaking a power magically hovering above or dwelling within the stone. Stonehenge, considered physically, is a mere circle of stones, but when human life invests this piece of the physical universe with religious value, aligning it with the stars, it takes on what Walter Benjamin calls the aura of place. The key to the aura is that it is a projection from persons onto place, not a property of place itself. The size and topology of a mountain, the kind of flora and fauna that inhabit it—these are properties of the mountain. The way the mountain takes on ritualistic or cult value to a native American tribe, like Mount Olympus for the Ancient Greeks, is not, strictly speaking, a property of the mountain but of the collective imagination of the tribe, of how the mountain *appears* to the tribe, of how it is experienced and valued. An aura is subjective or intersubjective. And it is specific to place; it cannot reside everywhere, for the sacred only makes sense in contrast with the profane, and some part of the world has got to be considered that, for the cult practice around certain places to make sense. Even Aboriginal peoples, for whom all nature is animistic (the living legacy of the "ancestors"), must see something as ordinary to make the contrast (perhaps they themselves?). Place, people, or events take on a special value by contrast with other places, people, or events that do not, or do not in the same way, in the same degree or from the same perspective.

The experience of place depends utterly on being there. To feel the aura of the sacred mountain, one must approach or ascend it, of the religious temple, or church, or holy place one must make the pilgrimage. The aura depends absolutely on being-present-to. As Woody Allen puts it, 90 percent of life is showing up. Aura does not project across distances; it is attached by the collective imagination indelibly to particular things. Aura in turn lends a specific piece of the world the sense of its absolute uniqueness from all other places, its "this-ness" apart from all else. A bush is a bush, until it burns with the God of Moses, and before it stands the man. Then it is absolutely unique: this bush, not another, is the bush one wants to see. As in the hotel that advertises "Moses slept here," making that hotel room where he lay down his head unique—auratic.

The aura takes on a very different valence in modern life, as religious and cult worship fall away in a secularizing modern Europe. Once Stonehenge was the site of cult worship, it now stands apart from that, vacant, a beacon to an invisible and inaccessible past. At this point, cult value (itself a kind of aura) turns into the aura of lost things, of that which once was and is now unreachable. We will likely never know what kind of worship took place there at Stonehenge in the past, but the stones remain runes of the sacred, which is now embodied, we feel, in their "script," a palimpsest of what once was.

The aesthetics of the Grand Tour (and here I am going far beyond Benjamin if loosely in his spirit) emerges in the eighteenth century as a kind of aesthetic replacement for cult worship. By this moment, many of the stops on the Grand Tour have lost their original purpose and are runes of a world that was. The aesthetics of the Grand Tour approach place as a set of things rescripted for aesthetic contemplation and rapture, for taste and pleasure taken in their beauty, fascination, and sublimity, such as the city of Venice that has existed largely as an inert self-representation since its descent into decadence in the eighteenth century and then overthrow by Napoleon in 1797. Venice is a living icon of the past, slowly sinking into the lagoon. Aura is for the Grand Tour autumnal evanescence and unique individuality. When Franz Liszt, poet/pianist of the cult of rarified and beautiful things, wrote his three volumes of the *Annees de Pelerinages* for solo piano; the place of pilgrimage or religious worship was not the road to Compostela in Spain, nor Lourdes nor the Bethlehem of the Crusades. It was the Villa d'Este where dry October leaves arabesque onto stones in soft light, and there is a touch of chill coming down from the Alps. Liszt's pilgrimage is to the great monuments and places of Europe, each disclosing to him a sublime presence made all the more poignant by transience. The Grand Tour is a cult practice on par with religion. One might even say the Grand Tour, along with the museum, is modern life's secular inheritance of religion in the form of aesthetic experience.[5]

Aura is about evanescence. Which may be very short. Monet paints the same haystacks at different moments in the day and in different seasons, showing how, at each moment, light saturates the haystack differently, with a distinctive glow of luminescent color. His impressionism is a way of capturing the haystack's this-ness at the moment when the momentary glow is prolonged by our absorption yet already passing. The "now" is profound because of its quiet arc of brevity. Absorption elongates time: One can stand in front of a painting not noticing the hours gone by just as a spring Sunday by the river may feel like a small eternity, as life slows across the long arc of a lazy afternoon. Time passes and we do not notice. This deepening of the *now* is in Impressionism matched by our sense that it is evoked through dabs of color, refusal of the hard edges of drawing, preference for the sketch, spontaneous, ambient blending of color that we the viewers have to bring to representational clarity through our own perceptual engagement. We bring the patches of color to life. This active visual labor allows us to participate in the creation of what we see, thanks to our spontaneity of perception (Kant). We animate the work and thereby become absorbed in it. But the fact that the work is simply dabs of color apart from our absorption in it creates a strong sense of its evanescence. It is a moment reanimated in the looking but felt to be like memory, blurred and already past. There is joy in this. In a famous debate between Sigmund Freud and Roman Rolland, Rolland bemoans the fact that all things must pass, and Freud responds by saying it is because of transience that life takes on its poignant value.[6] And so the aura of the haystack is its transient character of light and color, recaptured (or recreated) in paintings that both animate and call attention to the passing of what we see.

The Grand Tour was about travel through Europe and especially the Mediterranean, its point being to take in the great sites of the past in their indelible singularity. One stood before the sacred site as a neophyte, following the steps of those who came before. Guide books were essential. One simply *had* to follow Goethe in his approach to Venice, seeing it for the first time from an approach by boat along the Brenta River, past the grand palazzi designed by Palladio and sited on the river. Just as one had to sojourn in the *mezzogiorno* in summer's heat, when at midday life retreats indoors, into quiet and cool darkness, while landscape appears with the vastness of overmodulated ruins, recalling lost empire and lost time. "Oh, dear white children, casual as birds, playing amidst the ruined languages," W. H. Auden wrote in his homage to that part of the world.

Time lost is time all the more precious because its reflection—in painting or in the chipped and faded stones of the cathedral—remains luminous, a remnant of what once was a beacon of life passing into nothingness. Europe's discovery of the deep history of things was not only a discovery about progress toward a better modernity. It was the converse discovery of the relative inaccessibility of the past, of the eventual ruination of all things. In order to have this exalted experience of the hovering of time in the stalwart ruin, one had to literally be there in its presence, to stand before it at the right hour in the right season, restricting such experiences to what we would now call the 1 percent who had leisure time and money to afford such experiences. The reward was a memory of each and every individual thing, an *impression*.

This cult of individual things, places, and let's add *people*, seems to me the ultimate aesthetic expression of the cult of the individual first enshrined by John Locke's proclamation of individual liberty—the only right Locke assigns to human beings in virtue of nature (God) in the *Second Treatise of Government* of 1683. From the right to liberty arose the important concept of individual autonomy, which I explored in the previous chapter as a space of individual privacy, freedom from authority and self-governance. I believe the *cult of the individual* central to modern Europe and America finds its final gasp of expression in the Grand Tour and the aesthetics of the aura. For the Grand Tour is all about the individual with time and leisure becoming an individual pilgrim standing before the absolutely unique site where the aura was to be found, projected, or felt. This church, that palazzo, this mountaintop, that stretch of sea, this library, that monument, each of absolute value in itself as a site of worship. I think this is why Benjamin thought it so important to understand how and why the aesthetics of the aura were being replaced by a revolutionary aesthetics based on the principle of multiplicity or the collective. At stake in the aesthetic transformation was a replacement of bourgeois individualism with revolutionary solidarity and collectivity. The end of democratic liberalism.

Part II

There is an idea central to Marx, which Benjamin echoes in his essay, that it is the technological forces of production that are the key catalytic drivers of changes in the socioeconomic formation. As in the importance of the hand mill for feudalism, the sailing ship for early capitalism (mercantile capitalism), and also the birth of colonialism, the discovery of electricity, the invention of the steam engine and of the factory line for industrial capitalism, of digital technologies for the globalized culture of financial capital, and so on. Benjamin famously argues that it is the technologies of reproducibility that are the key drivers of aesthetic change—change so vast that at the time of his writing, in the dark ages of the 1930s, he believed he was bespeaking them in the form of early prophesy. The technology of reproducibility of interest to this essay is less Gutenberg and his printing press, and more the invention of the engraving and woodcut by artists just after the Renaissance, when the Grand Tour began to come into being and a stream of tourists wanted to bring home images of what they'd seen. Ironically, visual reproducibility served the purpose of keeping the aura of things in memory, thanks to this iota of visual remembrance (the engraving you took with you). The artists of Rome made engravings so that the man or woman on the Grand Tour could bring back a token of what they saw. To paint a scene for each and every tourist would have proved impossible, not to mention expensive, and so technological innovation suited. A single engraved or carved plate could generate multiple images, all the same (give or take since the first is always brighter and clearer than the hundredth).

Hence the rise of a market. These engravings gradually spread, and before one knew it, they allowed people unable to take the Grand Tour to have a whiff of what they'd missed. As a result, the Grand Tour gradually turned into a set of images of places rather than an encounter with place itself, and with this the aura of place, Benjamin believed, eviscerated. This culture of the image is parodied in a brilliant early film of Jean-Luc Godard, *Band of Outsiders* (in the English title), where the men go off to war, returning with a huge war chest of spoils, which turns out to consist entirely of images, as if image value is a currency both weaker than the original and yet stronger, since images are more like dollar bills, capable of endless circulation with the power of that (see my earlier discussion of Warhol in Chapter 8).

Benjamin's well-known idea is that because for reproducible objects there is no original; there can be no aura surrounding these objects. (He is also interested in the role of *tradition* in the life of the aura, which is not my theme here.) While theater has aura—since the audience is present to the performance of the play—prints, photography, and film do not and cannot. For there is no way that the audience for these media can actually be present to a sacred original, with its absolutely felt uniqueness and resonance. We do not huddle around the film as we do around the stones of Salisbury Plain. One could huddle around the film set while Clark Gable is being filmed, and I suppose breathe in his aura, but that is not the film one watches, which is a string of scenes filmed at different times probably on various sets and locations. And then assembled postproduction. That aesthetic object, Benjamin says, one is not present-to, hence film aesthetics can have no real aura. But loss is finally gain. Having junked the old cult of the aura, and with it the bourgeois European ideal of individuality, film is able to deliver the world free of nostalgia for the past, for what once was. It can instead show the world of the present and the future. And in a way that democratizes, since every print is the equal (give or take in quality) of every other and one doesn't have to have money and time to burn to view it as one does to get to Italy for six months and saunter around. Film is a medium for the collective, not the lucky few. And one that shouts out: you are all equal, you all may share equally in this new kind of aesthetic experience.

Benjamin is interested in a number of political values that are meant to derive from this sea change, some of which are askew from this chapter. Very loosely improvised from him, there are three. First, the refusal of the cult of individuality. Second, the end of elite culture that privileges the few able to partake of travel to the sacred places of the world. That is: the democratization of aesthetic experience. And third, an emphasis on the present and the future instead of effete nostalgia for what once was, for the aura of lost things.

Finally, film is seen by the masses, not by an individual or two standing in a church. It is a collective medium with the power to motivate collectivities, or so it was thought (and not without good reason). The older idea of taste was that individual experiences accrete over time into a common bond, a community of taste that then serves to form new experiences in its wake. The new idea, brought about by the growth of technology, is about *group experiences*, in the movie theater, which is why the great Russian filmmaker Dziga-Vertov begins his masterpiece of 1929, *The Man with the Movie Camera*, by showing an empty movie theater fill up with people, who are watching together, even if each viewer in the theater is individually absorbed in what is on screen to the point where the others recede from view. Which is why Dziga-Vertov ends his film by rapidly cutting between what is on screen and the audience who are together watching it. To remind us (we the viewers of his film) that we are watching *together*. More on this filmmaker shortly.

Benjamin's forward-looking and revolutionary notion of film was, it is well known, articulated when Weimar intellectuals, and I include Benjamin in this group, were exploring the political power of this then new medium, which was being put to use in the form of fascist propaganda, creating mass hysteria, delusion, a rallying cry around which a collective could be influenced and prodded to act, rather like the role of Fox TV today. Film was crucial to the making of a degenerate aura around Hitler, which happened with Leni Riefenstal's *Triumph of the Will*, a masterpiece of sickening sublimity turning the 1934 Nazi Nuremberg Rally (the year after Hitler was elected to power) into a paean of sublime praise for him. That documentary/fictionalizing film sets Hitler apart from all others and under a halo from the film's opening shots, taken from inside his plane of the world of cloud and sky thousands of meters above sea level through which his plane floats toward Nuremberg. The film begins with a slow pan through this ether of cloud that from the start becomes Hitler's complement or mirror. He inhabits the *Luft*; he is a man apart and above, who descends to be among us like a prophet or god as the plane lands. We see the hordes waiting for him before he steps outside of the plane and down to planet earth. Only then do we catch our first glimpse of him—a man descending from mystical certainty to lead mere mortals, set apart from all else yet epicenter of all. This is cinematic wizardry to vile effect. The masses aspiring to be near him become his electric current, his musical overtones. They are an extension of his will, its triumphant reverberation. Surrounding him is the crowd, the mass, which is meant to be the same mass watching the film and made ecstatic by its destiny.

The role of film in the growth and spreading of fascism terrified Weimar intellectuals. They understood that on the stage of history the force of film was vast, perhaps paramount. Benjamin believed this artificial halo around Hitler to be a fascist degradation of the aura, replayed through the film medium. He was not wrong about this. Benjamin was not alone in trying to get his head around its implications; this "aestheticization of politics" was perhaps the central concern of the Frankfurt School. And so, it became of paramount importance to consider and applaud the revolutionary potential of film rather than its propagandistic value (as if these things could entirely be separated).

Part III

I think that the film medium was too young at that time for any of these thinkers to grasp how the most basic terms of the medium prepare the remaking of the aura in a way that is not necessarily degenerate. What I want to suggest is that Ingrid Bergman is also auratic on screen, but hardly Hitler. In fact, film creates the conditions for the mass reproducibility of the aura. I argued this at length in my 2008 book, *The Star as Icon*.[7] The aura in film is not simply a matter of stylization, content, and technique, but derives directly from the film medium. This is because (to telescope the long argument from that book into a few sentences) film remakes the conditions of presence, of *being-present-to*. As Stanley Cavell writes in *The World Viewed*, while the actors, actresses, and mountains and valleys on the film screen are not scenes and people to which I am present—I cannot, for example, get them to acknowledge me, speak to me, call out my name, and so on—they are *aesthetically present to me*. Watching Cary Grant appear on screen, I feel he is there before me. And this is the crucial element of the aesthetics of film. That I simultaneously feel what I am watching is ethereal, mere light on screen, as if from a distant planet, and that the actor or actress is there before me in some luminous way. Aesthetically the actor or actress is, and is not, there on screen. On the one hand, all we really watch is light playing on a two-dimensional surface (the film screen). On the other hand, it is essential to film experience that we feel the actor or actress is there before me. It is simply that we are shielded from the actor or actress metaphysically, since they are of the past, and we the present. If I say hello Clark to the actor on screen, he will not answer, he cannot answer, he is not there. But he *feels* there.[8]

This wants a little amplification. Film and photography remake the experience of presence by turning the condition of *being-present* into an asymmetrical relation. Presence is ordinarily something that works both ways. If you are present to me (I can see you, hear you, reach out to touch you), you can in principle do the same with me. I may be hiding behind a chair or behind a one-way glass, but if I emerged, I would be present to you as you are to me. This symmetry is maintained throughout the Grand Tour. If I am present to a Titian painting in Venice, it is present to me (although it can't see me obviously). We share the same space. Similarly, Patrick Stewart playing Hamlet is actually in the theater with me; if I am attending the performance, we share the same space. We are symmetrically present, each to the other. Symmetry of perception and sharing of space are totally absent from film. For although Cary Grant seems to appear before me in *North by Northwest*, I cannot appear before him: he is absent, deceased, his performance was filmed in the past. This weird way in which Grant appears both present while, in fact, being of the past (when the image was shot) seemed to me in that book the very conditions for his appearance under the sign of an aura. Hence the popular idea of the film star—someone in the firmament whom we see from a "distance" yet simultaneously feel is present to us, as if in the form of a planetary gift.

Roland Barthes put the matter well in *Camera Lucida*. Studying a photo of his beloved, recently dead mother, a madness takes him over (as he puts it). Barthes feels she has emerged from the photo ghostlike or spectral and is there before him, as if he could speak to her. Yet, as soon as he reaches out to touch her, or opens his mouth to speak to her, the experience of her presence, *the seeming-presentness-of-her*, gives rise to its deflationary opposite. She is only an image on paper; she is not really there. She will never really be there. This double experience of figures and things appearing from the photo or from the film screen before us—seeming to really be there before us, while we also know all we are really seeing is photographic images or projected light—is enough, I argued in *The Star as Icon*, to re-create something of the aura in a way that makes it mass-producible. For we feel the distant stars of our firmament are there on screen before us by some strange beneficence, there before us like an incandescent faraway beam of light; even if their presence is illusory, they remain in the past. While film does not make me present to the actors and actresses and places on screen, it makes them present to me, as if suddenly a distant planet were miraculously in my living room. And their strange mode of incantation lends them the sense of absolute individuality. There is no one like Ingrid Bergman, Rosalind Russell, Cary Grant: each is what Cavell calls an individuality, separate from all others.

This means that for film two conditions for the aura obtain. First, film makes the people and things on screen appear before us: *we are present to them* in some asymmetrical but substantial way. That is, they are present to us.

Second, what appears before us are individualities: stars set apart from others, with the aura of the planetary (the distant star).

Perhaps the clearest instance of the cult of the star as she becomes present to the film viewer occurs in Alfred Hitchcock's *Rear Window*, and in a scene early in the film. The scene opens with the camera panning around the closed courtyard of a mundane New York apartment complex, peeping from midrange into the glass box of each tiny apartment to see what is happening within. This, we believe, is L. B. Jeffries's point of view, since he is the one with the broken leg who stares incessantly out of the window, spying on his fellow apartment dwellers like *bugs under glass* (a phrase from the film). Not incidentally Jeffries is a photographer, accustomed to viewing the world through lenses. But when the camera completes its circular tour of the courtyard and turns back into Jeffries's own apartment, we see that he is asleep. And so, we realize the point of view of the camera panning around these apartments could not possibly have been his. He is being observed close-up by another; this is the only conclusion we can draw. Which is shocking, as if this invisible person has stolen his point of view, claimed his consciousness. This will be the battleground of the film, fought over the ownership, authority, and safety of *point of view*. We do not know it yet. We wait a second in anticipation of discovering who is the source of this invisible point of view, who is looking at L. B. Jeffries while he sleeps. We wait only a microsecond when a shadow appears, gliding over him in a style mysterious, languid, sexy, just possibly sinister, as if by stealth. Only then do we see the classically blonde head. It bends over him until the camera angle impossibly switches and she is *bending out of the screen toward us*. Larger than life, her eyes glow with excitement. It is effervescently overstimulating, this uncanny emergence from the screen toward us that should not be happening but is, unnerving until the camera performs a switchback and shows us her lips touching his, shot from the side. It is their kiss now, not ours. We are relieved and robbed, overprepared and let down. The kiss is rapturous, their heads utterly filling the screen, their lips joining and gently pulling apart. One of the best in cinema, it is also part of a dialogue between them, she stealing up on him and doing things, he in a secret tense enjoying the passivity while aggressively defending his tough-guy independence. Soon enough we will realize his ambivalence around submission to this kiss because he will start a fight with her.

But first, after the kiss they talk:

"How's your leg?" she asks.
"It hurts a little."
"And your stomach?"
"Empty as a football."
"And your love life?"
"Um ... not too active."
"Anything else bothering you?"
"Mmmm ... Who are you?"

Her voice is sinewy, balmy, gentle in the way it caresses his body. The voice lingers as she continues:

Reading from top to bottom, Lisa, Carol, Freemont.

She speaks each of these words as she slides through the apartment turning on lights, one light for each word. She swirls about in her black-and-white chiffon dress and satin black shawl, set boldly against the dark evening's reddish glow. She is liquid, ecstatic, in complete control. She has stated her name, but as the endpoint of an action that is also her source: a self-illumination through light and movement. This is the bright-lighted presence of the star, the perfect harmony of appearance and word. She is dulcet flesh and filigree of light. At once distant and up-close, in a unique form of presence.

Without a concept of aura, there is *no coherent way to understand what a star is*. To understand what is called *star quality*. The aesthetics of the star are incoherent without some kind of concept of the aura/halo surrounding them. To repeat, this halo is created by a combination of two things. The essential structure of the medium that brings actors and actresses present to me while shielding me from them. And how the star is shot. Camera angles, lighting, make-up, and the rest all serve to articulate the Hollywood star and set her apart from others in the film. These techniques are very much also those that create the *voyeuristic stance* so many feminist film theorists have descried.[9] Hitchcock plays this for a racket in many of his films, including *Psycho*, where Norman Bates puts his dames in Cabin 1 so that he may study them through the same kind of keyhole we use to study the film and its female star—the eye of the camera. Norman's voyeuristic and murderous eye is ours. There is a retrograde tendency in Hollywood's use of the close-up, slowing of time, and focus on the burnished star, since when everything stops for her, she becomes the object of our gaze. We stare at her and gape.

In sympathy with Weimar minds, the film aura has played a major and, I will say, reactionary role in the history of the cult of the individual by remaking the unique individual in the form of the *Star*. For the mechanisms of reproducibility have simply allowed for the remaking of the aesthetics of the *aura* in a way that now makes it mass-reproducible. A corollary is this. There is no single, correct causal story of the history of the technological forces of production and the class struggle. Technological development cuts both ways, aesthetically and politically. About this, Marx was wrong. As was Benjamin in following him.

Part IV

My mistake in *The Star as Icon* was to think that *all* film partakes of the aesthetics of the aura when it is, in fact, Hollywood movies and the like, along with the dreaded propaganda films of the 1930s, that have the franchise on this particular aesthetic characteristic. Film has a range of aesthetic possibilities, the aura around person (Grace Kelly) and/or place (John Ford's Monument Valley) being only one. Which aesthetic possibility is realized depends on film syntax and story, on framing, editing, character, plot, and the like. It was precisely the Russian avant-gardes who refused the aesthetic cult of the aura, and with it of individuality over the collective. And for Benjamin, these were the filmmakers who signaled the new era, the ones he cared about and in the light of whose work he erected his theory. Benjamin witnessed a real alternative in avant-garde cinema, whose form and content stood against the history and cult of individual liberty (bourgeois) in the name of the collective. And he wrote in praise of it.

Then how does Russian avant-garde cinema refuse the cult of the aura, the cult of the star and, through the star, of individuality? There is no clearer example than Dziga-Vertov's silent masterpiece, *The Man with the Movie Camera* of 1929, the last film Vertov was able to make before Stalin shut down the avant-gardes. Featuring his brother Mikhail Kaufman as the cameraman (Vertov was born David Kaufman), and his partner in cinema and life, Elizaveta Svilova, as the film's astonishing editor, the story is nothing more or less than a day in the life of Odessa, from earliest dawn to evening darkness. The film was in fact shot in a number of cities but is meant to be Odessa alone. The only real character in the film is the city, which is dynamic, exuberant, intricate, astonishing, and always at work, while in no way an object of nostalgia, ruination, or aura. It is a collective. There are no lingering shots that keep the imagination focused on individuals set apart from others. The eye of the camera proceeds with a relentless brilliance, focusing on work, cooperation, the city as a collective in motion, speeding toward its historical future. Since there is no role for the past here, not even in the shots of death or dying, but simply the material force of life in all its aspects, there can be no role for the aura of past things. Nor is there any associated cult of beauty: the beautiful face of Garbo, the powerfully etched face of Cary Grant, the sinewy athleticism and comic intelligence of Katherine Hepburn.

Part of what ensures Dziga-Vertov's emphasis on the collective over the individual is the even rhythm of the shots. While the film intensifies in the manner of symphonic music, through visual fugue, prolongation, modulation, and full orchestral *tutti* within variation, it does not pick out any persons and highlight them as individual characters by slowing down and lingering on their close-up in a way that might set them off from others. Even the cameraman—whom we follow throughout the film as he labors to film the day, trudging up dangerous ladders with his heavy equipment in tow, positioning himself on the tops of buildings, trams, vertiginously between tram tracks, at the edge of the sea, and on and on—is not individualized. He is shown only in motion, doing his job, a laborer in the field of documentary. Nor does the camera linger on parts of the city to set them off in a glorious haze. The city pulses, bursting with energy, shifting in perspective continually.

Indeed, if there is one overriding theme of Vertov's film, it is that of *work*. The camera harps on industrial production and then leisure (relaxation from work). We see Svilova laboriously cutting and pasting strips of film in her studio, which then turn into cinematic magic as the film rushes toward experiment. The experimental character involves so many brilliant innovations developed by Vertov over a ten-year period of work that we feel we are in the world of technological wizardry, but in no way of the kind that obliterates subjects. Rather, invention intensifies the city-in-motion as time is speeded up to the point where telephone operators facilitate calls by manually making connections at a wildly speeded-up pace, or slowed to the point where suddenly one can concentrate on a thing that otherwise would have bypassed vision or remained at its periphery. Control over duration, among the central features of the film medium, is matched by the splitting of images as if the energy of the city were volcanically erupting, by shots through water or beer glasses, magnifying images, by freeze frames and stop motion. Rather than focusing on individual items set apart from others, the film finds likeness across machines, types of labor, kinds of people. It equalizes, is about equality, not individuality. Vertov harps on the revolving of wheels, whether on trams or in factories, associating them with the revolving cartridge of the cinema projector. This links cinema with industry, as if the filmmaker and editor were simply one kind of *laborer*, engaged in one kind of production situated among others. This sense of film being part of the city, among its forms of labor, is central to the story, which that of a cameraman filming within the city he is of. We never think of him as foreign, rather as an insider/outsider who sees by being part of things, while distant enough from the city to give it dynamic form. And we know little about him, identifying with him not as an individual character but a laborer in cinema.

Most important he is not set apart from others, as if occupying a separate and more exalted universe, in the manner of the Hollywood film star. The film does not slow down when he appears to highlight him differently from others. There is no place for the aura here. Only dynamic form and force.

The Russian avant-gardes did this by, among other things, inventing a completely different syntax of the close-up. The work of Sergei Eisenstein is perhaps clearest. *Potemkin* (1925), about the mutiny of a ship in the 1905 Russo-Japanese war. This minor historical event becomes the centerpiece of the film, when the citizens of Odessa rush to help the insurrectionary sailors, only to be mowed down by the Czar's forces on the Odessa steps, in perhaps the most famous sequence in cinema. Eisenstein depends on an extensive use of close-ups, which in Hollywood land are the conduit for the star. But his close-ups neither slow down the pace of the story by languidly lingering on the star, nor do they set the star apart from all others through set design and framing for us to gaze upon him/her as an object of attraction if not voyeurism. At one point, a mother realizes her child has been shot and picks him up, bucking the tide to walk resolutely up the steps toward the soldiers, joined by other women. She cries out, my son has been hurt; the response is she is fired on. Set apart, we might have thought she would elevate beyond others into the realm of the star but it does not happen. She is presented in action, a mother courageous and willing to face death for her child. That is all. We know, and need know, nothing else about her. And we do not dwell on her physical characteristics, turning her into an object of our gaze. The scene is far too propulsive for that.

Close-ups cut quickly from person to person, and each person is always shown focused on something outside the frame, not on us, nor languidly on nothing (waiting to be seen). Eyes point elsewhere than toward us, and our gaze is directed laterally outside the frame to what is invisible in the close-up shot—the larger action. In short, Eisenstein's close-ups are always employed *relationally*, as a way of showing us particular persons connected to the larger collective story. Cutting from one person to another intensifies relationality through montage. Moreover, there are many persons shown in close-up, not the special few. Film continually cuts from one to the next in the course of montage, that principle of cinematic counterpoint wherein one event is never completed without first cross-cutting to others. A woman is shot and mortally wounded, but before she falls, the film cuts to people rushing down the steps away from the police and then back, in an act of what in music is called prolongation. The montage effect is to prevent the mind from focusing exclusively on any one person or event, but *between many*. It is the larger story of *collective resistance and suffering*, and of state violence, that matters, not the individuals in themselves. The collective principle, central to film form, refuses a place for the aura.

Of course, these films were silent. Once dialogue enters, there has to be more individuality in cinema because the actors speak, their characters unfold, and so on. It is simply harder to maintain the absence of individuality. Which is as true of life as it is of film and a problem for the Marxist perspective. And so, the aura will inevitably return, if only in part.

Russian avant-garde films were taken by Benjamin as harbingers of aesthetic/revolutionary transformation. The causal result of the growth of new technological forces—of reproducibility. He thought them prophetic. Sadly, history has proved otherwise. And not only because Stalin shut down the avant-gardes at the end of the 1920s, but because film has many varieties. It clearly embraces both revolutionary and conservative aesthetics.

The tension between these general typologies of films—Hollywood versus avant-garde—can only be called political. It is a normative difference, with many films on both sides that don't entirely conform to these norms but sit in the middle. These genres represent distinct visions of moral life—of how persons should seek to live among others. And distinct visions of politics—of the correct dispensation of political justice. Both are political *in virtue of contributing to larger patterns of ideology*. One prompts the cult of the individual through the star and the aura of landscape and place. The other, collective life and its political solidarity. Of course, one can love *both kinds of films* without subscribing to either ideology exactly, or to a bit of both. This is called human nature.

Part V

Both ideologies are political insofar as they are articulated in the context of the triad: liberty, collectivity, and political economy (the state in relation to markets). But each with opposing emphasis, aspiration, and conclusion. And so, we return to the core idea of the book—that politics is about how art is set in this triad. And the answer is, variously. The question of collective representation within this triad is dramatically posed in our time with Black Lives Matter, Occupy Wall Street, and other eruptions of resistance that also want to become politically driven protest movements, challenging both state and market economy. Black Lives Matter seems to be catalyzing real change in the racist system. Let's hope so anyway. Occupy Wall Street I fear, not. The larger question of where individual freedom demands participation in the collective, and where both sit in relation to market economy and the state, is about as central a moral and political question as any person, group, or nation can face. To be fair, the fate of collective movements in our age, and where we individuals do and do not fit in, is one that art could hardly be expected to get right when it is so problematical in every other sphere of life. It is therefore understandable that art should stake its various positions on individual liberty, collective power, and market economy with risk, aspiration, and, sometimes, delusion. Art is simply an example of the precarious uncertainties of life in a world without adequate emancipation, where people disagree about, and fight over, nearly every aspect of politics and where public trust is under threat and fast eviscerating.

Notes

1 Introduction

1 Jean-Francois Lyotard, *The Postmodern Condition: A Report on Knowledge*, trans. Geoff Bennington and Brian Massumi (Minneapolis: Minnesota University Press, 1979).
2 Thomas Piketty, *Capital in the Twenty-First Century* (Cambridge: Harvard University Press, 2013).
3 The very pronouncement of the right to liberty was compromised by colonial embroilment. A colonial administrator, Locke wrote the Constitution of the Carolinas that mandated harsh penalties for runaway slaves, before moving to the West Indies, perhaps the harshest site of slavery in the world. Locke never renounced his position on the slaveholding world, and his ambivalence can be found in those chapters of the *Second Treatise* that deal with slavery. There, Locke wrestles with the question of whether slavery is ever justified given the natural right all men are meant to have to liberty in the state of nature. Rights are meant to apply universally and equally, and yet, Locke has to find a way to allow a crack in his thinking to justify slavery. This he does at the price of near incoherence. Locke is a perfect window into the gap between the articulation of natural rights central to the emancipation of modern Europe and Europe's embroilment in empire, which catalyzes the long articulation of concepts of race, inevitably racist, required for a set of nations dedicated to subjugating the rest of the world and extracting labor and goods from that world in the manner of theft.
4 Isaiah Berlin, *Four Essays on Liberty* (Oxford: Oxford University Press, 1969).
5 C. F. Immanuel Kant, *Critique of Judgment*, trans. J. H. Bernard (New York: Haffner Press, 1951), and David Hume, "Of the Standard of Taste," "Of Tragedy," and "Of the Delicacy of Taste and Passion," in *Selected Essays*, ed. Stephen Copley and Andrew Edgar (Oxford: Clarendon Press, 1998).
6 C. B. McPherson, *The Political Theory of Possessive Individualism* (Oxford: Oxford University Press, 1962).
7 See Theodor Adorno and Max Horkheimer, *Dialectic of Enlightenment*, ed. G. S. Noerr, trans. Edmund Jephcott (Stanford: Stanford University Press, 2002).
8 See Daniel Herwitz, *Cosmopolitan Aesthetics: Art in a Global World* (London: Bloomsbury, 2019).
9 See Daniel Herwitz, *Making Theory/Constructing Art* (Chicago: Chicago University Press, 1993), chs. 2 and 3.

10 Clement Greenberg, "Avant-Garde and Kitsch," in *Art and Culture* (Boston: Beacon Press, 1961), pp. 3–21.

11 Wittgenstein famously remarked that philosophy consists of "assembling reminders for a particular purpose." Ludwig Wittgenstein, *Philosophical Investigations*, trans. Elizabeth Anscombe (New York: Macmillan, 1958), #127.

12 For more on this, see Daniel Herwitz, *Aesthetics, Arts and Politics in a Global World* (London: Bloomsbury, 2017), chs. 1–3.

13 Herwitz, *Cosmopolitan Aesthetics*; and *Aesthetics, Arts and Politics*.

14 Herwitz, *Cosmopolitan Aesthetics*, ch. 2.

15 Ibid.

2 The Politics of Visibility: Lurie and Rancière

1 Jacques Rancière, *The Politics of Aesthetics*, trans. with intro. by Gabriel Rockhill, interview with Rancière by Rockhill, afterword by Slavoj Zizek (London: Bloomsbury, 2004), p. 59.

2 Louis Althusser, Etienne Balibar, Roget Establet, Pierre Marchery, and Jacques Rancière, *Reading Capital*, trans. Ben Brewster and David Fernbach (London: Verso, 2016).

3 I thank Miriam Ticktin for prompting me to reread Rancière. Her use of his writing in the critique of humanitarianism is much worth reading.

4 Rancière, *The Politics of Aesthetics*, p. 59.

5 T. J. Clark, *The Painting of Modern Life: Paris in the Art of Manet and His Followers*, rev. edn. (Princeton: Princeton University Press, 1999).

6 See Albert O. Hirschman, *Essays in Trespassing: Economics to Politics and Beyond* (Cambridge: Cambridge University Press, 1981); and *Crossing Boundaries: Selected Writings* (New York: Zone Books, 1998).

3 Art and the Mining of Diamonds: Kentridge, Modisakeng, and What Is Meant by Politics

1 A lively book on the gold and diamonds is Martin Meredith, *Diamonds, Gold and War: The British, The Boers and the Making of South Africa* (London: Simon Schuster, 2007).

2 Daniel Herwitz, *The Star as Icon* (New York: Columbia University Press, 2008). Also Daniel Herwitz, *Heritage, Arts and Politics in the Postcolony* (New York: Columbia University Press, 2012), ch. 6.

3 For a seminal discussion of the rise of modern art in Paris, see T. J. Clark, *The Painting of Modern Life: Paris in the Art of Manet and His Followers* (New York: Knopf, 1984).

4 C. F. Anne De Courcy, *The Husband Hunters: Social Climbing in London and New York* (New York: W&N, 2017).
5 Herwitz, *The Star as Icon*.
6 G. W. F. Hegel, *The Phenomenology of Spirit*, trans. with intro. and commentary by Michael Inwood (Oxford: Oxford University Press, 2018), especially the famous chapter on the master and slave.
7 C. F. Alexandre Kojève, *Introduction to the Reading of Hegel: Lectures on the Phenomenology of Spirit*, ed. Allan Bloom (Ithaca: Cornell University Press, 1980). And Frantz Fanon, *Black Skin, White Masks*, trans. Richard Philcox (New York: Grove Press, 1968).
8 T. J. Clark, *Farewell to an Idea: Episodes from a History of Modernism* (New Haven: Yale University Press, 1999), p. 22.
9 Arthur Danto, *The Transfiguration of the Commonplace* (Cambridge: Harvard University Press, 1981).

4 The Politics of the Witness: Georges Gittoes

1 K. L. Walton, "Transparent Pictures," *Critical Inquiry* 12(4), 1986.

5 Virulent Nationalism and the Politics of Offense: The NEA 4

1 Robert Hughes, *Culture of Complaint* (New York: Warner Books, 1993), pp. 172–3.
2 Ibid., p. 158.
3 Ibid., p. 102.
4 Albie Sachs, "Preparing Ourselves for Freedom," reprinted in *TDR* 35(1), 1991: 187.

6 Literature and the Politics of the Truth Commission: Dorfman and Coetzee

1 J. M. Coetzee, *Disgrace* (New York: Penguin, 1999). References to the book will be subsequently numbered in the text.
2 Although transitional justice is distinctive, one ought not to make too, too much of its distinctiveness. For every society that lives as a democracy contains within itself an ongoing conversation of democracy, in which dissent is crucial. Hence, every society contains within itself the seeds of "transition" of some kind or another.

3 Martha Minow, "The Hope for Healing: What Can Truth Commissions Do?", in Robert Rotberg and Dennis Thompson (eds.), *Truth v. Justice* (Princeton: Princeton University Press, 2000), p. 253.

4 Jacques Derrida, *On Cosmopolitanism and Forgiveness*, trans. Mark Dooley and Michael Hughes, preface by Simon Critchley and Richard Kearney (London: Routledge, 2001).

5 Ibid., p. 30.

6 Lyndsey Stonebridge, *The Judicial Imagination: Writing after Nuremberg* (Edinburgh: Edinburgh University Press, 2011), p. 16.

7 Places that have had truth commissions include Argentina, Bangladesh, Bolivia, Brazil, Canada, Chad, Colombia, Congo (Democratic Republic), Chile, the Czech Republic, Ecuador, El Salvador, Fiji, Germany, Ghana, Guatemala, Haiti, Kenya, Liberia, Mauritius, Morocco, Nepal, Nigeria, Panama, Paraguay. Peru, Poland, the Philippines, Rwanda, Sierra Leone, Solomon Islands, South Africa, South Korea, Sri Lanka, Timor-Leste (East Timor), Togo, Tunisia, Uganda, Ukraine, Uruguay, the United States, Yugoslavia (Federal Republic of).

8 Geoffrey Robertson, *Crimes against Humanity: The Struggle for Global Justice* (London: Penguin, 1999), p. 266.

9 Albie Sachs, *The Soft Vengeance of a Freedom Fighter* (London: Grafton Books, 1990).

10 For a spectacular example of TRC researchers unearthing previously hidden files before they were burnt by the authorities, see Lindy Wilson's documentary film *The Gugulethu Seven* (1999).

11 David Bunn, "On the Reluctance of Monuments," in Hilton Judin and Ivan Vladislavic (eds.), *Blank* (Rotterdam: Netherlands Architectural Institute, 1998).

12 For a wonderful story of the way the red sea becomes a sign of freedom in modern Europe, see Lydia Goehr, *Red Sea-Red Square-Red Thread: A Philosophical Detective Story* (Oxford: Oxford University Press, forthcoming). Also my "Coat of Many Colors," in *Race and Reconciliation* (Minneapolis: Minnesota University Press, 2003), ch. 2.

13 Derrida, *On* Cosmopolitanism and *Forgiveness*, p. 32.

14 Ibid., p. 33.

15 Ariel Dorfman, *Death and the Maiden* (New York: Penguin, 1994), p. 72. Subsequent references will be numbered in the text.

16 Cf. Fredric Nietzsche, "On Truth and Lying in Their Extra-moral Sense," *Untimely Meditations*, trans. R. J. Hollingdale (Cambridge: Cambridge University Press, 1999).

17 Herwitz, *Race and Reconciliation*, ch. 2.

18 Jacques Rancière, *Dissensus: On Politics and Aesthetics*, trans. Steven Corcoran (London: Continuum, 2010).

19 J. M. Coetzee, *The Lives of Animals* (Princeton: Princeton University Press, 1999).

7 Identity Politics in a Consumerist World

1 Charles Taylor, *Multiculturalism and the Politics of Recognition* ed. Amy Guttmann, commentary by Amy Gutmann, Anthony Appiah et al. (Princeton: Princeton University Press, 1992).
2 Nicholas Delbanco, private conversation.

8 Art Market Politics: Manet to Banksy

1 See T. J. Clark, *The Painting of Modern Life: Paris in the Art of Manet and His Followers* (Princeton: Princeton University Press, 1985).
2 C. F. Sander Gilman, "Black Bodies, White Bodies, Towards an Iconography of Female Sexuality in Late 19th-Century Literature, Art and Medicine," *Critical Inquiry*, 12, 1984: 204–42.
3 Clark, *The Painting of Modern Life*, where Clark reads Olympia as the body of the new, rising middle class.
4 Peter Burger, *Theory of the Avant-Garde*, trans. Michael Shaw (Minneapolis: Minnesota University Press, 2007).
5 Daniel Herwitz, *The Star as Icon* (New York: Columbia University Press, 2008).
6 G. W. F. Hegel, *Aesthetics: Lectures on Fine Art*, trans. T. M. Knox (Oxford: Clarendon Press, 1998).
7 Bianca Solonga, "Discovering Bansky in Bethlehem," *Lifestyle*, October 27, 2018, p. 5.
8 Ibid., p. 3.
9 Ibid., p. 9.

9 Autonomy as Negotiation: Mozart Reconsidered

1 Ted Cohen, *Serious Larks: The Philosophy of Ted Cohen*, ed. with an intro. by Daniel Herwitz (Chicago: Chicago University Press, 2018).
2 See my *Cosmopolitan Aesthetics: Art in a Global World* (London: Bloomsbury, 2019), especially chs. 5 and 6.
3 Ibid.
4 Jurgen Habermas, *The Structural Transformation of the Public Sphere*, trans. Thomas Burger and Fredrerick Lawrence (Cambridge: MIT Press, 1991).
5 Charles Taylor, *Sources of the Self: The Making of Modern Identity* (Cambridge: Harvard University Press, 2006).
6 Habermas, *Structural Transformation*, pp. 17–8.
7 All quotes from the Libretto of *The Marriage of Figaro* are translated by Lionel Salter.

8 Carol Hanisch, "The Personal Is Political," in *Notes from the Second Year: Women's Liberation*, 1970.

9 Roland Barthes, *The Grain of the Voice: Interviews 1962–1980*, trans. Linda Coverdale (New York: Hill and Wang, 1981).

10 The influence of Stanley Cavell should be clear here, especially *Pursuits of Happiness: Hollywood Genres of Remarriage* (Cambridge: Harvard University Press, 1981).

10 Film, the Individual, and the Collective

1 For more on this issue, see my *Cosmopolitan Aesthetics: Art in a Global World* (London: Bloomsbury, 2019), especially chs. 5 and 6. And the *locus classicus*: Benedict Anderson, *Imagined Communities* (London: Verso, 2010).

2 For more on the nineteenth century, see my *Cosmopolitan Aesthetics*.

3 Alexander Nehamas, *Nietzsche: Life as Literature* (Cambridge: Harvard University Press, 1985).

4 Walter Benjamin, "The Work of Art in an Age of Mechanical Reproducibility" (trans. Jephcott et al.), in *Walter Benjamin: Selected Writings, Vol. 3* (Cambridge: Harvard University Press, 2002), pp. 103–42.

5 For more on Venice, see Bruce Redford, *Venice and the Grand Tour* (New Haven: Yale University Press, 1996).

6 Sigmund Freud, "On Transience," *Collected Writings of Freud, Volume XIV*, trans. James Strachey (London: Hogarth Press, 1957), pp. 305–7.

7 Daniel Herwitz, *The Star as Icon* (New York: Columbia University Press, 2008).

8 Stanley Cavell, *The World Viewed* (Cambridge: Harvard University Press, 1971).

9 Laura Mulvey, *Fetishism and Curiosity* (Bloomington: Indiana University Press, 1996); and "Visual Pleasure and Narrative Cinema," reprinted in Movies and Methods, Volume II (ed. Bill Nichols) (Berkeley: California University Press, 1985), pp. 303–14.

Bibliography

Adorno, Theodor, and Max Horkheimer, *Dialectic of Enlightenment*, ed. G. S. Noerr, trans. Edmund Jephcott, Stanford: Stanford University Press, 2002.

Althusser, Louis, Etienne Balibar, Roger Establet, Pierre Marchery, and Jacques Rancière, *Reading Capital*, trans. Ben Brewster and David Fernbach, London: Verso, 2016.

Barthes, Roland, *The Grain of the Voice: Interviews 1962–1980*, trans. Linda Coverdale, New York: Hill and Wang, 1985.

Benedict, Anderson, *Imagined Communities*, London: Verso, 2010.

Benjamin, Walter, "The Work of Art in an Age of Mechanical Reproducibility," trans. Jephcott et al., *Walter Benjamin: Selected Writings, Vol. 3*, Cambridge: Harvard University Press, 2002.

Berlin, Isaiah, *Four Essays on Liberty*, Oxford: Oxford University Press, 1969.

Bunn, David, "On the Reluctance of Monuments," in *Blank*, edited by Hilton Judin and Ivan Vladislavic, Rotterdam: Netherlands Architectural Institute, 1998.

Burger, Peter, *Theory of the Avant-Garde*, trans. Michael Shaw, Minneapolis: Minnesota University Press, 2007.

Cavell, Stanley, *The World Viewed*, Cambridge: Harvard University Press, 1971.

Cavell, Stanley, *Pursuits of Happiness: Hollywood Genres of Remarriage*, Cambridge: Harvard University Press, 1981.

Clark, T. J., *The Painting of Modern Life: Paris in the Art of Manet and His Followers*, New York: Knopf, 1984.

Clark, T. J., *Farewell to an Idea: Episodes from a History of Modernism*, New Haven: Yale University Press, 1999.

Coetzee, J. M., *Disgrace*, New York: Penguin, 1999.

Coetzee, J. M., *The Lives of Animals*, Princeton: Princeton University Press, 1999.

Cohen, Ted, *Serious Larks: The Philosophy of Ted Cohen*, ed. with an intro. by Daniel Herwitz, Chicago: Chicago University Press, 2018.

Courcy, Anne De, *The Husband Hunters: Social Climbing in London and New York*, New York: W&N, 2017.

Danto, Arthur, *The Transfiguration of the Commonplace*, Cambridge: Harvard University Press, 1981.

Derrida, Jacques, *On Cosmopolitanism and Forgiveness*, trans. Mark Dooley and Michael Hughes, preface by Simon Critchley and Richard Kearney, London: Routledge, 2001.

Dorfman, Ariel, *Death and the Maiden*, New York: Penguin, 1994.

Fanon, Frantz, *Black Skin, White Masks*, trans. Richard Philcox, New York: Grove Press, 1968.

Freud, Sigmund, "On Transience," *Collected Writings of Freud, Volume XIV*,
    trans. James Strachey, London: Hogarth Press, 1957, pp. 305–7.
Gilman, Sander, "Black Bodies, White Bodies, Towards an Iconography of
    Female Sexuality in Late 19th-Century Literature, Art and Medicine,"
    Critical Inquiry, 12 (1984): 204–42.
Goehr, Lydia, *Red Sea-Red Square-Red Thread: A Philosophical Detective Story*,
    Oxford: Oxford University Press, forthcoming.
Greenberg, Clement, "Avant-Garde and Kitsch," in *Art and Culture: Critical
    Essays*, Boston: Beacon Press, 1961, p. 15.
Guyer, Paul, "The Origin of Modern Aesthetics: 1711–1735," in *The Blackwell
    Guide to Aesthetics*, edited by Peter Kivy, Oxford: Blackwell, 2004, pp. 32–5.
Habermas, Jurgen, *The Structural Transformation of the Public Sphere*, trans.
    Thomas Burger and Peter Kivy, New York: Burt Franklin, 1976.
Hanisch, Carol, "The Personal Is Political," in *Notes from the Second
    Year: Women's Liberation*, 1970.
Hannah, Arendt, *The Human Condition*, intro. by Margaret Canovan, Chicago:
    University Press of Chicago, 1958.
Hegel, G. W. F., *Aesthetics: Lectures on Fine Art*, trans T. M. Knox, Oxford:
    Clarendon Press, 1998.
Hegel, G. W. F., *The Phenomenology of Spirit*, trans. with intro. and commentary
    by Michael Inwood, Oxford: Oxford University Press, 2018.
Herwitz, Daniel, *Making Theory/Constructing Art*, Chicago: Chicago University
    Press, 1993.
Herwitz, Daniel, *Race and Reconciliation*, Minneapolis: Minnesota University
    Press, 2003.
Herwitz, Daniel, *The Star as Icon*, New York: Columbia University Press, 2008.
Herwitz, Daniel, *Heritage, Arts and Politics in the Postcolony*, New York:
    Columbia University Press, 2012.
Herwitz, Daniel, *Aesthetics, Arts and Politics in a Global World*, London:
    Bloomsbury, 2017.
Herwitz, Daniel, *Cosmopolitan Aesthetics: Art in a Global World*, London:
    Bloomsbury, 2019.
Hirschman, Albert O., *Essays in Trespassing: Economics to Politics and Beyond*,
    Cambridge: Cambridge University Press, 1981.
Hirschman, Albert O., *Crossing Boundaries: Selected Writings*, New York: Zone
    Books, 1998.
Hume, David, "Of the Standard of Taste," "Of Tragedy," and "Of the Delicacy of
    Taste and Passion," in *Selected Essays*, edited by Stephen Copley and Andrew
    Edgar, Oxford: Clarendon Press, 1998.
Kant, Immanuel, *Critique of Judgment*, trans. J. H. Bernard, New York: Haffner
    Press, 1951.
Kojève, Alexandre, *Introduction to the Reading of Hegel: Lectures on the
    Phenomenology of Spirit*, ed. Allan Bloom, Ithaca: Cornell University Press,
    . 1980.

Kracauer, Siegfried, *Theory of Film: The Redemption of Physical Reality*, New York: Oxford University Press, 1960.

Locke, John, *Second Treatise on Government*, Los Angeles: Enhanced Media, 2016.

Lyotard, Jean-Francois, *The Postmodern Condition: A Report on Knowledge*, trans. Geoff Bennington and Brian Massumi, Minneapolis: Minnesota University Press, 1979.

Marcuse, Herbert, *The Aesthetic Dimension*, trans. and rev. by Erica Sherover and Herbert Marcuse, Boston: Beacon Press, 1978.

McPherson, C. B., *The Political Theory of Possessive Individualism*, Oxford: Oxford University Press, 1962.

Meredith, Martin, *Diamonds, Gold and War: The British, The Boers and the Making of South Africa*, London: Simon Schuster, 2007.

Minow, Martha, "The Hope for Healing: What Can Truth Commissions Do?," in *Truth v. Justice*, edited by Robert Rotberg and Dennis Thompson, Princeton: Princeton University Press, 2000.

Mulvey, Laura, "Visual Pleasure and Narrative Cinema," reprinted in *Movies and Methods, Volume II*, ed. Bill Nichols, Berkeley: California University Press, 1985, pp. 303–14.

Mulvey, Laura, *Fetishism and Curiosity*, Bloomington: Indiana University Press, 1996.

Nehamas, Alexander, *Nietzsche: Life as Literature*, Cambridge: Harvard University Press, 1985.

Nietzsche, Fredric, "On Truth and Lying in Their Extra-moral Sense," *Untimely Meditations*, trans. R. J. Hollingdale, Cambridge: Cambridge University Press, 1999, pp. 57–124.

Piketty, Thomas, *Capital in the Twenty-First Century*, Cambridge: Harvard University Press, 2013.

Rancière, Jacques, *The Politics of Aesthetics*, trans. with introduction by Gabriel Rockhill, interview with Rancière by Rockhill, afterword by Slavoj Zizek, London: Bloomsbury, 2004.

Redford, Bruce, *Venice and the Grand Tour*, New Haven: Yale University Press, 1996.

Robert, Hughes, *Culture of Complaint*, New York: Warner Books, 1993.

Robertson, Geoffrey, *Crimes against Humanity: The Struggle for Global Justice*, London: Penguin, 1999.

Sachs, Albie, *The Soft Vengeance of a Freedom Fighter*, London: Grafton Books, 1990.

Sachs, Albie, "Preparing Ourselves for Freedom," reprinted in *TDR*, 35(1) (1991): 187.

Solonga, Bianca, "Discovering Bansky in Bethlehem," *Lifestyle*, October 27, 2018, p. 5.

Stonebridge, Lyndsey, *The Judicial Imagination: Writing after Nuremberg*, Edinburgh: Edinburgh University Press, 2011.

Taylor, Charles, *Multiculturalism and the Politics of Recognition*, ed. Amy Guttmann, commentary by Amy Gutmann, Anthony Appiah et al., Princeton: Princeton University Press, 1992.

Taylor, Charles, *Sources of the Self: The Making of Modern Identity*, Cambridge: Harvard University Press, 2006.

Walton, K. L., "Transparent Pictures," *Critical Inquiry*, 12(4) (1986): 801–8.

Wittgenstein, Ludwig, *Philosophical Investigations*, trans. Elizabeth Anscombe, New York: Macmillan, 1958.

Wolfgang Amadeus Mozart and Lorenzo Da Ponte, *The Marriage of Figaro*, selections from the libretto translated by Lionel Salter. Schiller, Fredrich, *On the Aesthetic Education of Man: In a Series of Letters*, ed. and trans. with an intro. by Elizabeth M. Wilkinson and L.A. Willoughby, Oxford: Clarendon Press, 1982.

Index

Abbey, W. 44
Adorno, T. 6, 11
"aeskesis" 28
aesthetic 27
aesthetic autonomy 169–70
aesthetic experience 176
aesthetic/experimental innovation 13
aesthetic judgments 9
aesthetic shock 12
aesthetic synergy 44
African National Congress (ANC) 39,
    43, 87, 95, 97, 101–2
agency 53, 54, 63; *see also*
    political agency
alchemy of attraction 46
Allende, S. 111
alluvial diamond fields 42
Althusser, L. 29
America 54
American Idol 45
America's Most Wanted 138
anti-bourgeois solidarity 7
antimony 55
Arabian Nights 31
Arendt, H. 2
art: blogs 1
    cultivates personal intimacy 7
    disturbational 54
    documentary 33
    Hegelian tradition of thinking 4
    human imagination 5
    installation 41
    as investment 151
    medium of 4, 41
    mining of diamonds and 41–62
    modern 45
    plastic 67
    political 4
    political spectrum of 7

populist-driven 16
radical powers of 2
utopian political aspirations for 2
valuation of currency 152
visual 41, 42
vivification 65
Art Basel 4
artistic achievement 36
art market politics 143–57
assumption 10
authoritarianism 77
autonomy 8, 84, 159–71
avant-gardes 1–2, 4, 6–7, 11–12,
    15–16, 18, 20
avant-garde thinking 59

Banksy 152–157, 193
Bergman, I. 46
Between Joyce and Remembrance
    (Kaplan) 105
Beuys, J. 130
Bharatiya Janata Party (BJP) 77
black Africans 42, 44
black labor 42
Blood and Tears (Gittoes) 69–70
Boer Republic 42
Boer War 32, 42

Cape Town 33, 36, 37
capitalism: industrial 1
    mercantile 1
case studies 5
charcoal 49
Chicago, J. 131–2
Chilean population 108
Chilean Truth Commission 100, 109
China 43
Churchill, W. 66
Civil War 32

Clark, T. J. 32, 57
class inequality 3, 134, 169
Coetzee, J. M. 89, 118
Cold War 130
Cole, E. 33
commodification 45
consciousness 52
constructivism 59
Constructivist photographer 54
Corcoran Gallery 82
corruption 39, 65
crime against humanity 97
cultural autonomy 84
cultural innovation 77
culture 11
    democratic 2
    of humanitarianism 3
Culture of Complaint (Hughes) 78

D'Amato, A. 79, 81–2, 86–7
Danto, A. 42, 58
Dean, J. 152
Death and the Maiden (Dorfman) 89,
    94, 109, 111
de Klerk, W. 43
democracies 38
democratic culture 2
democratic dispensation 38–9
democratic transition 49, 95
Derrida, J. 6, 105
dialectic 52
diamonds 42–3, 44
    aesthetics of 47, 53
    allure of 46
    beauty of 46–7
    characteristics of modern art 45–6
    dazzle of 46
    epitome of femininity 45
    mining of 51
Diana, L. 44
Die Winterreise (Schubert) 58
dignity 39, 51
Dinner Party (Chicago) 130, 132
discomfort 80

Disgrace (Coetzee) 89, 118, 121,
    122
display 45
disturbational art 54
documentary art 33
documentary film 41, 47
Dorfman, A. 89, 109
Duchamp, M. 79

Eckstein, S. 48, 51
Eichmann Trial 99
embattled spaces 163
Europe 1, 8
exhibitions 55
experimentation: fusion of 15
    individual 15
    plastic 12, 129
    visual 13

Fanon, F. 52
fate of democracy 40
Felix in Exile (Kentridge) 61
femininity 45
fetish of commodities 46
film 173–88
film star 46
Final Constitution 43
Finley, K. 77
First Treatise on Government
    (Locke) 120
First World War 1, 7, 12, 145
Fleck, J. 77
foreign investment 43
forgiveness-brand 106
Fountain (Duchamp) 79, 147
Fox TV 138
Freedom Charter of 1955 34
freedom of speech 163
Free Palestine (Lurie) 31, 39

Garbo, G. 46
Gentlemen Prefer Blondes (Hawk) 46
Germany 1, 8, 54
Gilded Age of American 45

Girl with Balloon (Banksy) 153
Gittoes, G. 63–73
global capitalism 41
global computer systems 63–4
globalization 2–3
gold 44, 47
Goldblatt, D. 33
gold mines 48
Goya's depictions of war 5
graffiti 36
Gramsci, A. 16, 18, 43, 150
Grands Magazins 143
Greenberg, C. 16
gross violations of human rights 126
group rights 133
Growth, Employment and
    Redistribution Act (GEAR)
    43–4, 53
Guernica (Picasso) 66
The Gugulethu Seven (Mbelo) 106

Habermas, J. 29, 163
Haussmann, G. 143
Hawks, H. 46
Hegel, G. W. F. 117
hegemony 16
Hinterhauser, M. 58
Hirschman, A. O. 38
Hitchcock, A. 146
HIV/AIDS 42, 77
Holzer, J. 133
homilies 58
Horkheimer, M. 11
Hughes, H. 77
Hughes, R. 78, 81
human degradation 51
humanity 98
human rights 3
Hyperallergic (blog) 1

idea of democracy 38
identity-based capital 139
identity politics 129–41
ideological prompts 58

impressionism 32
India 77
individual experiences 8–9, 173
individual experimentation 15
industrial capitalism 1
inequality 41
    class 3, 134, 169
infrastructure 39
Instagram 30
installation art 41
Interim Constitution South African
    43, 53, 94, 101–2
international community 97
International Monetary Fund 43
international notoriety 152
i-Phone 47
Iziko Museum 51, 56

Jackson, M. 16
Jefferson, T. 7, 9
Jesus Mocked by the Soldiers
    (Manet) 143
Johannesburg, Second City after Paris
    (Soho) 58

Kaplan, M. 105
Kelly, G. 44
Kennedy, J. F. 45
Kentridge, W. 47–8, 49, 50, 55–62
Kitchener, L. 42
Kojève, A. 52
Kruger, B. 133
Kwa-Zulu Natal 120

Land Act of 1913 42
Lefa La Ntate 51
LGBT rights 81
literature 89–127
Lives of Animals (Coetzee) 122
Locke, J. 7–8, 9
locus classicus 130
Lord of the Rings (Tolkien) 47
Lurie, D. 16–17, 30–7, 39–40, 65, 89,
    92, 125, 152

Luxemburg, R. 6
Lyotard, Jean-Francois 2

Mandela, N. 43
Manet, E. 36, 143
Mapplethorpe, R. 78
Marcuse, H. 6
Marikana Strike 44
Marriage of Figaro (Mozart and Da
    Ponte) 162, 165
Marx, K. 1, 3, 13
master–slave dialectic 52
Mbelo, T. 106
McPherson , C. B. 9
melancholy, Cape Town 33
me-moir 136
mercantile capitalism 1
Miller, T. 77
Mine (Eckstein) 48, 49, 50, 53
miners 43
mines: in Australia 46
    in Canada 46
    in Russia 46
    in South Africa 46
    violence of 44
Minow, M. 96
mismanagement 39
modern architecture 32
modern art 45–6
modernity 32
Modisakeng, M. 47, 51
Mofokeng, S. 33
Monroe, M. 46
moral adages 58
Morning after Dark 37
mountain's shoelace 37
Mozambique car bombing 100
museological allure 45
mythologization of heritage 38

Namibia 42, 46
National Endowment for the Arts
    (NEA) 77–9
*National Endowment for the Arts
    v. Finley* 77

national heritage 162
nationalization 43
national narratives 110
National Party 43
nation-building exercise 96, 116
natural rights 7–8
Nazi crime 98
Nazi nationalism 54
NEA 4 77–80, 82–5, 87–8
Nietzsche, F. 11, 75, 116, 174
nondemocratic states 38
nondiscriminatory/violent 76
nonretributive justice 101
Norval Foundation 55
novel 41

Occupy Wall Street 64
Olympia (Manet) 143
One Dollar Bills (Warhol) 148–9
opportunities 39, 52
"Ostranie" 13

*The People Shall Share in the Country's
    Wealth* (Lurie) 35
The Perfect Moment
    (Mapplethorpe) 78
Phenomenology of Spirit (Hegel)
    118, 159
Philosophy of Right (Hegel) 118
photo: formal arrangement 34
    tightly indexed 66
    visual arrangement 36
    wallet-sized pictures 36
photographer 36, 54
photography 40;
    performance 136
Picasso's *Guernica* 5
Piketty, T. 3
Piss Christ (Serrano) 78
Plaatjie, S. 43
plastic art 67
plastic experimentation 12, 129
political agency 54, 56, 63
political art 4
political regimes 97

political rhetoric 56
political statement 56
*The Political Theory of Possessive
    Individualism* (McPherson) 9
political transition 43
politics: art in 6, 22
    art market 143–57
    concepts of 2
    courts 7
    cultural 23
    currency of art 1
    embraced 1
    eschews 7
    of financial capital 3
    genuine 6
    identity 129–41
    issue-based 3
    of offense 75–88
    political concepts 6
    racial 3
    as resistance 29
    single guiding 6
    of Truth Commission 89–127
    of visibility 27–40
    of witness 63–73
    writing on art 2
posters 36
Postmodern Condition (Lyotard) 2
The Preacher (Gittoes) 69
Prevention of Terrorism Act 96
pricelessness 45
private life 173
Promotion of National Unity Act 53
propaganda posters 58
proportionality 102
Psycho (Hitchcock) 146
public gesture 34
public infrastructure 39
"pursuit of happiness" 9

radical alternatives 2
radical experimentalism 63
radical transformation 1
raises political consciousness 13
Ramaphosa, C. 39, 44

Rancière, J. 2, 28–30, 37, 82
Rawls, J. 29
Reading Capital (Althusser) 29
reconciled society 118
reconciliation 106, 117
refugee camp 42
Renaissance fresco 10
Republic of South Africa 44
restorative justice 101
Rettig Commission 111
Rhodes, C. 42
Rhodesian proportion 42
rights 39, 44
Riis, J. 32
Ring of the Nibelungs (Wagner) 47
Robertson, G. 100
Rodchenko, A. 12–13
Rorty, R. 6
Russian Constructivists 55
Russian Revolution 7, 12, 59

Sachs, A. 100–1
Schadeberg, J. 33
Schubert, F. 58
Second Amendment 71
Second Treatise of Government
    (Locke) 7
Second World War 38, 55, 75, 85,
    98, 130
self-consciousness 7
sensibility 9
Serrano, A. 78
Sherman, C. 133
Smuts, J. 44
social mobility 39
soft vengeance 100
*The Soft Vengeance of a Freedom
    Fighter* (Sachs) 101
solidarity 133
Solonga, B. 155
South Africa 34, 42, 43, 48, 54
    art 42, 47
    democracy 39–40
    democratic transition 43
    international debt 43

miners 44
  transition 94
  workers union in 46
South African Constitution 44, 53
Spero, N. 133
Standard Bank 51
Statue of Liberty 32
Steiglitz, A. 32

Taylor, C. 133
theory-driven innovation 63
Titian painting 10
township 34
transient relationship 34
transitional dyad 110
transitional justice 96, 101
Transvaal 42
truth 137
Truth and Reconciliation Commission
  (TRC) 97–101, 104–8, 118
Truth and Reconciliation Committees
  43, 53, 56–7, 91–2, 94, 96–7

ultimate justification 97
uncertainty 59
Undercity (Lurie) 31, 34
utopian emancipation 1

Venus of Urbino (Titian) 143
"Verfremdung" 13
violence: of mines 44

virulent nationalism 75–88
visibility 30
visual art 1, 4–5, 41, 42, 47
  capacity 17
  language 4
  medium/media of 5
  philosophy and 59
  political aspirations for 4
  political power of 6
visual experimentation 13
visual installation 41
visual texture 42
Vooruitzigt 42

Walled-Off Hotel (Banksy) 154
wallet-sized pictures 36
wall paintings 36, 37
Walton, K. 66
Warhol, A. 148
weak revolution 43
Weimar artists 5
Weinberg, P. 33
White Light (Gittoes) 71–3
Winston, H. 46, 47
Wittgenstein, L. 30
women 46
Woodstock, Lower Main Road
  (Lurie) 35
Writing the City (Lurie) 30

Zeitz MOCAA 55

www.ingramcontent.com/pod-product-compliance
Ingram Content Group UK Ltd.
Pitfield, Milton Keynes, MK11 3LW, UK
UKHW020734280225
455688UK00012B/654